CHILD NUTRITION AND PRIMARY EDUCATION

Child Nutrition and Primary Education

By

Surendra Nath Misra
Manaranjan Behera

ANMOL PUBLICATIONS PVT. LTD.
NEW DELHI - 110 002 (INDIA)

ANMOL PUBLICATIONS PVT. LTD.
4374/4B, Ansari Road, Daryaganj
New Delhi - 110 002
Ph.: 23261597, 23278000
Visit us at: www.anmolpublications.com

Child Nutrition and Primary Education

First Published, 2004

ISBN 81-261-2070-3

PRINTED IN INDIA

Published by J.L. Kumar for Anmol Publications Pvt. Ltd., New Delhi - 110 002 and Printed at Mehra Offset Press, Delhi.

CONTENTS

FOREWORD

Primary education is a major indicator of social development. The founders of Indian Constitution, while formulating the Constitution piously hoped that in 10 years time (meaning there by 1960) all children below the age of 14 would be provided with free and compulsory education. Unfortunately, in spite of the Directive Principles of our Constitution two-third of the children in the age group of 5 to 9 do not know how to read and write nor attend any school. Further, those who join the primary schools, only two third continue beyond primary school. The situation is worse in rural areas. Nation Sample Survey Report indicates that in rural areas as many as 69 per cent girls and 43 per cent boys do not enroll themselves in any school. NSS Report of 1995 shows that in the age group of 6 to 11, as many as 78 million children did not attend any school.

Extreme poverty and social discrimination are the major causes of illiteracy. Several programmes have been launched to attract children to schools. The Mid-day Meals Programme is a major programme launched all over the country, not only to attract children into the embrace of primary schooling, but also, to provide nutritional support for generating necessary interests, both physical and psychological, among the children to ensure their presence in the schools. The Mid-day Meals programme is thus, a multi-dimensional programme aimed at reducing dropouts, provide nutritional support and educating children. Much before the programme was designed as a National Programme, the government of Tamil Nadu introduced it as a state sponsored programme under the name of Noon-Meals programme.

The Planning Commission, in fitness of things, very rightly wanted to study the working of the programme in an educationally developed state and compare the same with an educationally backward state. For this purpose the two states chosen are Tamil Nadu and Orissa and the comparative study was entrusted to

Nabakrushna Choudhury Centre for Development Studies, Bhubaneswar. The entire study was organised under the stewardship of Prof. S. N. Misra who was designated as Director of the Project. Prof. S. N. Misra certainly did a painstaking job and the present report is an outcome of his sincere effort and scholastic abilities.

I express my sincere thanks to Sri M.K. Kaw, former Principal Advisor and presently the Secretary, Department of Education, Ministry of Human Resource Development. Government of India, Sri K.K. Bakshi, Principal Advisor (Education), Dr. V.P. Garg, Joint Advisor (Education) and their colleagues in the Education Division of Planning Commission for entrusting the study to this Centre.

I express my deep sense of gratitude to Prof. B. Mishra, Chairman of the Centre for his help and guidance in conducting the study. I also thanks Dr. (Mrs.) S.Laxmi, Professor of Economics, Bharati Dasan University, Tiruchirapally for her help in conducting the field survey in Tamil Nadu.

I shall fail in my duty if I do not express my sincere and heartfelt thanks to Dr. R.C. Panda, Secretary, Rural Development and Sri M.A. Gourishankar, Secretary, School Education Department, Government of Tamil Nadu, Sri M. M. Mohanty, Secretary, School and Mass Education, Government of Orissa for their unstinted help and support in the conduct of the Study.

I sincerely hope, the findings of this study will help, not only the Planning Commission and the State Governments of Orissa and Tamil Nadu, but also the policy makers in shaping the future programmes for University Primary Education.

Gyana Chandra Kar
DIRECTOR
Nabakrushna Choudhury Centre for
Development Studies, Bhubaneswar-751013.

ACKNOWLEDGEMENTS

Children are the future of mankind. When children grow with all their potential the nation prospers. Education and health, inter alia, are the two basic requirements of children, these primal needs are found to be more basic and urgent for school going children as we go down to the level of primary schools. The nation is committed to achieving universalisation of elementary education covering children in the age group of 6 years and 14 years. But here at this level, one comes across a paradoxical situation of more enrolment of students in the primary school on the one hand and a large-scale dropout of children from schools on the other. As a result, there is poor retention and attendance of children in schools. This paradoxical situation has put a big question mark on the efficacy of universal primary education in the Country. Among the factors identified for such a malady are the large-scale poverty, malnutrition and undernutrition amongst the school going children. The parents of most of the children are not only poor, but also, have very low level of income. They fail to meet the required calorie intake of their children. Besides, food eaten by the children lack essential nutrients. On account of poverty, undernutrition and malnutrition, children lack zeal, enthusiasm and interest for study. Learning becomes uninteresting and attending school is considered to be a sheer waste of time. It is found that most of the primary school going children do not get two square meals a day in their homes. Often they attend school without any food. In majority cases they get only one square meal a day and that too is deficient of vital nutrients. On account of this, their physical and mental growth is adversely affected. This reduces their quest for learning and prevents them to pursue education on a continuous and sustainable basis. This is one of the main causes for growing dropout and poor retention of children in schools. It is, therefore, suggested that the children of this vulnerable age group be provided with some supplementary food in schools so as to upkeep their spirit of learning and interest in education. To overcome this, the Government of India introduced Nutritional Support to Primary Education programme (Mid-day Meals scheme) in the year 1995. India was not the first country to be credited with the launching of the programme in 1995. The school lunch programme was implemented by several developed and developing countries of the world much earlier than India's experiment with this programme. Even in India, before launching of the programme by the Central Government, the Tamil Nadu government made an experiment with the school lunch programme as early as 1956, under the able leadership of K. Kamaraj, the then Chief Minister of the State. The programme, as it exists in different parts of the country, varies from state to state both in content and in form. While in some states like Orissa and Tamil Nadu, cooked food is provided, in other states like Andhra Pradesh, Uttar Pradesh and Himachal Pradesh etc. only 3 kilograms of foodgrains per child per month is provided on the basis of 80 per cent of attendance in the school. A few states like Delhi, however, provide processed food like sweet bread to the children in the school lunch programme. The objective of the programme is that with supplementary nutritious food given in the school lunch programme, the children will be more interested to attend school and take interest in study and education.This would help to reduce dropouts among the children, which in turn, help increase retention of children in the schools.

Orissa and Tamil Nadu have introduced cooked food for school-going primary children in the schools as both the states are primarily agricultural states and rice is the staple food for the majority of people in both the states. In view of this, the present study is mainly confined to two states; Orissa and Tamil Nadu for purpose of comparison. Planning Commission while sponsoring the study to the NKC Centre for Development Studies also suggested for a comparative study of the programme covering the two states.

During the course of the study, assistance, support and guidance have been received from several quarters and from a number of institutions and individuals. Since it is not possible to name all of them here in this brief acknowledgement, still some of them who directly and overwhelmingly contributed for the completion of the project from beginning to the final stage deserve to be mentioned here.

A comparative study of Nutritional support to Primary Education (Mid-day Meals scheme) in Orissa and Tamil Nadu was sponsored by Planning Commission and was conducted by Nabakrushna Choudhury Centre for Development Studies, Bhubaneswar, Orissa with a grant in-aid of Rs. 2,38,350/- for carrying out the research study. In this connection, we express our sincere thanks to Sri M.K. Kaw, former Principal Adviser, Planning Commission and presently the Secretary Dept. of Education, Ministry of Human Resource Development, Government of India for taking all initiatives and piloting the study in different states of the country.

We also offer our sincere and heartiest thanks to Sri K.K. Baksi, Principal Advisor (Education), Planning Commission and Dr. V.P. Garg, Joint Advisor (Education) for Providing timely guidance, logistic support and relevant materials as and when required for the completion of the project.

We take this opportunity to profusely thank to Dr. Ramesh Ch. Panda, IAS, Secretary, Rural Development Department, Government of Tamil Nadu, Thiru M.A. Gowrishankar, IAS, Secretary, School Education Department, Tamil Nadu, Thiru R. Narayanasamy, Director of Elementary Education, Tamil Nadu for providing all literature, study material and information about Tamil Nadu. Besides, they also provided necessary guidance from time to time for the successful launching of the project. We also take this opportunity to express our sincere gratitude to Sri Madan Mohan Mohanty, IAS, Secretary (School Education) Government of Orissa, Sri R.N. Pani, IAS, Director of Elementary Education, Sri Digambar Mohanty, IAS, Director, Secondary Education for providing all necessary information and material for the study.

We are particularly very thankful to our esteemed Director. Prof. G.C. Kar for taking interest and giving all possible guidance for the successful implementation of the project. In spite of his busy schedule of work at the Centre, he spared his valuable time for scrutinising, reviewing and improving the manuscript by contributing his vast knowledge and experience on the subject. I particularly express my deep gratitude to him for writing the foreword to this project, which speaks of his interest and keen observation on the subject.

We are also thankful to Prof. B. Misra, Chairman of NKC Centre of Development Studies, for taking keen interest on the subject and offering his valuable suggestions and comments for improving the draft at every stage of the preparation of the report.

We express our sincere thanks to Sri C. Thangavelu, IAS, Collector, Madurai, Sri Bibhu Nayyar, Collector, Villupuram, Tamil Nadu, Sri, Pradipta Kumar Mohapatra, IAS, Collector, Puri and Sri, Deoranjan K. Singh, IAS, Collector, Rayagada, Orissa for their help cooperation, support and assistance in the course of the study.

We express our thanks to Prof. (Mrs.) S. Laxmi and her team of project staff of Bharati Dasan University, Tiruchirapalli, Tamil Nadu for undertaking the responsibility of conducting the field survey in Madurai and Villupuram.

We take this opportunities to thank all the respondents both in Orissa and Tamil Nadu consisting of students, parents, teachers, educated/literate persons, panchayat representatives, social activists/NGO's and local government officials for responding calmly and coolly to large volley of questions put by the project staff. The replies received from them helped us to prepare the final draft. We take this opportunity to offer our thanks to Sri Hemanta Kumar Padhan, Research Assistant and the other project staff engaged temporarily in the project, Sri Satyajit Tripathy, Sri Ashok Kumar Nayak, Sri Srikanta Sarangi and Sri Ramesh Sahoo, for sincerely undertaking the field study.

Finally, all the colleagues in the Centre deserve our sincere thanks for the support they have shown for the study. We particularly thank Sri Labanyendu Mohan Das for undertaking the computer part of the project report neatly and efficiently.

Prof. S.N. Misra
Dr. Manaranjan Behera

CHAPTER-1

INTRODUCTION

Children are the mirror of a nation and hope of the world. Unless children develop, no nation can prosper, hence, investment in child development is the need of the hour. Large number of children around the world, particularly in poor countries, are found to be undernourished and malnourished. These children are to be supported by food, adequate in quantity and rich in quality. Unless they get the right quantity and proper quality of food, their physical and mental development will not be improved. Absence of nutritious food results in several diseases and physical deficiencies among children. They will be disinterested in reading. Their attendance in school will decline. Their body development will not be there. Hence, supply of nutritious food is essential to create interest and zeal for reading amongst children. Food persuades children to attend school regularly and in large numbers.

Understanding the need for nutritious food for children, many developed and developing countries took the initiative for providing food to the school children, and countries like U.S.A., Japan, China and Great Britain provided free lunch to school children particularly in elementary schools.

India has a large child population. According to 1991 Census Report, children accounted for about 31 crore in the age group of 0-14 years. The number of children enrolled in schools of the age group 6-14 years in India is 15.15 crore in 1996-97. Further, most of the children enrolled in the schools are found to be very poor. They fail to get two square meals a day. Even a majority of them manage with just one meal in a day. The food they eat not only lacks nutrition, but it is also unbalanced. The condition of the SC/ST children is still precarious. They show no interest in studies. Their attendance in school is poor. They do not continue reading in schools and dropout from schools in the early part of their career. Since their parents are poor, they express their inability to provide them with food. They compel them to work in some low paid works even at the tender age.

To prevent this, different types of Mid-day Meals programmes have been introduced in the country at the Primary School level in different time-periods. In 1925, the National Programme of Nutritional Support to Primary Education or the Mid-day Meals programme was introduced in India on a modest Scale by Madras Corporation. In pursuance of the recommendations made by National School Health Committee, the Government of India launched the Mid-day Meals in 1962-63 as an important supplementary feeding programme under the Ministry of Education. But, because of the various problems associated with the previous Mid-day Meals programme, the government of India was compelled to revise the programme. The revised National Programme is 'Nutritional Support to Primary Education', which was launched on 15th August, 1995 to give a boost to universal elementary education in terms of increasing enrolment, retention and attendance in primary classes by supplementing nutritional requirements of children attending Primary Schools.The programme has commenced in almost all the states and Union Territories of India. Cooked meals are being provided in six states, viz, Gujarat, Jammu and Kashmir, Kerala, Madhya Pradesh, Orissa, Tamil Nadu and in one Union Territory, i.e., Pondicherry. In Delhi, Processed food (sweet bread) is being supplied through Modern Food Industries. The rest of the states and Union Territories are distributing food grains. Students securing more than 80% of attendance are given 3 kgs of food-grains each per month.

In the year 1995-96, as many as 3.35 crore children of 2.25 lakh schools covering 2999 blocks were benefited under the present Mid-day Meals (MDM) Scheme in the country. The programme was expanded to cover 5.57 crore primary school going children in about 5 lakh schools, spread over 4426 blocks in the country during 1996-97. The actual expenditure of the scheme was Rs. 441.21 crore in 1995-96, whereas, the revised outlay for 1996-97 was Rs.1050.00 crore.

Importance Of The Study:

The study was undertaken in two states, viz.,Orissa being an educationally backward and Tamil Nadu, being an educationally advanced state. The total literacy rate of Orissa was 49.09 percent as per 1991 census, which was less that that of Tamil Nadu (62.66 per cent) as well as national average (52.21 per cent). If female literacy rate would be taken into consideration, this was 34.68 per cent in Orissa, whereas, the same for Tamil Nadu was 51.33 and for India it was 39.29 per cent. Thus, from literacy point of view, Orissa was found to be an educationally backward state and Tamil Nadu an educationally advanced state of India. Further the dropout rate of students at primary level. in Orissa was much higher than Tamil Nadu and the national level. In 1996-67, the dropout rate of students in Primary Schools in Orissa was 47.6 per cent. On the other hand it was only 15.1 per cent in case of Tamil Nadu in the aforesaid year. At the national level dropout in the said year was 42.8 per cent. From the enrolment side also, the position of Orissa was not good. The gross enrolment ratio in Class I-V was 89.3 per cent in Orissa in 1996-97, whereas, the same for Tamil Nadu and India were 106.2 per cent and 90.5 per cent respectively.

In order to prevent dropout among children and to further improve enrolment in primary schools, state intervention in the form of free lunch programme was considered to be more desirable. Besides, the Mid-day Meal programme has further the advantage of meeting one time food requirement of the children with nutritional support to their diet for creating interest and zeal among them to attend school regularly.

Both Orissa and Tamil Nadu had the advantage of providing cooked food in the school lunch programme. The cooked food served in the primary schools has the merit of improving regular attendance in the school. Since both the states are primarily agricultural states, cooked food with requisite nutrition was considered to be more suitable than dry lunch prevalent in some parts of the country. It is against this background that a comparative study of school lunch programme covering mainly primary school going children of I to V classes in Orissa and Tamil Nadu as suggested by Planning Commission, was considered more plausible. The project is a humble attempt in that direction.

Objectives Of The Study:

The objectives of the study are as follows:

i. To compare the success or failure of Mid-day Meals Scheme in improving enrolment, retention, dropout and attendance in Primary Schools in Orissa with that in Tamil Nadu.

ii. To examine what socio-cultural, administrative, managerial and financial factors and circumstances are responsible for the success or failure of the scheme.

iii To find whether the scheme introduced in the state has some weaknesses and needs any modification suitable to the socio-cultural peculiarities of the region.

iv. To study more specifically the related questions like inadeqanacy of implementation, administrative failure in reaching the benefits, lack of convergence of the schemes, etc.

Methodology:

The study has been undertaken both by secondary and primary sources of data and information. Although secondary sources of materials are considered to be more important, yet some thrust is put on primary level data and materials. The objective is to corroborate secondary sources of information with that of field level investigations and findings.

The primary sources of data and information are collected through sample surveys and interviews. Multi-stage sampling method is followed to select the samples in both the states of Orissa and Tamil Nadu.

In the first stage, two districts one educationally advanced and the other educationally backward are selected from each state. For the selection of districts in Orissa, all the 30 districts of the State are arranged in ascending order of their literacy rates as per 1991 Census (Tablle-1.1). The educationally advanced district is selected randomly from among the last five districts having high literacy rates. Similarly, for selecting an educationally backward district, the first five districts having low literacy rates are taken into consideration. In this case also, random procedure is adopted for selecting the educationally backward district. On the basis of this procedure, Puri is elected as an educationally advanced district while Rayagada is selected as an educationally backward district. The similar procedure is in the case of Tamil Nadu while selecting the districts. On the basis of the procedure outlined above, Madura district is considered as the educationally advanced district of Tamil Nadu while Villupuram ranks as the educationally backward district (Table-1.2).

In the second stage, the selection of blocks from the sample districts is made. In block selection, the blocks of Puri and Rayagada districts of Orissa are arranged in ascending order of their literacy rates which can be seen from Table-1.3 and Table-1.4. For selecting the educationally advanced blocks, we have selected randomly one block from Puri district and the other from Rayagada district from the last five blocks having higher literacy rates. Similarly, for selecting the educationally backward block, one block from Puri district and the other from Rayagada district have been selected from the first five blocks exhibiting lower percentage of literacy. On the basis of this procedure, the two blocks selected from Puri district are Satyabadi (educationally advanced) and Puri Sadar (educationally backward). Similarly in Rayagada district, the blocks selected are Kolnara (educationally advanced) and Rayagada (educationallly backward).

In Tamil Nadu, the same procedure has been adopted in selecting the blocks from Madurai and Villupuram districts. The blocks selected from Madurai district are Madurai-East Block (educationally advanced) and Alanganuller Block (educationally backward (Table-1.5). The educationally advanced and educationally backward blocks selected from Villupuram district are Koliyanur and Thirunavalur respectively (Table-1.6).

In the third stage, selection of schools is made. From the Primary Schools operating in different panchayats under the block, five schools coming under five different panchayats are selected at random for the purpose of our study. The details about the schools, coming under Satyabadi and Puri Sadar blocks of Puri district and, Kolnara and Rayagada blocks of Rayagada district can be seen from Annexure-1.1. Similarly, in Tamil Nadu, the schools that have been selected from Madurai East and Alanganuller blocks of Madurai district and, Koliyanur and Thirunavalur blocks of Villupuram district can be seen from Annexure-1.2.

The last and ultimate stage is the selection of sample units. From each school, 5 students and their parents, one panchayat Representative, one NGO\Social worker and one educated villager are selected randomly for the study. On the basis of this, both in Puri and Rayagada districts covering four blocks, a total number of 100 students, 100 parents, 20 teachers, 20 panchayat representatives, 20 NGO\ Social workers and 20 educated villagers have been surveyed through well structured questionnaires meant for each category of respondents. Further, 20 officials involved in the operation of Midday Meals Scheme (10 from each district) have also been interviewed (Annexure-1.1).

Similar procedure has also been adopted in Tamil Nadu. The total number of students, parents, teachers, Panchayat representatives, NGO\Social workers, educated villagers and officials surveyed for the purpose of the study are same as that of Orissa (Annexure-1.2). On the basis of the methodology pursued for the study, the field survey was undertaken first in Orissa covering two districts during July, 1999 to September, 1999. The printed questionnaires prepared for seven categories of respondents were canvassed by trained field investigators specially recruited for the purpose.

In Tamil Nadu, the same questionnaires were canvassed to respondents by locally recruited field investigators in both the districts. To avoid difficulties in communication due to language, interpreters from Bharati Dasan University, Dept of Economics Tiruchirapally were recruited. In Tamil Nadu, the field study was undertaken during the period October,1999 to December, 1999.

The data so collected were then processed and put in the form of primary tables. Later final tables were prepared taking into consideration the objective of the study, for purpose of analysis and interpretation.

Limitations Of The Study:

The study has the following limitations:

:i. As already mentioned, the Nutritional Support to Primary Education or Mid-day Meals Scheme was introduced in the country on 15th August 1995. So to know the impact of Mid-day Meals Scheme data on enrolment, attendance retention and dropout, have been collected with regard to the above variable from the sample schools of Orissa and Tamil Nadu for the time period 1989-90 to 1998-99, covering the period of a decade.

ii. In the study, government or semi-government primary schools having Class-I to V both in Orissa and Tamil Nanu where there is the programme of noon-meals have been surveyed. Schools like National Child Labour Project School managed by Labour and Employment Department, Ashram Schools run by Panchayati Raj Department and Tribal Welfare Department and schools for disabled children run by Women and Child Welfare Department, where also noon-meal programme is operating are not taken into consideration for lack of time and accessibility.

iii. In Orissa and Tamil Nadu, Primary School going children (Class-I to V) have been interviewed for the study purpose as the Mid-day Meals Scheme is meant for primary school stu dents at national level. But, Tamil Nadu is an exception.Along with the Primary School Students, Mid-day Meal is given to the students of class-VI to X and the entire extra burden is borne by the State Government. In this study primary school children of class I to V getting the benefit of Mid-day Meals are only studied.

The entire study is divided into seven chapters.

The first chapter introduces the subject matter, examines the scope of the study, and discusses the objectives and methodology of the study. It thus serves as a prologue.

In the second chapter, Socio-economic profile of Orissa and Tamil Nadu, and the sample districts and blocks are analysed. The chapter also deals with characteristic features of the respondents, viz., Students, Parents and Teachers, whose roles are important for purpose of study.

The third chapter examines the evolution, structure, organisation and operation of Mid-day Meals Scheme in Orissa and Tamil Nadu.

The impact of Mid-day Meals Scheme on enrolment, retention, attendance, and dropout of students in Orissa and Tamil Nadu are examined in the fourth chapter.

In fifth chapter, Socio-cultural, administrative, managerial and financial factors influencing Mid-day Meals Scheme both in Orissa and Tamil Nadu are analysed.

The sixth chapter finds out the weaknesses on Mid-day Meals Scheme and gives suggestions to overcome the weaknesses.

The last chapter summarises the main findings of the study and draws policy conclusions on the basis of the findings. It is in the form of an epilogue.

TABLE-1.1

DISTRICTS ARRANGED IN ASCENDING ORDER OF TOTAL LITERCY RATES IN ORISSA

SL. No.	*Name of the District*	*Total Literacy Rate (As Per 1991 Census)*
1.	Nabarangpur	18.62
2.	Malkangiri	20.04
3.	Koraput	24.64
4.	Rayagada	26.01
5.	Nuapada	27.52
6.	Gajapati	29.37
7.	Kalahandi	31.08
8.	Kandhamal	37.23
9.	Mayurbhanj	37.88
10.	Bolangir	38.63
11.	Boudh	40.98
12.	Sonepur	42.62
13.	Deograrh	44.45
14.	Keonjhar	44.73
15.	Ganjam	46.72
16.	Baragarh	47.65
17.	Angul	51.53
18.	Sambalpur	51.56
19.	Jharsuguda	52.64
20.	Sundargarh	52.97
21.	Dhenkanal	54.91
22.	Nayagarh	57.20
23.	Balasore	57.64
24.	Jajpur	58.00
25.	Bhadrak	60.54
26.	Puri	63.30
27.	Kendrapara	63.61
28.	Cuttack	65.44
29.	Jagatsinghpur	65.78
30.	Khurda	67.72
	Orissa	49.09

Source: Censes of India, 1991 Census.

TABLE-1.2

DISTRICTS ARRANGED IN ASCENDING ORDER OF TOTAL LITERACY RATES IN TAMIL NADU

Sl. No.	*Name of the District*	*Total Literacy Rate (As per 1991 Census)*
1.	Villupuram	45.36
2.	Dharmapuri	46.02
3.	Tiruvannamalai	53.07
4.	Salem	53.31
5.	Periyar	53.80
6.	Dindigul Anna	56.68
7.	Pudukkottal	57.63
8.	South Arcot Valladur	58.59
9.	North Arcot Ambedkar	60.87
10.	Tiruchirapalli	61.22
11.	Ramanathapuram	61.59
12.	Kamarajar	62.91
13.	Pasumpon Muthuramalingathevar	63.04
14.	Tirunelveli Kattabomman	65.58
15.	Thanjavur	66.02
16.	Nagapattinum	66.17
17.	Coimbatore	66.35
18.	Chengalpatta-MGR	66.38
19.	Madurai	66.41
20.	Niligiris	71.70
21.	Chidambaranag	73.02
22.	Madrsas	81.60
23.	Kanniya Kumari	82.06
	Tamil Nadu	62.66

Source: Census of India, 1991.

TABLE-1.3

BLOCKS ARRANGED IN ASCENDING ORDER OF TOTAL LITERACY RATES IN PURI DISTRICT

SI.No.	*Name of the Block*	*Total Literacy Rate (As per 1991 Census)*
1.	Krushnaprasad	52.37
2.	Bramhagiri	54.37
3.	Puri Sadar	56.80
4.	Kakatpur	60.23
5.	Kanas	61.45
6.	Astaranga	61.66
7.	Gop	63.61
8.	Pipili	63.89
9.	Satyabadi	65.43
10.	Nimapara	65.64
11.	Delang	66.77
	Puri District	63.30

Source: Govt. of Orissa, D.E. &.S., District Statistical Handbook, Puri (1995).

TABLE-1.4

BLOCKS ARRANGED IN ASCENDING ORDER OF TOTAL LITERACY RATES IN RAYAGADA DISTRICT

SI.No.	*Name of the Block*	*Total Literacy Rate (As per 1991 Census)*
1.	Kasipur	13.20
2.	Rayagada	15.90
3.	Chandrapur	16.40
4.	K.Singhpur	18.89
5.	Gudari	19.27
6.	B.Cuttack	21.01
7.	Muniguda	21.47
8.	Gunupur	23.16
9.	Kolanara	26.03
10.	Ramanguda	28.34
11.	Padmapur	34.51
	Rayagada District	26.01

Source: Govt. of Orissa, D.E. & S., District Statistical handbook, Rayagada (1995).

TABLE-1.5

BLOCKS ARRANGED IN ASCENDING ORDER OF TOTAL LITERACY RATES IN MADURAI DISTRICT

SI.No.	Name of the Block	Total Literacy Rate (As per 1991 Census)
1.	Sedapatti Block	47.46
2.	Chellampatti Block	47.58
3.	Kottampatti Block	50.00
4.	Kallikudi Block	54.87
5.	Alanganallur Block	56.35
6.	Usilampatti Block	57.27
7.	Mellur Block	57.39
8.	Vadipatti Block	59.47
9.	Tirumangalam Block	59.67
10.	T.Kallupatti Block	59.92
11.	Madurai East Block	62.06
12.	Madurai West Block	65.33
13.	Tirupparangunram Block	67.86
	Madurai District	66.41

Source: Census of India, 1991.

TABLE-1.6

BLOCKS ARRANGED IN ASCENDING ORDER OF TOTAL LITERACY RATES IN VILLUPURAM DISTRICT

Sl.No.	*Name of the Block*	*Total Literacy Rate (As per 1991 Census)*
1.	Kalrayan Hills	15.29
2.	Ulundurpet	37.70
3.	Rishivandiam	37.78
4.	Thirunavalur	40.23
5.	Thiyagadurgam	40.60
6.	T.V.Nallur	41.63
7.	Mugaiyur	42.47
8.	Kallakurichi	45.55
9.	Melmalayanur	46.75
10.	Tirukoilur	46.80
11.	Kanai	47.71
12.	Merkanam	47.74
13.	Vallam	47.77
14.	Olakkur	47.79
15.	Sankarapuram	47.98
16.	Chinnasalem	48.12
17.	Mailam	50.01
18.	Gingee	50.51
19.	Vikkiravandi	51.93
20.	Vanur	51.96
21.	Kandamangalam	52.68
22.	Kolianur	54.36
	Villupuram District	46.02

Source: Census of India, 1991.

CHAPTER-2

SOCIO-ECONOMIC BACKDROP

This chapter is divided into three sections. The first section deals with the socio-economic background of Orissa and Tamil Nadu. The second section analyses the profile of the sample districts and blocks. In the third section, characteristic features of the sample respondents, viz., students, parents, teachers, panchayat representatives, educated villagers, NGO/social workers and officials, are analysed.

Section-I

ORISSA

1. Geographical Setting

Orissa is a rural oriented, agricultural based and one of the most backward states of the Country. It is situated between 17°.5 East to 22°.5' North latitude, and between 81°.5' and 88° East longitude with a vast coastal belt. The whole area of the state lies in the tropical zone. It is surrounded by West Bengal in the north-east, Madhya Pradesh in the west, Andhra Pradesh in the south-east and the Bay of Bengal in the east. The state comprises 1,55,707 sq.kms. of area, which is 4.74 per cent of the total geographical area of the Country.

2. Administrative Structure

The state has 30 revenue districts, 58 sub-divisions, 170 tehasils, 314 blocks, 5,263 gram panchayats and 51,057 villages apart from 123 urban bodies, 32 municipalities and 70 Notified Area Councils (NACs). There are 211 parliamentary constituencies and 147 assembly constituencies in the state. The number of police stations to look after the law and order situation in the state is 446..

3. Soil And Climate

The land mass of Orissa can be classified into three categories, viz., low (25.6 per cent), medium (33.6 per cent), and uplands (40.8 per cent) with various types of soils like red, yellow, red-loamy, alluvial, coastal alluvial, laterite and black soil with low and medium texture, distributed in ten types of agro-climatic zones.

The climatic condition of a state plays a vital role, as it is the most important determinant of agricultural productivity, soil fertility and natural resources of the region. In Orissa, the climatic condition is hot, moist and humid.The state is divided into six different climates such as, Hot and Moist, Hot and Most Sub-humid, Hot and Humid, Warm and Humid, Warm and Moist, and Hot and Dry Sub-humid. The climatic condition of the state is very favourable for agriculture with an average temperature of 40° C and the normal annual rainfall of 1502 mm.

4. Demographic Features

Orissa has a population of 3.17 crore, which is 3.74 per cent of the total population of the Country according to 1991 Census. The average annual growth rate of population was 2.06 per cent in the decade 1981-91 and it was 2.17 per cent per annum in the decade 1971-81. This indicates that the population of the state is declining at a very slow rate. Further, the density of population is 203 persons per square kilometre of area in 1991, which was 169 persons per square kilometre of area in 1981.

Out of the total population in Orissa, 50.74 per cent are males and 49.26 per cent are females.The sex ratio of the state indicates that it is 971 per 1000 males in 1991 census, which was 981 per 1000 males in 1981 Census. This implies that the number of females per 1000 males is declining in the state, which is cause for concern.

In the state, most of the population lives in rural areas. As per 1991 Census, 86.62 per cent of the total population lives in rural areas as against 13.38 per cent in urban areas. The caste-wise distribution of the total population indicates that the state has higher percentage of ST population than SC population. The percentage shares of ST and SC population 22.21 per cent

TABLE - 2.1

OCCUPATIONAL CLASSIFICATION OF WORKERS IN ORISSA, TAMIL NADU AND INDIA, 1991 CENSUS

Sl. No.	Type of Workers	Orissa Male	Orissa Female	Orissa Total	Tamil Nadu Male	Tamil Nadu Female	Tamil Nadu Total	India Male	India Female	India Total
1	Cultivators	4,110,982	487,518	4,598,500	4,215,235	1,448,855	5,664,090	88,480,942	22,221,404	110,702,346
		(47.58)	(15.04)	(38.70)	(26.42)	(17.59)	(23.41)	(39.44)	(24.75)	(35.24)
2.	Agricultural labourers	1,937,971,	1,038,779	2,976,750	4,171,571	3,724,724	7,896,295	46,164,747	28,432,997	74,597,744
		(22.43)	(32.04)	(25.05)	(26.14)	(45.22)	(32.64)	(20.58)	(31.67)	(23.75)
3.	Household Industry	225,998	98,405	324,403	447,079	355,877	802,956	4,555,016	2,249,005	6,804,021
		(02.62)	(03.04)	(02.73)	(02.80)	(04.32)	(03.32)	(02.03)	(02.51)	(02.17)
4.	Other Workers	2,215,992	261,990	2,477,982	7,040,632	1,395,093	8,435,725	82,457,879	11,370,503	93,828,382
		(25.64)	(08.08)	(20.85)	(44.12)	(16.94)	(34.87)	(36.75)	(12.67)	(29.87)
5.	Total Main Workers	8,490,943	1,886,692	10,377,635	15,874,517	6,924,549	22,799,066	221,658,564	64,273,909	285,932,493
		(98.27)	(58.20)	(87.33)	(99.48)	(84.07)	(94.23)	(98.79)	(71.60)	(91.02)
6.	Marginal Workers	149,828	1,355,299	1,505,127	82,954	1,312,323	1,395,277	2,705,223	25,493,654	28,198,877
		(01.73)	(41.80)	(12.67)	(00.52)	(15.93)	(05.77)	(01.21)	(28.40)	(08.98)
	Total	8,640,771	3,241,991	11,882,762	15,957,471	8236872	24,194,343	224,363,807	89,767,563	314,131,370
		(100.00)	(100.00)	(100.00)	(100.00)	(100.00)	(100.00)	(100.00)	(100.00)	(100.00)

** Excluding Jammu & Kashmir.*

Note: Figures in the parentheses indicate percentage to the corresponding total

Source: Census of India, 1991.

and 16.20 per cent respectively as per 1991 Census.

The occupational distribution of population shows that the total number of workers in the state is 11.88 millions consisting of 87 per cent main workers and 13 per cent marginal workers as per 1991 Census. The percentage shares of cultivators, agricultural labourers and workers engaged in household industries to total workers are 38.70, 25.05 and 2.73 respectively. This indicates that the percentage of workers engaged in agriculture (excluding livestock, forestry, fishing and other activities) is 63.75. Further, out of the total workers, 72.72 per cent are male workers and 27.28 per cent female workers (Table-2.1). The work participation rate in Orissa is 37.53 per cent with 53.7 per cent male work participation rate and 20.79 per cent female work participation rate.

5. Literacy Rate

From Table-2.2, it can be seen that the total literacy rate of Orissa according to 1991 Census is 49.09 per cent as against the national average of 52.21 per cent.

TABLE - 2.2

SEX AND CASTE-WISE LITERACY RATE IN RURAL AND URBAN AREA OF ORISSA, TAMIL NADU, 1991 CENSUS

Sl. No.	*Region*	*Orissa* SC	ST	TOTAL	*Tamil Nadu* SC	ST	TOTAL	*India* SC	ST	TOTAL
1.	Rural									
	M	51.22	33.38	60.00	54.47	32.38	67.18	45.95	38.45	57.90
	F	19.39	9.30	30.7 9	30.30	17.80	41.84	19.46	16.02	30.60
	T	35.45	21.29	45.46	42.50	25.24	54.59	33.25	27.38	44.70
2	Urban									
	M	62.10	52.91	81.21	72.58	56.32	86.06	66.60	66.56	81.10
	F	32.30	27.73	61.18	51.68	37.94	69.61	42.29	45.66	64.10
	T	47.80	40.85	71.99	62.24	47.29	77.99	55.11	56.60	73.10
3	Total									
	M	52.42	34.44	63.09	58.36	35.25	73.75	49.91	40.65	64.10
	F	20.74	10.21	34.68	34.89	20.23	51.33	23.76	18.19	39.30
	T	36.78	22.31	49.09	46.24	27.89	62.66	37.41	29.60	52.10

Note: M = Male, F–Female, T–Total

Source: Census of India, 1991.

The literacy rate of males and females in the state are 63.09 per cent and 34.68 per cent respectively. The sex-wise literacy rate of Orissa is also lower than that of the national average. As far as caste-wise literacy rate is concerned, in Orissa, the SC population has a higher literacy rate (36.78 per cent) than that of the ST population (22.31 per cent). Again, if we look at the rural and urban literacy rates in the state, it indicates that the urban literacy rate (71.99 per cent) is much higher than the rural literacy rate (45.46 per cent).

6. State Income and Poverty

The state income or Net State Domestic Product (NSDP) at factor cost in Orissa was Rs. 21,46,279 lakh at current prices in the year 1995-96. The per capita NSDP during the year was Rs. 6,236/-, which was less than the per capita national income (per capita Net National Product), i.e. Rs, 9,578/-. Further, as per the estimates made by the Modified Expert Group of Planning Commission, the percentage of population living below the poverty line was 48.6 consisting of 49.7 per cent in rural areas and 41.6 per cent in urban areas in Orissa in 1993-94. But all these figures were quite more than the national average. At national level, the percentages of population living below the poverty line in rural, urban and combined area were 37.3, 32.4, and 35.9 respectively.

7. Land Utilisation Pattern

The land utilisation pattern of Orissa as revealed from Table-2.3 shows that the total geographical area of Orissa was 15571 thousand hectares in the year 1995-96. Out of the total geographical area, the percentage share of forest land was 36.75 as against 22.44 in India in the year 1993-94. The net area sown in the state was 39.88 per cent of the total geographical area, whereas, at national level, it was 46.60 per cent. The percentage share of gross cropped area to total geographical area was 62.09 per cent. This shows that the share of area sown more than once was 22.21 per cent.

TABLE - 2.3

LAND UTILISATION PATTERN OF ORISSA AND TAMIL NADU

(Area in 1000 hect.)

Sl. No	Items	*1995-96 Orissa* Area	*1995-96 Orissa* Percentage to total geog--raphical area	*1995-96 Tamil Nadu* Area	*1995-96 Tamil Nadu* Percentage to total geog-raphical area
1.	Total geographical area	15571.00	100.00	13004	100.00
2.	Forest land	5722.00	36.75	2143	16.46
3.	Barren and uncultivable land	553.00	3.55	490	3.77
4.	Misc. tree and groves	715.00	4.95	221	1.70
5.	Permanent pastures	514.00	3.30	125	0.96
6.	Cultivable waste	435.00	2.79	348	2.68
7.	Land put to non-agricult--ural use	858.00	5.51	1912	14.70
8.	Current fallows land	210.00	1.35	1293	9.94
9.	Other fallows land	354.00	2.27	1130	8.69
10.	Net area sown	6210..00	39.88	5342	41.08
11.	Area sown more than once	3458.00	22.21	925	7.11
12.	Total cropped area	9668.00	62.09	6267	48.19

Source: 1) For Orissa, Orissa Agricultural Statistics, 1995-96. P-5.
2) For Tamil Nadu, Statistical Hand Book of Tamil Nadu, 1997, P-78.

8. Land Holding and Land Operation

Skewed distribution of land holding is a great obstacle for agricultural development. Table-2.4 shows that, in Orissa, the total area under land holding was 52,95,782 hectares and the total number of landholders were 39,47,947. As a result, the area per holding was a meagre 1.34 hectares. Out of the total landholders, 53.66 per cent were marginal and 26.22 per cent were small landholders. The percentage share of semi-medium, medium and large landholders were 15.03, 4.70 and 0.38 respectively. This shows that the percentage marginal and small landholders to the total was 80 per cent in Orissa.

TABLE - 2.4

AREA AND NUMBER OF DIFFERENT OPERATIONAL HOLDINGS IN ORISSA AND TAMIL NADU, 1990-91

Sl. No.	Type of Operational Holdings	Orissa			Tamil Nadu		
		Area	Number	Area per Holding	Area	Number	Area per Holdings
1.	Marginal (below 1 hect.)	1045050 (19.73)	2118429 (53.65)	0.49	2117826 (28.34)	5848096 (73.11)	0.36
2.	Small (1 to 2 hect.)	1426171 (26.93)	1035308 (26.22)	1.38	1794471 (24.01)	1274515 (15.93)	1.41
3.	Semi-Medium (2 to 4 hect.)	1560846 (29.47)	593522 (15.03)	2.63	1686514 (22.57)	617605 (7.72)	2.73
4.	Medium (4 to 10 hect.)	1011831 (19.11)	185522 (04.70)	5.45	1301124 (17.41)	227594 (2.85)	5.72
5.	Large (10 and above)	251884 (04.76)	15166 (0.38)	16.61	573742 (7.68)	31122 (0.39)	18.44
	All Categories	5295782 (100.00)	3947947 (100.00)	1.34	7473677 (100.00)	7998932 (100.00)	0.93

Note: Figures in the parentheses indicate percentage to the corresponding total.

Source : a) For Orissa, Agricultural Census, Board of Revenue, Cuttack.
b) For Tamil Nadu, Directorate of Economic and Statistics, Chennai.

9. Agriculture

Agriculture is the most important sector in Orissa. Nearly 88 per cent of the total population depends on agriculture. In 1996-97, it contributed 31 per cent to the State Domestic Product. The principal food crops that are produced in Orissa are rice, wheat, maize, ragi, gram, and arhar, and the non-food crops are groundnut, sesamum, cotton, jute, sugarcane, chillies and ginger. The total area under foodgrain production was 56297 hundred hectares, which was 89.24 per cent of the total cultivable area in 1995-96. Out of the total area under foodgrain production, 71.79 per cent was used for rice production, 0.08 per cent for wheat, 1.13 per cent for ragi and 2.64 per cent for arhar.

The yield rate of foodgrains in Orissa was 9.0 quintals per hectare in the 1996-97, which was less than the national yield rate of 16.0 quintals per hectare. The rate of rice in Orissa was 9.9 quintals per hectare, whereas, the national yield rate was 18.8 quintals per hectare.

Thus, rice, being the major crop in Orissa, has a very low yield rate of 9.9 quintal per hectare. This could be due to the lack of adequate irrigation facilities, lack of wide spread use of HYV seeds, and lack of adequate use of fertilisers. The percentage of net area irrigated to net area sown in Orissa was 32.8 in 1992-93, which was less than the national average, i.e. 32.5 per cent. The area under HYV crops in the state was 3143.12 thousand hectares in 1996-97 constituting 38.26 per cent of the gross cropped area. Regarding the consumption of fertilisers in Orissa, it was found in 1996-97 that the per hectare consumption of fertilisers of gross cropped area was only 30.52 kgs as against 77.5 kgs at national level.

10. Industry

In the field of industry, the position of Orissa at all India level is very poor. By the end of 1993-94, Orissa had 287 large and medium industries with an investment of Rs. 1432.93 crore and employment potential of 76.38 thousand persons. With regard to number of small-scale industries, it was 52,709 by the end of 1996-97. The total environment and employment opportunity generated by the small-scale industries were Rs. 908.93 crore and 3.65 lakh persons respectively.

As per the Annual Survey of industries, the percentage of factory workers to total all India factory workers in Orissa in the year 1994-95 was only 2.19. The per capita gross output in industry in 1993-94 in the state was Rs. 2874.90, which was less than the national average, i.e. Rs. 5705.70. During the same year, the per capita value added by manufacturer was Rs. 611.80 in Orissa, whereas, at all India level, it was as high as Rs. 1195.30. In terms of net value added, the position of Orissa was at the bottom amongst the fourteen major states of India.

11. Transport

Roads and railways, the two major means of transport, facilitate the economic development of an economy to a great extent. Roads are the major means of transportation in Orissa. The length of surface road per 1000 sq.km of area in 1994-95 was 267 km in Orissa as against 358 km at the national level. The percentage of villages connected with all weather roads in the same year was 40 in Orissa, which was less than the national average, i.e., 48. Again, the number of registered motor vehicles per 1000 persons in 1993-94 was 16.38 in Orissa, whereas, at national level, it was 30.51. With regard to the vehicle density per sq km of area, the number was 3.5 in Orissa and 10.4 in India.

As far as railways is concerned, Orissa lags far behind the other Indian states. The existing railway lines in Orissa pass through the fringes of the state leaving the central areas untouched. The railway route length in the state per 1000 sq.km of area comes to 14.06 km in 1996-97 as against 19.08 km at national level. Again, the railway route length per lakh of population in 1996-97 was 6.31 km. in the state and this figure was also less than the national average i.e., 6.69 km. This inadequacy has restricted the pace of industrial development in the state. Thus, in the field of transport, Orissa's position is below the national average.

12. Banking

A stable banking system is essential for the all round development of any nation. The total number of banks in Orissa was 2160 in 1996, which was 3.39 per cent of the total number of banks of the country. Again the population per bank in Orissa as on March 1998 was 16.2 thousand as against the national average of 14.8 thousand. This indicates that per bank population in Orissa was higher than the national average. The credit-deposit ratio in Orissa in the same year was 45.2 per cent, which was lower than the national credit-deposit ratio, i.e,, 55 per cent. Again, average per bank deposit in Orissa was only Rs. 332 lakh in 1996-97, which was much below the national average of Rs. 796 lakh in the same year. Moreover, average per bank credit in Orissa was Rs.163 lakh as against Rs. 444 lakh in India. It is clear from the above data that the banking section performance in Orissa is far from satisfactory.

13. Education

Education is one of the most important indicators of economic development. The state Government. in Orissa has been investing a lot of money on education in order to achieve universalisation of education. In the year 1992-93, Government of Orissa spent Rs. 630.54 crore on education head. As per the report of Ministry of Human Resource Development (1995) the percentage of educational expenditure to total governmental expenditure was 19.8 per cent in 1994 in Orissa. In the same year, the educational expenditure as a percentage of State Domestic Product was 5.4. per cent. Furthermore, the per capita expenditure on education in 1995-96 was Rs. 295/- in the state (Table-2.5).

In the year 1997-98, the total number of primary schools, middle schools, high schools and general colleges in the state were 42104, 12406, 6072 and 1031 respectively. Table-2.5 represents that the number of primary schools per 1000 population and per 100 sq km of area were 1.33 and 27.04 respectively. With regard to middle schools, the respective numbers were 0.39 and 7.97.

In Orissa, the pupil-teacher ratio in primary schools was 36.07 and, in middle schools, it was 34. But, as per the standard norm of the government, the pupil-teacher ratio is 40. This shows that the pupil-teachers ratio is less than the standard norm in Orissa. This might be due to the poor enrolment of students. As per 1991 Census, the percentages of population attending schools in the age-group 6-10 and 11-13 were 54.3 and 59.4 per cent respectively. On the other hand, the same respective figures at national level were 51.2 and 63.8.

Moreover, the dropout rate of students in Orissa is found to be very high. As per the calculation made by the office of the Director of Public Instructions, Bhubaneswar, the dropout rate of students at primary level in the year 1997-98 was 47 per cent. The dropout rate of girls was 50.5 per cent, which was more than the dropout rate of boys, i.e., 44.2 per cent. In the year 1988-89, the Planning, Monitoring and Statistics Division, Ministry of Human Resource Development (Department of Education), Government of India, New Delhi made the calculation of dropout rates of various states, and according to that calculation, the dropout rate at primary stage in Orissa was 38.97 per cent, which was less than the national average, i.e., 47.97 per cent. However, the result that has been achieved so far is not very encouraging.

14. Health Services

The health services in Orissa are not very satisfactory. The Government of Orissa has not met the criteria of the Central Government i.e., one sub-centre per 3000 population in tribal areas and one sub-centre per 5000 population in other areas, for providing health services to the people. The required number of sub-centres by 1991 was 6568 as against the existing 5927 number of sub-centres.

As on March 1997, the total number of Government medical institutions in Orissa was 1629 consisting of 3 medical college hospitals, 31 district headquarters hospitals, 21 sub-divisional hospitals and 1436 Community and Primary Health centres. The number of beds and doctors in the Government medical institutions were 13677 and 4888 respectively. The respective bed-population ratio and doctor-population ratio were found to be 1:2315 and 1:7255. in addition to the 1629 Government medical institutions, the number of Ayurvedic institutions in the state was 533, which includes 5 hospitals and 528 dispensaries in the year 1996-97. In the same year, the number of Homeopathic institutions was 467 consisting of 4 hospitals and 463 dispensaries.

Moreover, the per capita budgetary expenditure of the government in 1997-98 was Rs. 67.80, which was less than the per capita budgetary expenditure on health services at national level, i.e., Rs. 95.70.

15. Nutrition

The nutrition schemes like Anganwadi (ICDS) and Mid-day Meals are in operation in Orissa. The Anganwadi scheme is taking care of children below 6 years of age in the state. The basic objective of this scheme is to help child in its physical and mental growth. Cooked food is provided to the children under the scheme. In 1997-98, there were 28351 Anganwadi centres in the state with 1651.33 thousand beneficiaries getting nutritional benefit. An amount of Rs.51.74 crore was spent by the government on the Anganwadi centres for providing health care services covering supplementary nutrition, immunisation, pre-school education, health check-up, and health education to children of age group 0-6.

Mid-day Meals Scheme was launched in 1995 in the state. It was operating in 40697 primary schools covering 450045 number of students in 1998-99. The primary aim of the scheme is to increase enrolment, attendance and to reduce dropout rates in primary schools. Under the scheme, cooked food is given to students. The state government allotted Rs. 42.52 crore during 1997-98. However, the total expenditure was only Rs. 37.94 crore.

TAMIL NADU

1. Geographical Setting

Like Orissa, Tamil Nadu is also rural based and agriculture oriented sate, but it is considered as an advanced state of India. Geographically, the state is located in the southern most part of the Indian sub-continent. It lies between 8°. 5' and 13°. 35' North latitude and between 76°.15' to 80°.20' East longitudes. The total geographical area of the state is 130,058 sq.kms. which accounts for 4 per cent of the total geographical area of the Country. The state shares its boundaries with Kerala, Karnataka and Andhra Pradesh. The Indian ocean lies in its southern periphery and Bay of Bengal lies in its eastern periphery.

2. Administrative Structure

Tamil Nadu constitutes 29 revenue districts, 66 revenue divisions, 104 municipalities, 384 panchayat unions, 635 town panchayats, 12,584 village panchayats and 17,273 revenue villages. The state has 39 parliamentary constituencies and 235 assembly constituencies. There are 1189 police stations and 134 police outposts in the state to maintain the law and order situation.

3. Soil And Climate

Tamil Nadu also represents various types of soils such as red loamy (South Arcot, Salem, Dharmapuri, Coimbatore, Madurai, Thanyavur, etc.), Laterite soil (Nilgiri), black soil (Chengalpattu, South Arcot, North Arcot, Salem, Dharmapuri, Madurai, etc), Sandy coastal alluvium (Ramanthapuram, Nagapattinum, South Arcot, etc.), and red sandy soil (Coimbatore and Nilgiri). Tamil Nadu has a coastal belt full of water resources. Cauvery is the main source of water in the state.

As far as climatic condition is concerned, Tamil Nadu has four seasons, namely, South-west Monsoon, North-east Monsoon, winter and hot winter. The normal annual rainfall is 923 mm. The temperature in Tamil Nadu differs between plain areas and hill areas. In plain areas, the maximum temperature is 45.2° C and minimum is 11.9° C and, in the hill areas, the maximum temperature is 27.1°C and the minimum is 1.0° C.

4. Demographic Features

According to 1991 Census, the total population of Tamil Nadu was 5.59 crore, which was 4.84 crore in 1981 Census. The average annual growth rate of population was 1.43 per cent during the decade 1981-91. In the decade 1971-81, the average annual growth rate was 1.75 per cent. This indicates that population growth rate in the state decreased in the decade 1981-91 over the decade 1971-81. Thus, in terms of population, the number is much higher in Tamil Nadu than that in Orissa, but in terms of growth rate of population, the rate is comparatively much less in Tamil Nadu.

Out of the total population in the state, the percentages of male and female population in the state were 50.66 and 49.34 respectively. In Tamil Nadu, the sex ratio is 974 females per 1000 males as per 1991 Census, but it was 977 per 1000 males in 1981 Census. A comparison of both the states with regard to sex ratio indicates almost the same picture. According to 1991 Census, 65.85 per cent of the total population live in the rural areas and the rest 34.15 per cent live in the urban areas. As far as caste-wise distribution of population concerned, Tamil Nadu has 19.18 per cent of SC population and 1.03 per cent of ST population.

The number of total workers in the state as per 1991 Census was 24.19 millions consisting of 65.96 per cent males and 34.04 per cent females. Out of the total workers, the percentage shares of main and marginal workers were 94.23 and 5.77 per cent respectively. This shows that the percentage of main workers in Tamil Nadu is more than the national average. Further, cultivators, agricultural labourers and workers engaged in household industries constitute 23.41, 32.64 and 3.32 per cent of the total workers. Thus, cultivators and agricultural labourers together constitute 56.05 per cent. (Table-2.1). Regarding work participation rate, it is 43.31 per cent in Tamil Nadu, which is higher than the national average (37.46 per cent). The male and female work participation rates are 56.39 and 29.89 per cent respectively in the state. The sex-wise work participation rate is also higher in Tamil Nadu than the national average (51.55 per cent for males and 22.25 per cent for females).

5. Literacy Rate

Tamil Nadu is considered to be one of the highly literate states in the Country. As per 1991 Census, the literacy rate in the state was 62.66 per cent, which was much higher than the national literacy rate of 52.21 per cent. The sex-wise literacy rate indicates that the male literacy rate of the state was as high as 73.75 per cent and the female literacy rate was 51.33 per cent. The literacy rates of SC and ST were 46.24 per cent and 27.89 per cent respectively. Again, if we look at the rural and urban literacy rate, it was 54.59 per cent for rural areas and 77.99 per cent for urban areas (Table-2.2).

6. State Income and Poverty

In Tamil Nadu, the Net State Domestic Product (NSDP) at factor cost in the year 1995-96 was Rs. 5971809 lakh at current prices and the per capita NSDP was Rs. 10222/-. This indicates that the per capita NSDP in Tamil Nadu was more than the per capita Net National Product (Rs. 9578/-). On the other hand, the percentage of population living below the poverty line in the year 1993-94 was more or less same as the national average. It was 35.3 per cent in Tamil Nadu and 35.9 per cent in India. In the rural and urban areas of Tamil Nadu, the percentages of population living below the poverty line were 32.5 per cent and 39.8 per cent respectively.

7. Land Utilisation Pattern

Tamil Nadu had 13004 thousand hectares of geographical area out of which the forest land constituted only 16.48 per cent in the year 1995-96. The percentage of net area sown to total geographical area was 41.08 in the state. But the percentage of gross cropped area was 48.19 per cent indicating the fact that the percentage of area sown more than once was very less, i.e., 7.11 per cent (Table-2.3).

8. Land Holding and Land Operation

The total number of landholders in Tamil Nadu in 1990-91 was 79,98,932 possessing 74,73,677 hectares of land. This means the area per holding was 0.93 hectare. Again in Tamil Nadu, the percentages of marginal and small landholders were 73.11 per cent and 15.93 per cent respectively. Thus, the combined percentage share of marginal and small landholders was 89.04, which was more than that of Orissa. On the other hand, these marginal and small landholders accounted for only 52.35 per cent of the total operated land. The percentage shares of semi-medium, medium and large landholders were 7.72, 285 and 0.39 respectively (Table-2.4).

9. Agriculture

Like Orissa, agriculture in Tamil Nadu also plays a very important role. According 1996-97, agriculture and allied sector contributed 19 per cent to the State Domestic Product. The principal food crops that are produced in Tamil Nadu are rice, cholam, (jowar), cumbu (bajra), ragi, black gram, red gram and other pulses, and in non-food crops, the crops produced are groundnut, sesamum, coconut, cotton, sugarcane, chillies, etc. The total area under foodgrain production was 53.28 per cent of the total cropped area and, in the rest 46.72 per cent of the total cropped area, non-foodgrains were produced in the year 1995-96. In the foodgrain production, rice had maximum area, i.e., 31.13 per cent of the total cropped area. Similarly, in non-foodgrain, groundnut had maximum share of 14.89 per cent of the total cropped area. In Tamil Nadu, HYV seeds have been used quite impressively. The total area under HYV crops was 3100 thousand hectares in 1996-97, which was 48 per cent of the gross cropped area.

As far as yield rate is concerned, Tamil Nadu is far ahead of Orissa as well as the national average. The yield rate of foodgrains was 17.9 quintals per hectare as against the national yield rate of 16.00 quintals per hectare. Similarly, the yield rate of rice was 26.7 quintals per hectare, which was much higher than the national yield rate of 18.8 quintals per hectare.

The higher yield rate might be due to cultivation of HYV crops, better irrigation facilities and adequate use of fertilisers. The net area irrigated to net area sown in Tamil Nadu was 46.4 per cent in 1992-93, which was higher than the national average. The consumption of the fertilisers of gross cropped area in 1996-97 in the state was 114.8 kgs/hect, as against 77.5 kgs/hect. at national level.

10. Industry

Tamil Nadu is considered to be one of the highly industrialised states of India. By the end of 1993-94, the total number of registered factories in the state was 18099 with an investment of Rs. 41984.54 crore and employees of 1152.74 thousand. Regarding small-scale industries, there were 263845 number of registered small-scale industries in the state by 1996-97. The fixed capital on various assets put in operation in these units was Rs. 6395 crore, and the employment opportunities generated by the above industires were 25.22 lakh persons.

The data collected from the Annual Survey of Industries show that 13.21 per cent of the total all India factory workers were in Tamil Nadu in the year 1994-95. The per capita gross output in industires in the year 1993-94 was Rs. 10292.60, which was much higher than the national average (Rs. 5705.70). Similarly, the per capita value added by manufacturer in Tamil Nadu was Rs. 1995.80 as against the national average of Rs. 1195.30 in 1993-94.

11. Transport

Roads and railways are the major means of transportation in Tamil Nadu. The length of surface road per 1000 sq.km. of area in 1994-95 was 1064 km. in Tamil Nadu, which was almost 4 times that of Orissa. The percentage of villages connected with all weather roads in 1994-95 was 71 in the state as compared to 48 at the all India level. In 1993-94, the number of registered motor vehicles per 1000 persons was 37.16 in Tamil Nadu, which was higher than the national average.

The railway route length in the state per 1000 sq.kms. area and per one lakh population were 30.75 km. and 6.68 km. respectively in the year 1996-97. As far as the geographical area of the state is concerned, the state is well connected with railway lines.

12. Banking

The banking sector performance is much better in Tamil Nadu as compared to many other Indian states. The total number of banks in the state was 4642, which was 7.28 per cent of the total banks in the Country in 1996. As on March 1998, the population per bank was 12.9 thousand in Tamil Nadu, and this was less than the national average. This indicates that, in Tamil Nadu, the density of banks is higher than the national average. The credit deposit ratio as on March 1998 was 96.1 per cent, which was higher than the credit deposit ratio in the Country. Again, average per bank deposit and per bank credit in 1996-97 were Rs. 732 lakh and Rs. 707 lakh respectively in the state. This shows that Tamil Nadu is in a better position in the banking sector as compared to the national average.

13. Education

Tamil Nadu is considered to be one of the educationally advanced state of India. On education head, the Government of Tamil Nadu spent Rs. 1472.20 crore in 1992-93, which was more than two times of the total expenditure on education by Orissa Government. The percentage of educational expenditure to total governmental expenditure in 1994 in Tamil Nadu was 21.3 per cent. But educational expenditure as a percentage of State Domestic Product was 4.4 per cent. The per capita expenditure on education in 1995 was quite high in Tamil Nadu, i.e., Rs. 369/- (Table-2.5).

TABLE - 2.5

VARIOUS INDICATORS OF THE DEVELOPMENT OF EDUCATION IN ORISSA AND TAMIL NADU

Si. No	*Indicators*		*Orissa*	*Tamil Nadu*
1.	*2*		*3*	*4*
1.	No. of Primary Schools, 1997-98		42104	30796
2.	No. of Middle Schools, 1997-98		12406	5473
3.	No. of Students in Primary Schools, 1997-98 (in Thousand)		4005	4626
4.	No. of Students in Middle Schools, 1997-98 (in thousand)		1384	2576
5.	Pupil-teacher Ratio in Primary Schools, 1997-98		36.07	40.00
6.	Pumpil-Teacher Ratio in Middle Schools, 1997-98		34.00	40.00
7.	No. of Primary Schools per 1000 Population		1.33	0.55
8.	No. of Middle Schools per 1000 Population		0.39	0.10
9.	No. of Primary Schools per 100 sq.kms		27.04	23.68
10.	No. of Middle Schools per 100 sq.kms		7.97	4.21
11.	Percentage of Population attending schools in the age group 6-10, 1991 census	T	54.3	77.4
		M	60.6	79.8
		F	48.0	74.8
12.	Persentage of Population attending Schools in the age group 11-13, 1991 census	T	59.4	74.4
		M	69.2	79.9
		F	49.5	68.5
13.	Dropout Rate of Students at Primary level, 1997-98	T	47.0	15.09
		M	44.2	13.99
		F	50.5	16.18
14.	Per capita expenditure on education, 1995-96		Rs. 295.00	Rs.369.00
15.	Educational expenditure as a percentage of total governmental expenditure (1994)		19.8	21.3
16.	Educational expenditure as a percentage of State Domestic Product (1994)		5.4	4.4

Note: T= Total, M=Male and F= Female

Source: 1) SL.No. 1 to 10, collected and complied from the data in Economic Survey of Orissa (1998-99) for Orissa and for Tamil Nadu, School Education Policy Note on Demand No. 17-Education, 1999-2000, Govt. of Tamil Nadu.
2) SL. No. 11 and 12, Census of India, Bhubaneswar Office.
3) SL..No. 13, for Orissa, DPI Office, Bhubaneswar and, for Tamil Nadu, Office of the Director of Elementary Education, Chennai.
4) SL.No. 14, Statistical Outline of Orissa (1997), Directorate of Economics and Statistics, Bhubaneswar.
5) SL.No. 15 and 16, India, Ministry of Human Resources Development, 1995.

The number of primary and middle schools in the state were 30796 and 5473 respectively in 1997-98. Further, in 1995-96 the number of high schools, higher secondary schools and general colleges were 3419, 2490 and 280 respectively. The number of students per teacher in primary and middle schools are same, i.e., 40. Population-wise the number of primary and middle schools in Tamil Nadu were 0.55 and 0.1 per thousand population respectively. But the number of primary schools per 100 sq.km. of area was 23.68 and, in case of middle schools it was 4.21 (Table-2.5).

With regard to the enrolment of students, the position of Tamil Nadu is much better. As per 1991 Census, the percentage of population attending schools in the age-group 6-10 was 77.4. which was more than the national average of 11-13, the percentage of population attending school was 74.4 as against 63.8 at national level. Further, the dropout rate of primary school students in Tamil Nadu was very less, i.e., 15.05 per cent in 1997-98. The estimate of Human Resource Development Department also shows that the dropout rate in the state in 1988-89 was less, i.e., 21.41 per cent, whereas, the same at national level was 47.93 per cent.

14 Health Services

The position of Tamil Nadu in health services is found to be much better. The government of Tamil Nadu has already met the government of India norm of one Primary Health centre for every 30-thousand/20-thousand population in the plain/hill areas and one health sub-centre for every 5-thousand/3-thousand population in the plain/hill areas.

In the year 1996-97, the state had 23 district hospitals, 138 taluk hospitals, 69 non-taluk hospitals, 1420 Primary Health centres including 68 Community Health centres and 8682 health sub-centres. The total number of allopathic medical institutions in the state was 10,664. The number of population per bed and per doctor were 1:1341 and 1:7124 respectively. Further, the number of homeopathic institutions was 34 consisting of 1 hospital and 33 dispensaries. With regard to Ayurvedic institutions, the number was 475, which includes to 2 hospitals and 473 dispensaries.

The per capita budgetary expenditure of the state government on health services in 1997-98 was Rs. 116.70. As compared to national average (Rs. 95.70), the per capita expenditure on health services in Tamil Nadu was found to be more.

15. Nutrition

Nutrition schemes like Balwadi, Anganwadi and Noon-meal are operating in Tamil Nadu. The main objective of Anganwadi scheme in the state is to improve the nutritional and health status of children in the age-group 0-3 years. On the other hand, the objective of Balwadi scheme in the state is to provide all the basic amenities necessary for the physical and mental development of a child of 0-5 years of age. In the year 1999-2000, the total number of Anganwadi centres in the state was 10,477.

The Noon-meal scheme has been launched by the state Government since 1982. Tamil Nadu is the first Indian state to start this programme for school going children. The total number of schools covered under the scheme was 39,517 in 1995-96 and the total number of students covered was 43,29,226 by the year 1998-89.

Tamil Nadu Government has a separate budgetary provision for nutrition on social services head. During the year 1996-97, the total budgetary provision on nutrition was Rs. 406.59 crore, which was 2.97 per cent of the total budgetary provision of the state.

The analysis of the socio-economic profile of Orissa and Tamil Nadu show that Tamil Nadu is comparatively more advanced not only in the field of education but also in the fields like agriculture, industry, transport, banking and health services. Similarly, the work participation rate, literacy rate and per capita NSDP in Tamil Nadu are much more than that of Orissa. The poverty ratio in Orissa is very high as compared to Tamil Nadu. So, it would be very interesting to make a comparative study of Mid-day Meals Scheme between a backward state Orissa and an advanced state Tamil Nadu.

Section-II

This part of the chapter deals with the various socio-economic profile of different districts and blocks covered under the study in both the states viz., Orissa and Tamil Nadu.

PROFILE OF THE STUDY AREAS (ORISSA)

1. Districts Profile

This part of the chapter deals with the various socio-economic profile of different districts and blocks covered under the study in both the states viz., Orissa and Tamil Nadu. The socio-economic profile of the two sample districts in Orissa indicates that there is a great deal of disparities and difference among the various indicators in the two districts.

Puri is a coastal district of Orissa, located in the eastern part of the state. It is situated nearly 60 kms away from the state capital Bhubaneswar. The total geographical area of the district is 3051 sq.kms. The district has 1 subdivision and 11 blocks. On the other hand, Rayagada is a hilly district full of mountains and forests, and is situated in the southern part of Orissa. The total geographical area of the district is 7584 sq.kms. There are 2 sub-divisions and 11 blocks in the district. Puri is situated in the alluvial plain with a forest coverage of 0.18 per cent of the state's total forest area. The forest area in Rayagada is 7.01 per cent of the state's total forest area.

According to 1991 Census, Puri has a total population of 13.5 lakhs with 50.77 per cent males and 49.23 per cent females. While Rayagada, in the said year, had a total population of 7.14 lakhs with 49.71 per cent males and 50.29 per cent females. The density of population in 1991 in Rayagada was 94 per sq.km and, in Puri, it was 427 per sq.km This clearly indicates that Puri is a more thickly populated district than Rayagada. As per 1991 Census the sex ratio in Puri was 970 as against 1012 in Rayagada.

So far as SC and ST population are concerned, the proportion was 18.83 per cent in Puri district as against 70.37 per cent in Rayagada district. There is, thus, a larger concentration of SC and ST population in Rayagada district as compared to Puri district. Being tribal dominated block, Rayagada district needs more welfare schemes to support its population.

The rural-urban population distribution indicates that there is not much difference among the two districts in terms of percentage of urban population to total population. In 1991, Puri had 12.52 per cent of the population living in urban areas, whereas, in Rayagada, 12.51 per cent of the total population lived in urban areas.

On the literacy front, Puri district is far ahead of Rayagada district. According to 1991 Census, Puri had a literacy rate of 63.30 per cent, which was one amongst the highest in the state. On the other hand, the literacy rate in Rayagada was only 26.01 per cent. In Puri district, the male literacy rate was 76.83 per cent and female literacy rate was 49.41 per cent, and the literacy rates among SC and ST population were 42.51 per cent and 38.94 per cent respectively. On the other hand, in Rayagada, the male literacy rate was 36.53 per cent and female literacy rate was 15.63 per cent. The literacy rate among SC and ST population in Rayagada was 21.46 per cent and 10.39 per cent respectively. These figures clearly indicate that Rayagada is an educationally backward district of the state.

The land use pattern of the two districts shows a remarkable difference. Out of the total land area of 2.71 lakh hectares in Puri district, 1.35 lakh hectares (49.9 per cent) represent the net area sown. Similarly, in Rayagada, out of the total land area of 5.03 lakh hectares, 1.20 lakh hectares (24.0 per cent) are net area sown according to 1994-95 data.

On the irrigation front, Puri is much better placed than Rayagada. During 1994-95, Puri had 1.84 lakh hectares of irrigated land as against only 45 thousand hectares of irrigated land in Rayagada.

In 1995-96, the yield rate of paddy crops in Puri district was 22.21 kg per hectare (for Satyabadi block and Puri Sadar block it was 18.91 and 18.68 kg/hectare respectively). On the other hand, in Rayagada district the yield rate was 25.16 kg per hectare (for Kolnara and Rayagada block it was 25.25 and 30.09 kg/hectare respectively). This indicates that the yield rate in Rayagada per hectare is higher than Puri. But the production of paddy crops in quintals was much higher in Puri (27.6 lakh quintals) than Rayagada (10.9 lakh quintals)

As far as industrial development is concerned, Puri lags a behind Rayagada in terms of productive capital investment, employment opportunities created and net value added by manufacture. In the year 1994-95, there were 25 industrial units in Puri with 486 employees, Rs. 37,388 thousand productive capital investment and Rs. 37,772 thousand net value added by manufacture. During the same period. Rayagada had 20 Industrial units with 4681 employees and Rs. 25,61,006 thousand productive capital investment and Rs. 8,28,611 thousand net value added by manufacture. Thus Puri stands far behind Rayagada in industrial front.

The number of students admitted to primary schools in the year 1998-99 in Puri was 1.88 lakh students. On the other hand, in Rayagada, total students admitted in the same year was 74 thousand.

In the year 1998-99, Puri district had 1443 number of primary schools as against 1323 in Rayagada district. The number of teachers in Puri was 2701 and, in Rayagada, it was 3231 teachers. Similarly, the number of teachers per school in Puri was 1.87 whereas, in Rayagada it was 2.44 only. Again the teacher-pupil ratio in Puri district was 69.44 students per teacher, and in Rayagada district the number of students per teacher was 23.00 only.

TABLE - 2.6

DISTRIBUTION OF SCHOOLS PER 1000 POPULATION AND PER 100 SQ.KM OF AREA IN PURI AND RAYAGADA DISTRICTS OF ORISSA, 1998-98

District	*Number of Primary Schools Per 1000 population*	*Number of Primary Schools per 100 sq.km*
PURI	1.11	47.3
RAYAGADA	1.85	17.44

Source: Compiled from data collected from DPI Office, Bhubaneswar.

The figures in Table 2.6 indicate that, as far as density of primary schools per 1000 population is considered, Rayagada is ahead of Puri. But if the number of schools per 100 sq.km of area is taken into consideration then Puri is ahead of Rayagada by a great margin. Further, the educational infrastructural facilities available in Puri are better than that of Rayagada, which explains the high literacy rate in the district.

2. Block Profile

The two blocks selected in Puri and Rayagada also exhibit different socio-economic traits.

In Puri district, Puri Sadar block (educationally advanced) has a geographical area of 260.82 sq. kms. and Satyabadi block has a geographical area of 183.09 sq. kms. On the other hand, in Rayagada district, Rayagada block has a geographical area of 531.25 sq.kms, whereas, Kolnara block has total geographical area of 365.63 sq.kms.

According to 1991 Census, Puri Sadar block had a total population of 1.15 lakhs which included 59 thousand males (51.00 per cent) and 56 thousand females (49.00 per cent). Similarly in Satyabadi block, the total population during the same period was 92 thousand including 47 thousand males (50.82 per cent) and 45 thousand (49.18 per cent) females. On the other hand, in Rayagada block, in the same period, the total population was 80 thousand, out of which the male and female population were 39 thousands (49.08 per cent) and 41 thousands (50.92 per cent) respectively. Further, in Kolnara block the total population was 59 thousand, out of which male and female population were 29 thousand (49.50 per cent) and 30 thousand (50.50 per cent)respectively. The above figures indicate that in both the blocks of Puri, the number of female population is less than that of male population, whereas, the reverse is true in case of Rayagada district. The sex ratio in Puri Sadar block was 961 and in Satyabadi block it was 968 in 1991 Census. On the other hand, in Rayagada block it was 1037, and in Kolnara block it was 1020.

As far as density of population is concerned, Puri is far ahead of Rayagada district. The block figures indicate that, in Puri Sadar block, the density of population was 441 per sq. km and, in Satyabadi block, it was 500 per sq. km. On the other hand, in Rayagada block it was only 150 per sq. km and in Kolnara block, it was 166 per sq. km as against the district average of 94 per sq. km.

The caste-wise distribution of population indicates that, in both the blocks of Rayagada district, there is a large concentration of backward caste population. On the other hand, in both the blocks of Puri district there is the preponderance of other caste population. In Puri Sadar block, the share of SC and ST population was 17.65 per cent of the total population and the other caste population was 82.35 per cent of the total population. Similarly in Satyabadi block, the total share of SC and ST population was 20.38 per cent of the total population and the rest 79.61 per cent belonged to other caste population. Moreover, in Rayagada block, the share of SC and ST population was 84.98 per cent of the total population and the rest 15.02 per cent was other caste population. In Kolnara block, 77.88 per cent of the total population belonged to SC and ST caste and the rest 22.12 per cent belonged to other caste population.

As far as literacy rate is concerned, Puri Sadar block had a total literacy rate of 56.80 per cent (SC— 32.98 per cent, ST— 19.50 per cent). Similarly in Satyabadi block, the total literacy rate was 65.43 per cent (SC— 43.78 per cent, ST—34.60 per cent). On the other hand, in Rayagada block, the literacy rate was 15.90 per cent (SC—17.81 per cent, ST—8.23 per cent) and, in Kolnara block, literacy rate was 26.03 per cent (SC—28.26 per cent, ST— 13.60 per cent).

On the education front, in Puri Sadar block in the year 1998-99, the total number of primary schools was 116 with 16887 number of students and 298 teachers. In the same period, Satyabadi block had 96 schools with 11292 students and 263 number of teachers. On the other hand,. in Rayagada block during the same period, there were 167 primary schools with 10679 students and 294 teachers and in Kolnara block there were 117 primary schools with 5847 students and 280 teachers.

TABLE-2.7

DISTRIBUTION OF SCHOOLS, STUDENTS AND TEACHERS IN THE SAMPLE BLOCKS OF PURI AND RAYAGADA DISTRICTS, 1998-99

Sl. No.	*Name of Blocks*	*Teacher-pupil ratio in Primary Schools*	*No of Primary Schools per 100 sq.km*	*No of Primary Schools per 1000 Population*
1.	Satyabadi	43	52	1.05
2.	Puri Sadar	57	44	1.009
3.	Kolnara	21	33	1.97
4.	Rayagada	36	31	2.09

Source: Compiled from the data collected from the respective block offices.

Table 2.7 reveals that both the blocks in Rayagada show a better picture than the blocks in Puri as far teacher-pupil ratio, number of primary schools per 100 sq. km and schools per 1000 population are concerned.

Lack of infrastructural facilities in the schools at primary level reduces the quality of education in the blocks of Rayagada. However, compared to Rayagada, infrastructure facilities in Puri are somewhat contributing better towards improvement in the quality of education.

PROFILE OF THE STUDY AREAS (TAMIL NADU)

1. District Profile

Like Orissa, the sample districts in Tamil Nadu, viz., Madurai and Villupuram, show differences in the socio-economic characteristics.

Madurai district is located in the southern part of the state. The district has a total geographical area of 6565 sq. kms. On the other hand, Villupuram district is located in the north-eastern part of the state. This is a coastal district with a total geographical area of 7595 sq. kms.

According to 1991 Census, Madurai district had a total population, the percentage of males was 50.91 per cent and females was 49.09 per cent. The district has less percentage of backward caste population. The combined SC and ST population in 1991 was 5 lakhs, which was 14.27 per cent of the total population.

On the other hand, in Villupuram district, the total population was 28 lakhs. Out of this the percentages of males and females were 50.79 and 49.21 respectively. Unlike Madurai district, Villupuram has a higher percentage of backward caste population. The combined SC and ST population in the district was 8.0 lakhs, which was 29.04 per cent of the total population. Table 2.8 gives a detailed caste-wise distribution of population in both the districts.

TABLE-2.8

CASTE-WISE DISTRIBUTION OF POPULATION IN MADURAI AND VILLUPURAM DISTRICTS OF TAMIL NADU, 1991 CENSUS

(Figures in Percentages)

DISTRICT	*SC*	*ST*	*OTHERS*
MADURAI	14.60	0.37	85.03
VILLUPURAM	27.27	1.77	70.96

Source: Census of India, 1991.

The sex ratios in both the districts depict almost a similar situation. In Madurai district it was 964 and in Villupuram district it was 968 females per 1000 males. As far as density of population is concerned. Madurai has a higher density of population as compared to Villupuram district. In the year 1991, the density of population in Madurai district was 525 persons per sq. km. as against 363 persons per sq. km in Villupuram district.

As per 1991 Census, Madurai district has a total working population of 15.18 lakhs, which was 43.99 per cent of the total population. Out of the total working population, 9.80 lakhs (64.5 per cent) were male working population and 5.8 lakhs (35.5 per cent) were female workers. The male and female work participation rate were

55.78 per cent and 31.77 per cent respectively. On the other hand, in Villupuram district the working population in 1991 was 12.50 lakhs, which was 36.23 per cent of the total population. In Villupuram district, out of the total working population, 7.73 lakhs (61.86 per cent) were male workers and 4.77 lakhs (38.14 per cent) were female workers. This indicates that in Villupuram 55.24 per cent and among females it was 35.16 per cent. The work paticipation rate among males was 55.24 per cent and among females it was 35.16 per cent. This indicates that in Villupuram district, the female work participation rate is higher than that of Madurai district.

As far as occupational distribution of population is concerned, the 1991 Census data reveal that, in Madurai district, 14.55 lakhs (95.86 per cent) of the total workers were main workers and the rest 63 thousands (4.14 per cent) were marginal workers. Similarly, in Villupuram district, in the same year 11.42 lakhs (91.39 per cent) of the total workers were main workers and the rest 1.08 lakhs (8.61 per cent) were marginal workers. The above figures indicate that in Villupuram the percentage of marginal workers was higher than that of Madurai district.

In Madurai district, the total forest coverage during 1995-96 was 13.56 per cent of the total land area as against only 9.93 per cent in Villupuram district. In the same year, the net area sown in Madurai district was 1,62,776 hectares i.e., 43.50 per cent of the total land mass as against 3,68,065 hectares i.e., 50.96 per cent of the total land mass.

On the literacy front, the two districts Madurai and Villupuram exhibit wider variations. According to 1991 Census, in Madurai district, the total literacy rate was 66.44 per cent as against only 48.36 per cent in Villupuram district. The male and female literacy rate in Madurai district were 77.74 per cent and 54.74 per cent respectively as against 60.92 per cent male and 35.38 per cent female literacy rate in Villupuram district. A comparison of the two districts indicates that both in terms of male as well as female literacy rates, Madurai is far ahead of Villupuram district.

Moreover, according to 1998-99 data, Madurai district had a total number of 1038 primary schools with 1,75,562 number of students.On the other hand, in Villupuram district during the same period, there were 1697 primary schools with 3,24,279 students. Table 2.9 shows that Villupuram district is ahead of Madurai district in terms of number of primary schools per 1000 population and per 100 sq. kms of area. However, so far as the quality of education, the infrastructure facilities and the awareness about education among general public are concerned, Villupuram district is lagging far behind Madurai district.

TABLE-2.9

DISTRIBUTION OF SCHOOLS PER 1000 POPULATION AND PER 100 SQ.KM OF AREA IN MADURAI AND VILLUPURAM DISTRICTS OF TAMIL NADU, 1998-99

District	*No of Schools (primary) per 1000 population*	*No. of Schools (primary) per 100 sq.km.*
Madurai	.30	15.80
Villupuram	.62	22.34

Source: *Compiled from the data collected from the District Elementary* Education Office of the respective districts.

2. Block Profile

The two sample blocks selected in each district of Tamil Nadu also depict wide variations in terms of population, literacy rate as well as on the education front.

In Madurai district, the two blocks selected are Madurai East and Alanganuller block. The Madurai East block has a total geographical area of 199.21 sq.kms. as against 160.05 sq. kms. of total geographical area in Alanganuller block. In Villupuram, the two blocks selected are Koliyanur and Thirunavalur blocks. The total geographical areas of the two blocks are 197.05 sq. km. and 186.00 sq. kms. respectively.

According to 1991 Census data, Madurai East block had a total population of 1.22 lakhs, which was 3.54 per cent of the district's total population. Similarly Alanganuller block had a total population of 96 thousands which was 2.78 per cent of the total population of the district. The caste-wise distribution of population indicates that the combined SC and ST population in both the blocks of Madurai district was almost same. In Madurai East block, the combined SC and ST population accounted for 20.21 per cent of the total block population. Similarly in Alanganuller, it was 21.55 per cent of the total block population. But in absolute figures, Madurai East block had a higher SC and ST population than Alanganuller block.

On the other hand, in Villupuram district, Koliyanur block had a total population of 1.27 lakhs (4.61 per cent of the district population) and Thirunavalur block had a total population of 99 thousands (3.60 per cent of the total district population). The caste-wise analysis indicates that Thirunavalur has a higher percentage of SC and ST population as compared to Koliyanur block. The combined SC and ST population in Thirunavalur was 30.96 per cent of the total population of the block, while that of Koliyanur block was 26.30 per cent of the total population of the block. The above analysis clearly indicates that the selected blocks in Villupuram district have a higher SC and ST population than the sample blocks of Madurai district.

The sex ratios in all the blocks of both the districts depict a similar picture. In Madurai East block and Alanganuller block the ratios were 973 and 971 respectively, and in Koliyanur and Thirunavalur block, the respective ratio were 970 and 971 females per 100 males.

As far as density of population is concerned, in Madurai East block it was 614 per sq. kms. and in Alanganuller block it was 599 per sq. km. On the other hand, in Koliyanur block it was 646 and in Thirunavalur block it was 533 per sq. km. The data clearly indicates that the advanced block, of both the districts have a higher density of population than the backward blocks of the districts. Again, among the advanced blocks, Koliyanur block has a higher density of population than Madurai East Block.

With regard to literacy rate, in Tamil Nadu like Orissa, all the blocks show more disparities in literacy rates. In Madurai East Block, the total literacy rate was 62.06 per cent. In this the male literacy rate was much higher at 74.02 per cent than female literacy rate of 49.86 per cent. Similarly in Alanganuller block, the literacy rate was

56.35 per cent with a male literacy rate of 69.60 per cent and female literacy rate of 42.73 per cent. The caste-wise analysis of literacy rates in both the blocks indicates that the literacy rate among ST population is higher in both the blocks than that of SC literacy rate. In Madurai East block SC and ST literacy rates were 42.40 per cent and 52.17 per cent respectively and, in Alanganuller block, SC literacy rate was 44.16 per cent and ST literacy rate was 56.50 per cent. A comparison of both the blocks indicates that the literacy rate among backward caste (SC & ST) is higher in the backward block of Alanganuller. However, the overall literacy rate of all castes is higher in Madurai East block.

On the other hand, in Koliyanur block of Villupuram district, the literacy rate was 54.36 per cent with 67.56 per cent male literacy rate and 40.73 per cent female literacy rate. Similarly in Thirunavalur block, the total literacy rate was as low as 40.23 per cent with 54.36 per cent male literacy rate and only 25.69 per cent female literacy rate. The caste-wise analysis of literacy rates in the two blocks of Villupuram district depicts a complete different picture than that of the sample blocks of Madurai district. In both Koliyanur and Thirunavalur blocks, the SC literacy rates are higher than that of ST literacy rates, whereas, the reverse is true in case of the sample blocks of Madurai district. In Koliyanur block, SC literacy rate was 41.27 per cent as against 32.71 per cent of ST literacy rate. Similarly in Thirunavalur block, SC literacy rate was 28.37 per cent as against 21.09 per cent ST literacy rate. So from literacy point of view both the blocks of Madurai district stand far ahead of its counterpart in Villupuram district.

On the education front, in Madurai East block in the year 1998-99, there were 78 primary schools with a total number of 17760 students and 196 teachers. In Alanganuller block. in the same year there were 54 primary schools with 11682 students and 279 teachers. On the other hand, in Koliyanur blcok of Villupuram district there were 76 primary schools with 12279 students and 333 teachers and, in Thirunavalur block, there were 89 primary schools with 11527 students and 238 teachers.

Table 2.10 gives a comparative picture of all the sample blocks in Tamil Nadu with respect to the teacher-pupil ratio, number of primary schools per 100 sq. kms. and number of primary schools per 1000 population. It can be observed from the table that there is not much variation so far as the education indicators of all the blocks are concerned except in Madurai East block, where the teacher-pupil ratio is as high as 90.61 and, in Thirunavalur block, where the number of primary schools per 1000 population is as high as 0.90. In respect of all other indicators, it is more or less same in all the blocks. However, a close observation of the available data reveal that literacy rates are much lower in both the blocks of Villupuram district compared to that of Madurai district.

TABLE - 2.10

DISTRIBUTION OF NUMBER OF SCHOOLS PER 1000 POPULATION AND PER 100 SQ. KM. OF AREA IN THE SAMPLE BLOCKS OF MADURAI AND VILLUPURAM DISTRICTS OF TAMIL NADU, 1998-99

Blocks	*Teacher-pupil raio in Primary Schools*	*No. of Primary Schools per 100 sq. km.*	*No. of Primary Schools per 1000 Population*
Madurai East	90.61	39.15	0.64
Alanganullar	41.87	33.74	0.56
Koliyanur	36.87	38.57	0.60
Thirunavalur	48.43	47.85	0.90

Source : Data compiled and collected from the Elementary Education Office of the respective blocks.

Thus, the profile of the sample districts and blocks of Orissa and Tamil Nadu show that there is a great deal of disparities and differences in the performances of the various socio-economic indicators in the sample areas. The districts/blocks, which are backward from literacy point of view, are also backward in other counts. The opposite is the case for educationally advanced districts/blocks.

Section-III

CHARACTERISTIC FEATURES OF SAMPLE RESPONDENTS

1. Students

The total number of sample students interviewed was 100 in each state, viz., Orissa and Tamil Nadu. Since, a total number of 20 schools were surveyed in each state, therefore 5 students were selected from each school on the basis of random sampling.

In Orissa, out of the 100 students interviewed, 23 students belonged to the age-group of 5 to 9 years, 55 belonged to the age-group of 9 to 11 years and the rest 22 belonged to 11 and above age group. Similarly, in Tamil Nadu, 56 students belonged to the age-group of 5 to 9 years, 38 students belonged to 9 to 11 years and the rest 6 students belonged to the age group of 11 years and above.

Out of the 100 students interviewed in Orissa, 12 belonged to class I, 9 belonged to class II, 25 belonged to class III, 16 belonged to class IV, and the rest 38 belonged to class V. Similarly in Tamil Nadu, 16 belonged to class I, 7 belonged to class II, 31 belonged to class III, 15 belonged to class IV and 31 belonged to class V.

The caste-wise distribution of student respondents indicates that, equal weightage was given to all students irrespective of castes and sexes both in Orissa and Tamil Nadu. In Orissa the number of SC, ST and other caste students interviewed was 25,32 and 43. Similarly, in Tamil Nadu, 42 SC students, 2 ST students and 56 other caste students were interviewed. Further, out of the total students in Orissa, 61 per cent were boys and 39 per cent were girls. Similarly, in Tamil Nadu, 59 per cent were boys and 41 per cent were girl students.

Moreover in Orissa, out of the 100 students interviewed, 51 per cent of the students belonged to the family having monthly income of below Rs. 1250/- and the rest 49 per cent belonged to the income level higher than Rs. 1250/- per month. On the other hand, in Tamil Nadu 63 per cent belonged to the family having monthly income of below Rs. 1250/- and the rest 37 per cent belonged to income higher than Rs. 1250/- per month.

2. Parents

Just like the case of students, the total number of sample parents interviewed was 100 in each state, of Orissa and Tamil Nadu. The respective parents of each student selected were interviewed during the fieldwork.

In Orissa, out of the 100 parents interviewed, 25 parents belonged to the age-group of 18 to 26 years, 56 belonged to the age-group of 26 to 42 years and the rest 19 belonged to the age group of 42 and above. Similarly, in Tamil Nadu, 31 parents belonged to the age group of 18 to 26 years, 56 belonged to 26 to 42 years and rest 13 belonged to the age group of 42 years and above. The caste-wise distribution of parent respondents indicates that, in Orissa, the number of SC, ST and other caste parents interviewed was 25, 32 and 43 respectively. Similarly in Tamil Nadu, 42 SC, 2 ST and 56 other caste parents were interviewed.

While conducting the field survey the data relating to literacy level, occupation of parents and their economic conditions was collected since these are the factors that have maximum influence on the education of the child. In Orissa, out of the 100 parents interviewed, 40 per cent were illiterate, 34 per cent were literate up to middle level and the rest 26 per cent had made it to the high school and college level. Similarly in Tamil Nadu, 49 per cent were illiterate, 31 per cent were literate up to middle level and the rest 20 per cent were literate up to the high school and college level.

As far as occupations of the selected parents are concerned, in Orissa, 24 per cent belonged to farming, 11 per cent belonged to business, 8 per cent belonged to service, 40 per cent belonged to labour class and the rest 17 per cent belonged to other activities like housewife, cooking etc. Similarly, in Tamil Nadu, 12 per cent were engaged in farming, 4 per cent in business, 1 per cent in service, 62 per cent in labour work and the rest 21 per cent in activities like housewife, weaving, etc. Again, out of the total parents interviewed in Orissa, 51 per cent had a monthly family income of below Rs.

1250/- and the rest 49 per cent had a family income above Rs. 1250/ per month. Similarly in Tamil Nadu, 63 per cent of parents had a family income below Rs. 1250/- per month and the rest 37 per cent had a monthly income of above Rs.1250/-.

3. Teachers

A total number of 20 teachers (one from each sample school) were interviewed in each state. All the teachers selected both in Orissa and in Tamil Nadu belonged to the age group of 30 to 50 years of age. In Orissa, out of the 20 teachers interviewed, 16 were males and 4 were females. Similarly, in Tamil Nadu, 11 male teachers and 9 female teachers were interviewed. Further, out of the 20 teacher interviewed in Orissa, 75 per cent had high school level qualification along with other professional training, 15 per cent were graduates with professional training, and 10 per cent were post-graduates with professional training Similarly, in Tamil Nadu, 50 per cent of the teachers had SSLC qualifications, 15 per cent had PUC qualification, 10 per cent were graduates and 25 per cent were post-graduates along with other professional training.

4. Panchayat Representatives

During the field survey,. 20 panchayats were covered in each state. For each sample school, one representative (sarapanch or ward member) was interviewed. In Orissa, out of the 20 panchayat representatives, 60 per cent belonged to the age group of 20 to 40 years and the rest 40 per cent were in the age group of 40 years and above. Similarly, in Tamil Nadu, 30 per cent belonged to 20 to 40 years of age and the rest 70 per cent belonged to 40 years and above. The caste-wise distribution of these respondents indicate that, both in Orissa and in Tamil Nadu,. 40 per cent of them belonged to backward castes (SC and ST) and 60 per cent belonged to other castes. As far as educational qualifications of these respondents are concerned, in Orissa, 10 per cent of these respondents were illiterates, 25 per cent had middle education, 45 per cent had high school education and the rest 20 per cent had college level education. On the other hand, in Tamil Nadu 25 per cent were literates up to middle level education, 65 per cent up to high school level and the rest 10 per cent were college level literate.

5. Educated Villagers

A total number of 20 educated villagers were selected in each of the states on the basis of random sampling. While selecting their respondents, their educational qualifications were given more importance along with other factors. In Orissa, out of the 20 educated villagers interviewed, 60 per cent belonged to the age group 20 to 40 years and the rest 40 per cent belonged to the age group of 40 years and above. Similarly, in Tamil Nadu, 80 per cent belonged to 20 to 40 years of age and the rest 20 per cent belonged to the age group of 40 and above. The caste-wise distribution of educated villagers shows that, in Orissa, 45 per cent of the respondents belonged to backward castes (SC+ST) and the rest 55 per cent belonged to other castes. Similarly in Tamil Nadu, 40 per cent belonged to backward castes (BC+MBC) and 60 per cent belonged to other castes. Moreover, 55 per cent of the educated villagers in Orissa had high school level education and the rest 45 per cent had college level education. On the other hand, in Tamil Nadu, 20 per cent had high school and 80 per cent had college level education.

6. NGO/Social Workers

Like educated villagers and panchayat representatives, NGO/ social workers were also interviewed from the area where the sample schools was located both in Orissa and Tamil Nadu. A total number of 20 NGO/social workers were selected from each state randomly.

The age-wise distribution of the NGO/social workers indicates that both in Orissa and Tamil Nadu, 55 per cent of the workers belonged to 20 to 40 years of age and the rest 45 per cent belonged to 40 year and above age group. In Orissa, 35 per cent of the workers belonged to backward castes (SC and ST) and the rest belonged to other castes and,. in Tamil Nadu, 55 per cent belonged to backward castes (BC+MBC) and 45 per cent belonged to other castes. As far as educational qualifications of these workers are concerned, in Orissa, 40 per cent of the workers had high school level education and the rest 60 per cent had college level education. On the other hand, in Tamil Nadu, 45 per cent had high school level education and the rest 55 per cent had college level education.

7. Officials

20 officials involved in the operation of Mid-day Meals Scheme either directly or indirectly were selected on the basis of random sampling method from each state. From each sample district, 10 officials were interviewed. The opinions of the officials regarding operation, management, administration, etc. of the scheme were given due importance in the course of analysis.

CHAPTER-3

EVOLUTION, STRUCTURE, ORGANISATION AND OPERATION OF MID-DAY MEALS SCHEME

Childhood is a period of rapid physical and mental growth and development. Children are building up new tissues constantly and replacing old ones. Their nutritional requirements are higher per unit of body weight than those of adults. Good food, adequate in quality and quantity, is essential to stimulate and maintain their growth. If children do not receive the nourishment they need, undernutrition and malnutrition of some kind or other will inevitably result, depending on the type and quantity of nutrients lacking in the diet. A malnourished child is dull, restless, unhappy, irritable and listless. Malnutrition not only affects health of children but also their attendance and performance in the school. Hungry and malnourished children do not learn or learn badly.

Realising these staggering dimensions of the malady of malnutrition in childhood, Governments worldwide have embarked on several nutrition and health intervention programmes. One such programme is the widely operating school lunch or Mid-day Meals programme. The effort in this direction of providing free lunch to the children in schools is not of recent origin. It dates back to 1865, when Frenchman Victor Hugo started the scheme in France on a free and payment basis. In 1868 it was enacted that all communities in France should establish school fund committees to provide meals for the poor and needy children. The school lunch programme was developed rapidly in England in the 1900's. The first "School Meals Act" was passed in the year 1906. Countries like U.S.A (1946), Indonesia (1969), China (1957), Ireland (1933), Japan (1889), and England (1900) also gave priority to the Mid-day Meals programme in their respective countries. But the real fight against malnutrition gained its momentum during and after the Second World War.

Studies in India confirm that malnutrition is prevalent among school children belonging to poor and rural population. It is in this background, measures to enhance the nutritional status of school-age children gained popularity in India. The pride of starting the free Mid-day Meals scheme in the elementary schools in the country goes to Madras Corporation. The scheme was started as a humble measure in Madras City tu feed 500 children in the year 1925. But it was K. Kamraj, the late Chief Minister of Tamil Nadu, who had the distinction of introducing the scheme in Tamil Nadu as early as 1956 for the first time in independent India. But the real fight against mal-nutrition took acceleration during the late 50's and early 60's. When most of the Indian states, like Karnataka (1961), Orissa (1959), Kerala, Punjab, Rajasthan, Andhra Pradesh (1962), M.P (1965), and Bihar (1968), etc. adopted the scheme as part of their educational system.

Initially in most of the states, the scheme was running through organisations like CARE and UNICEF, who used to supply Bolgar, Wheat/Balahar, Milk powder, Corn powder, Wheat flour, Jaggery, etc. They covered only the children of school age population Though the scheme was not very popular, but that was the only concrete step taken towards fighting malnutrition at national level till 1995 when the present type of Mid-day Meals Scheme was launched.

Malnutrition not only prevails among school age children but also amongst the pre-school age children (0-6 years of age). Children of this age group are most vulnerable and require a iot of care and attention. Since there was no such programme to take care of the children of this age group, the Government of India launched schemes like I.C.D.S. (Anganwadi), Nos-I.C.D.S. (Balwadi) to take care of children of this age group. Anganwadi scheme covered the age group of 0-3 years and Balwadi covered the age group of 0-6 years. But in some states like Orissa where Balwadi is not in operation any more, the Anganwadi scheme is extended to cover children below 6 years of age.

In India, the nutritional support programme has an inverse para-medical structure. The upper part of the pyramid belongs to school going children of 6-11 years of age, who are taken care of by the school lunch programme. The middle and lower part belongs to the pre-school going children of 0-6 years of age, who are taken care by the Anganwadi and Balwadi schemes.

Since the project is to have a comparative study about the Nutritional support to primary education in Orissa and Tamil Nadu, discussions take place on all the nutritional support programmes running in the two states. But more emphasis has been given on the Mid-day Meals Scheme launched in 1995 by the Central Government. Before explaining the Mid-day Meals Scheme, we should explain the evolution of school lunch programme in Orissa and Tamil Nadu along with other nutritional programmes operating in the two states.

EVOLUTION OF THE SCHOOL LUNCH PROGRAMME

1. Orissa

The school lunch programme was an integral part of the "Expanded Nutrition Programme "(ENP) in the state of Orissa.The ENP was sponsored in 1959, jointly by FAO, WHO, UNICEF, and Government of India for a period of two years. Only 240 villages were covered under the scheme. Apart from ENP, CARE an American NGO, took steps towards supplying proteinous foods like Milk Powder, Bolgar Wheat, Corn Powder, etc., to school going children during the 1960's. Their coverage was limited. However, that was the only source of fighting malnutrition till the advent of Anganwadi and Balwadi schemes. Again these two schemes covered only the children, who were below 6 years of age. There was no programme to fight malnutrition among school going children until 1995, when the Mid-day Meals Scheme was launched at the national level. The new Mid-day Meals Scheme covered the entire state barring a few urban areas. According to 1989-99, data, the scheme covered a total number of 45,03,045 students in 40,697 schools in the State. The Mid-day Meals Scheme has immensely benefited the poor and needy children of the State, particularly in rural and backward areas. The State Government has deployed personnel right from the block level till the state level. The Scheme has made people more aware about the necessity of nutritious food at the school-going age.

2. Tamil Nadu

In Tamil Nadu, the evolution of the scheme dates back to 1925 when Madras Corporation started a scheme to feed 500 children in the Madras City. But it was K. Kamraj, who had the destinction of introducing Mid-day Measl Scheme for the first time in the State. The basic objective was to enroll more children in the schools and to reduce dropout rates at the primary level. Under the Kamraj model, milk powder, care food, wheat etc. were given, though it was not very popular, yet it made the beginning of providing food to children in Tanil Nadu. Tamil Nadu Government in 1982-83 budget session announced the launching of free nutritious Noon Meal programme to provide 400-odd calories to 56 lakh poor children under the age group of 2-10 years. The scheme was named "Chief Minister's Nutritious Noon Meal programme" and better known as the M.G.Ramachandran model of Mid-day Meals Scheme. On September 15,1982, it was extended to cover children in urban areas and cities, adding an increment of 69.5 lakh new beneficiaries. Under the M.G.R Noon Meal Scheme, cooked food was provided to children from I to X standard. The advent of the new Mid-day Meals Scheme launched in 1995 gave a fillip to the School Lunch Programme in Tamil Nadu, as the M.G.R model was already operating in the State successfully since 1982. Under the new scheme, the State Government received 100 grams of rice per student per day from the Central Government which reduced the State expenses. So the new scheme could be regarded as the extension of the old M.G.R model of Mid-day Meals Scheme. The major plus point of the Tamil Nadu Mid-day Meals Scheme is that it created several new jobs exclusively for looking into the distribution of Mid-day Meals in schools. A Government handout read "this single largest employment programme for rural areas in independent India in the last 35 years, has brought about a revolutionary change in the rural landscape..."

Apart from the Mid-day Measl Scheme, the other nutritional support programmes in operation in the two states are Anganwadi scheme under the I.C.D.S project and Balwadi scheme under the non-I.C.D.S project. Both the schemes were launched to cater to the nutritional demand of children below 6 years of age. Below a comparative look of the two schemes in both the states, i.e., Orissa and Tamil Nadu, is given.

ANGANWADI SCHEME

ORISSA AND TAMIL NADU — A COMPARISON

The focus in planning for the pre-school child is important for many reasons. In India the total population of the pre-school age children according to 1991 census constitutes 18 per cent of the total population. This population is most vulnerable and exacting segment of the total population from all counts. viz., nutrition, health care, and education. That is why Anganwadi Centres under the Integrated Child Development Project were started. The basic objectives of the scheme are:

- To improve the nutritional and health status of children in the age group of 0-3 years.
- To lay the foundation of proper psychological, physical and social development of child.
- To reduce the incidence of mortality, malnutrition and school dropout.
- To enhance the capability of mothers to look after the normal health and nutritional needs of the child.

The beneficiaries under the scheme are expectant and nursing mothers, other women (15-45 years) and children less than 3 years of age. The services they receive are: health check up, immunisation, supplementary nutrition, and health education.

In Orissa, the scheme was started in the year 1975, where as in Tamil Nadu, it was started in the year 1985. In Orissa, the Women and Child Development Department and in Tamil Nadu, the Department of Social Welfare is responsible for the smooth functioning of the scheme. In Orissa, the scheme is operating in 279 project blocks, out of which, 267 are rural and 12 are urban blocks. Out of 30 districts, 18 are covered fully and 12 are covered partly. In Orissa, the scheme has a vast coverage, whereas, in Tamil Nadu, it has only 3 projects. In Orissa, since the Balwadi scheme is out of operation, the Anganwadi scheme has been extended to cover children up to 6 years of age. But in Tamil Nadu, the scheme is exclusively looking after children up to 3 years of age. The scheme is funded by the state governments of both the states. The two states deploy their machinery to look after the proper functioning of the scheme in their respective states. The Central Government does the funding for infrastructure requirements.

As far as food items are concerned, the two, Orissa and Tamil Nadu, differ in certain respects. In Orissa the food items given per child per day are as follows; Wheat (80 grams), Ragi (14 grams), Jaggery (20 grams) and Iron fortified salt (5 grams). In the preparation of this, transport cost of 10 paisa is also included therein. In Tamil Nadu, children below 3 years are divided into two groups, i.e. 6-24 months and 24-36 months. For children in the age group of 6-24 months, supplementary food is provided. The composition of 1 kilogram of supplementary food consists of the following: Wheat (200 grams), Ragi (200 grams), Toasted Bengal gram (150 grams). Green gram (200 grams), and Jaggery (250 grams). Each child in this group is provided a 'food ball' of 80 grams out of this composition of supplementary food meant for them. For children of 24-36 months the Anganwadi Centre provides cooked meals. This is given on the basis of per child per day. The Composition is: Rice (80 grams), dal (10 grams), oil (1 ml), and others (18 paisa).

The State Governments, in both the states, are responsible for the supervision of the proper functioning of the scheme in the states. In Orissa, the Department of Women and Child Development and in Tamil Nadu the Department of Social Welfare are entrusted with the task of looking after the monitoring and supervision of the scheme in their respective states. The Government of Orissa and Tamil Nadu have deployed a number of personnel for this purpose, which can be seen from chart-3.1 and 3.2.

If we analyse the Organisation chart, we can see that in Orissa, the Secretary-cum-Commissioner of Women and Child Development Department is the highest official looking after the scheme and he is assisted by a Deputy Secretary, Asstt. Director and Project Co-ordinator. The Project Coordinator is the head of the I.C.D.S Project in the State. He takes all policy decisions regarding the scheme in the State. He is assisted by the Programme Officer (at the district level), who supervises the project at the district level. At the Block level Child Development Project Officer (C.D.P.O.) is the key functionary. At the sector level, the supervisor is the main authority and he supervises 17 to 20 Centres, which constitutes one sector. And finally at the Anganwadi Centre, there is an Anganwadi worker and a helper. The job of the Anganwadi worker is to provide education to children below 6 years and to supply food and medicines to them. She gets a salary of Rs. 500 (for above matric) or Rs. 438 (for under matric). There is one helper in the centre, who gets a salary of Rs. 260 per month. She helps the Anganwadi Worker in discharging her duties.

In Tamil Nadu, the Commissioner of Social Welfare is the head at the state level. He is assisted by one Additional Director, one Joint Director of Social Welfare and three Deputy Directors— one for Women Welfare, one for Anganwadi Centre and one for Health. At the District and Block level, the structure is same as that of Orissa. The District Programme Officer is the head assisted by a Child Development Project Officer (C.D.P.O) at the Block level. Unlike Orissa, in Tamil Nadu, there are two supervisors at the Sector level, viz, grade one and grade two supervisors. The former does extensive supervision and the latter does intensive supervision. At the Centre level, there is an Anganwadi worker helped by two helpers, who prepare the meals for the children whereas, in Orissa, there is only one helper in the Anganwadi Centre.

In Orissa, the organisational set up is justified to some extent as the State handles 279 projects in the state covering more than 18 Districts, whereas, Tamil Nadu has a very vast Administrative set up but handles only 3 projects in the entire state.

BALWADI SCHEME

The Balwadi scheme in India was started under the non-1C.D.S. project. A Balwadi centre is to be opened in a village where Anganwadi centre is not functining. An active Voluntary Organisation or Mahila Samiti was allowed to open a Balwadi centre in a village where there is no Anganwadi centre or Non-Formal Education centre. The main objective of the Balwadi centre is to provide all the basic amenities to a child (0-6 years of age), which is necessary for the physical growth and mental development both at home and outside. However, this age limit varies from state to state. In Orissa, it is 0-6 years while in Tamil Nadu it is 0-5 years of age.

The objectives of the Balwadi scheme are:

1. To help children in their physical growth by undertaking health check ups from time to time.
2. To provide follow up measures with medical aid from the nearest health centres.
3. Provision of balanced meals or supplementary nutritive diet to the children.
4. To help the child to learn the art of social adjustment with a view to develop healthy relationship with other children.

The Balwadi centres were opened keeping the above objectives in mind. All children in Balwadi were given meals once in a day.

The Balwadi Scheme was introduced in Orissa in the year 1981.The State Women and Child Development Department was looking after the project. The Commissioner-cum-Secretary was the head of the Department and was assisted by a Deputy Secretary and Director Social Welfare at the State level. At the District level, the Collector was the head who was assisted by the Block Development Officer (B.D.O) at the Block level. At the Centre level, the Voluntary Organisation or the Mahila Samiti, whoever handles the project, was the authority for the proper functioning of the centre (chart-3.3). There were 121 Balwadi centres in the State until 1998 March, when the Government decided to close down the scheme in the state due to shortage of funds. Due to the closure of the Balwadi Scheme in Orissa, the Anganwadi gained more popularity and all the Balwadi centres were taken over by the Anganwadi project.

Balwadi Scheme was also introduced in Tamil Nadu in the year 1981. From 1981-1998, the programme was adopted under Tamil Nadu Integrated Nutrition Programme (T.I.N.P.). The Programme was funded by World Bank through the Central Government. In Tamil Nadu, the Balwadi centre takes care of children below 5 years of age, i.e., 0-60 months, whereas, in case of Orissa it was 0-72 months, In Balwadi Centres of Tamil Nadu, the school timing is from 9.00 A.M. to 4.00 P.M. with lunch break from 12.30 P.M. to 1.30 P.M. In Tamil Nadu, children up to 60 months have been divided into two groups — 0-36 months and 37-60 months. From 0-36 months children are given 100 grams of food in the form of a 'food ball'. The composition of the food ball is: fried wheat flour (41 grams), fried groundnut powder (12 grams), fried soya powder (12 grams), Jaggery (20 grams), and fried ragi powder (15 grams). From 37-60 months, children were given cooked food. The composition is: rice (80 grams), dal (10 grams) and vegetables, spices and oil (18 paisa). Once in a week the children of this age group are provided with an egg. The Balwadi centres are mostly located in rural areas. The average strength of a centre is 25 to 40 children, which was same as that of an Anganwadi centre. The Tamil Nadu government deploys a number of personnel, who are responsible for the proper functioning of the scheme in the state. The personnel involved can be seen from the organisational chart-3.4 As can be seen from the chart, the Project Co-ordinator is the organisational head of the scheme in the State. He is responsible for the scheme at the state level and takes all policy decisions. He is assisted by three Joint Coordinators (Nutrition, Communications and Training), two Deputy Directors (Nutrition and Health), one Accounts Officer and one Administrative Officer. The District Project Nutrition Officer (D.P.N.O.) is the implementing officer for all Balwadi centres in the District and is responsible for its success and failure. The Community Nutrition Instructress (C.N.I) is responsible for drawing and disbursement of salary and implementation of the scheme. She takes extensive supervision after intensive supervision is undertaken by the supervisors. In a block, there are nearly 21 such instructresses. The Community Nutrition Supervisor takes intensive supervision at the block level. Their main function is to collect food material, undertake weight of children, maintain records of vital statistics, facilitate immunisation, etc. Then there is a Community Nutrition Worker (C.N.W), who is supposed to know the socio-economic features of 1500 people and above, covering mainly three villages. She maintains a total of seven registers, each keeping details of anti-natal care, post-natal care, survey register, medical register, register for women working group, adolescent girls working group and child working group. The C.N.W. takes care of children of 0-36 months, while there is a Child Welfare Organiser (C.W.O.), who takes care of children of 37-60 months. Then there are two helpers at the centre level, who prepare meals and distributed them among the children. They are known as Child Welfare Assistants. It is interesting to note that in Tamil Nadu most of the officials involved right from the block level till the centre level are females. The Tamil Nadu Government by doing so has created a lot of employment opportunities for women in the State, whereas in Orissa, only at the Balwadi centre level women were involved in the scheme.

From the foregoing observation it is clear that both the schemes Anganwadi and Balwadi play an extremely important role in the physical and mental development of the children below 6 years of age. Both the schemes enable the Nutritional Support Programme to become a continuous process starting from 0 to 11 years of age, which is very important from the Country's point of view.

In Orissa, while Anganwadi plays a major role, in Tamil Nadu, Balwadi holds the key in the development of the child. Further, in Tamil Nadu, both the schemes are operating, whereas in Orissa, only Anganwadi is operating. Balwadi covers children in the age group of 0-5 years and Anganwadi covers children in the age group of 0-3 years in Tamil Nadu. This implies that, in Tamil Nadu, Anganwadi comes under Balwadi. That means, in Tamil Nadu, there are two different sets of schemes running for the same target group, i.e., children between 0-3 years of age. Hence, there is scope for the convergence of the two schemes in Tamil Nadu. However, the same scope is not available in Orissa, as there are no Balwadi schemes. The question of convergence, however, is dealt separately in a subsequent chapter.

MID-DAY MEALS SCHEME

The national programme of Nutritional Support to Primary Education launched by the Government of India on 15th August 1995 is a landmark in the direction of spreading education in the country at the elementary level. On that day, Shri P.V. Narasimha Rao, the then Prime Minister of India, inaugurated the Mid-day Meals Scheme in a school in Bahadurgarh sub-division of Rohtak District in Haryana.

The present type of Mid-day Meals Scheme could be regarded as one of the first organised and official attempt at the national level to fight malnutrition among school going children in India. Subsequent central Governments have also carried out the programme in the country with support from the respective state governments.

The important objectives of the national programme of Nutritional Support to primary education, popularly known as Mid-day Meals scheme, are as follows:

1. To promote physical growth and sound health of children by providing an adequate meal in the school which will meet at least one third of the daily requirement of calories and nutrients.
ii. To enable children to attend the primary school regularly.
iii To increase the enrolment of children in the primary schools.
iv. To prevents children dropouts from primary schools, which has become cause of concern in the recent years.
v. To help children understand the relationship between food, nutrition, a health and happy life.
vi. To increase the ability of the children to study well by improving their concentration and perseverance.
vii. To provide opportunities to children for social interactions and encourage them to shun differences among themselves due to caste and colour while participating in school lunch on a common platform.
viii. To inculcate good habits and proper dealings among school going children of tender age.

The beneficiaries under the scheme are children in the age group of 6-11 years. In other words, the target group under the new scheme are the school going children at the primary level. Although in Tamil Nadu, the scheme has been extended to cover all children between I and X standard, yet, in Orissa the main emphasis is on primary school going children of I to V class.

Under the present scheme, the state governments receive 100 grams of rice from the central government on per day per student basis, the central government also give Rs. 25/- per quintal of rice as transport cost from the F.C.I. godown to the block office or the centres where the scheme is in operation. Recently, this has been increased to Rs. 50/- per quintal in case of Orissa.

The Mid-day Meals programme consists of three essential components, viz., Procurement, Management and Distribution. All the state governments have deployed their personnel to look after the above mentioned functions. Each state Government at the state level, has entrusted the task of managing the scheme to a department, and this department is responsible for the functioning of the scheme in that state. But the major part of the function is done by the district and block level officials involved in the scheme.

The organisational chart-3.5 and 3.6 give the details of the personnel involved in the scheme in Orissa and Tamil Nadu respectively. The functions of the officials engaged in the operation of Mid-day Meals Scheme both in Orissa and Tamil Nadu are given below.

1. Orissa

The State Women and Child Development Department looks after the Administration and Management of the scheme in Orissa. It is the apex body for the management of the scheme in the State. The department along with its other activities handles the Mid-day Meals Scheme. All the policy decisions are taken by the department, which is located in the State Capital, i.e., Bhubaneswar.

At the district level, the District Collector is responsible for the overall management of the scheme in the district. All monetary transactions regarding the scheme are done by him. He authorises the D.S.W.O (District Social Welfare Officer) to undertake the purchases of dal, spices and other essentials required for the noon-meal programme in the district. The D.S.W.O assists the Collector in undertaking supervision activities. After the purchase of food items by D.S.W.O., they are given to the Civil Supplies Department under his jurisdiction who later supply the food items to the schools through Marketing Inspector (M.Is). The Marketing Inspector undertakes the job of transporting these items to the blocks or to the schools directly from the F.C.I godown. Apart from these officials at the district level, there is the Project Director D.R.D.A (District Rural Development Agency), who sanctions the payments to the cooks and helpers in rural areas. For urban areas, this money directly comes from the Women and Child Development Department.

At the block level, the Block Development Officer (B.D.O) is responsible for the implementation of the scheme. The BDO along with other developmental activities manages the operation of the MDM scheme in the block. The block office keeps all records of the food items supplied to the schools including the salary of cooks and helpers, The block office ensures timely supply of food items, so that, distribution of food to children in the school is not affected. BDO is assisted by the Social Education Organiser (S.E.O), who keeps monthly records of all expenditures on noon-meal programme in the block. The Sub-Inspector (S.I) does all the supervisory functions at the ground level. He visits schools, checks the enrolment and attendance records maintained due to Mid-day Meals programme in the schools.

At the school level, the persons involved in the scheme in Orissa are the Head master/Teacher, cook and helper of the school. The cook and helper are not treated as government officials as in the case of Tamil Nadu. The Head master/Teacher receives the foodgrains, undertakes storage of food items and maintains proper records of the stock of food materials for audit and inspection. It is the duty of the teacher to see that cooking is not hampered due to shortage of food materials or for want of personnel responsible for cooking. Normally the honorarium of cook and helper is Rs.200/- and Rs. 100/- respectively in Orissa, which is contrary to the situation prevailing in Tamil Nadu where it is comparatively higher. Mostly poor women and widows of the locality are appointed as cooks and helpers in Orissa. In Orissa, in each village where the scheme is in operation, there is a Village Food Committee or a Village Education Committee, who help in the smooth running of the scheme. The committe members meet once a month monitor the operation of the scheme in the locality. The teacher who handles MDM is also a memeber of these committees.

In Orissa, all the personnel involved in the scheme, consider the scheme as an additional duty over and above the normal responsibilities discharged by them. It is considered by them as an extra burden. But that is not the case in Tamil Nadu. In Tamil Nadu, the state government has created a separate department, manned by personnel exclusively for the job. On the other hand, Mid-day Meals programme in Orissa is looked after by a department, which along with other activities only oversees the programme.

2. Tamil Nadu

The structure of MDM in Tamil Nadu is given below.

Unlike Orissa, where the entire operation of the scheme is looked after by a single department, in Tamil Nadu, the scheme is implemented by both Director of Social Welfare and the Commissioner of Municipal Administration at the state level. The former looks after the scheme in rural areas, whereas, the latter monitors the scheme in urban and municipal areas. Both the Departments are responsible for the proper functioning and implementation of the scheme. They grant funds to the collectors who maintain records about the operation of scheme and take policy decisions regarding improvement in the performance of MDM.

The Collector is the organisational head of the scheme at the district level. He takes all decisions regarding MDM besides supervision at the district level. He arranges meetings of the officials involved in the scheme and entertains petitions and appeals regarding Mid-day Meals for an amicable solution. P.A. (Project Development) and P.A to Collector (Noon Meal) assist him. The P.A (PD) is the administrative head at the district level. He looks after all the administrative aspects of the scheme and helps the Collector in discharging his duties. The P.A. Noon Meal is the controlling authority of the programme. All activities relating to MDM are looked after by him.

At the block level, the Block Development Officer (B.D.O.) is the highest authority. He looks after the Noon Meal programme along with other programmes implemented in the blocks. He is ultimately responsible for any mismanagement of the scheme in his block and answerable to the Collector. He is the drawing officer for the Noon Meal programme. In Tamil Nadu, the B.D.O. is assisted by a Noon

Meal Manager. The Noon Meal Manger is a goverment servant. This post is created exclusively to manage the scheme at the block level in Tamil Nadu, whereas, in Orissa, there is no such post created to look after MDM. The salary of the Noon Meal Manager is 5000-150-6000 per month. He is the disbursing officer for Noon Meal in the block. He is responsible for procurement and distribution of food items. All the food items are supplied by the Tamil Nadu Civil Supplies Corporation. He prepares the budget, fixes the target and takes steps towards achieving these targets. He provides contingency to Noon Meal Organisers for purchase of firewood and vegetables. Auditing and accounting functions are also performed by him.

At the school level, there is a Noon Meal Organiser, who is also a government official. This post is created to avoid teachers' involvement in the scheme. The NMO gets a consolidated salary of Rs. 820/- with exgratia D.A. Her job is to receive all the food materials supplied by the Civil Supply Corporation. She is responsible for the safe keeping of food items. She also takes an active part in the preparation and distribution of the meal by the cook and helper. In contrast to this, in Orissa, the teachers are involved in the operation of the scheme. In Tamil Nadu, the Noon Meal organiser is helped by a cook and a helper. There is one cook for 200 students in a primary school and two cooks if the total enrolment strength exceeds 200 in the school. The cook gets a salary of Rs. 520/- with exgratia D.A. and the helper gets a salary of Rs. 450/- with exgratia D.A. The cook prepares the meal and distributes it to students, while the helper helps the cook in cooking the food items, undertakes the cleaning of utensils and assists in the distribution of food, In Tamil Nadu both these posts are government jobs. The posts of Noon Meal Manager, Noon Meal Organiser, cook and helper are mostly reserved for ladies in the state of Tamil Nadu.

Like Orissa, there is a Parent-Teacher Committee in each survey village in Tamil Nadu where the scheme is operating. Their main function is to supervise the implementation of Noon Meal Scheme in the locality. They help the Noon Meal Organiser in the storage of food items and in the solution of other problems.

The study foregoing thus brings out the following essential elements for the comparison the Mid-day Meals Scheme in both the states:

(i) In Tamil Nadu, the Mid-day Meals Scheme is administered by a separate department created for the purpose, whereas, in Orissa, the scheme is implemented by the existing welfare department which in addition to several official responsibilities shoulders the responsibility of Mid-day Meals Scheme.

(ii) In Tamil Nadu, separate posts like noon-meal offcer, noon-meal manager, noon-meal organiser, cook and helper are created. They are all treated as government servants enjoying certain facilities of the government. In Orissa, no such separate posts are there. Though there is the provision for cooks and helpers yet, they are not governemnt servants.Their salary remains very low as compared to the salary of cooks and helpers in Tamil Nadu.

(iii) In Tamil Nadu the teachers are in no way involved in the scheme. The entire job of Mid-day Meals Scheme is looked after by Noon-Meal Organiser. As a result of this, teacher's time is fully utilised for taking classes and teaching the students.On the other hand, the teacher in charge of MDM is unable to utilise more time for teaching students. A major part of his time is consumed in procuring food items from FCI, distributing food items for cooking, and purchasing fire-wood, vegetables and spices for the preparation of noon meals, Besides, he maintains all the records of receipts and expenditure of food items for audit and inspection. He is also accountable for lapses, if any, in the implementation of the programmes by authorities above him.

OPERATION OF THE SCHEME

Under the present Mid-day Meals Scheme, cooked food is supplied to students at the primary level. The teacher (in Orissa) or the Noon Meal Organiser (in Tamil Nadu) was supplied with food material by the state government. The central government provides rice free of cost to the state government for the purpose. It is the duty of the teacher of the Noon Meal Organiser to prepare the meals through the cook and the helper and distribute it among the students during the lunch hour on all working days. In Orissa, food is not given on holidays and Sundays, while in Tamil Nadu, food is given on holidays except Sundays. In Orissa, food is given to all students enrolled in the school, while in Tamil Nadu food is given according to the feeding strength determined by the concerned authority, Every year (July-Aug.), Extension officer, Noon Meal Manager and other officials of the block visit each and every school consecutively for 3 days. They observe attendance in the morning of each day and number of students taking the meals. On the basis of the budgetary allocation and on the basis of the inspection of schools, the feeding strength is determined in Tamil Nadu, Under the Scheme, food is given to all students from class-I to class-V in Orissa, in case of Tamil Nadu it is from class-I to class-X.

In Orissa, initially 100 grams of rice and 10 grams of dal were supplied, but in 1998, the State Government decided to increase the quantity to 125 grams of rice and 15 grams of dal. Again in April 1999, the State Government decided to reduce the quantity of rice to 100 grams per day per students.

The quantity of food items given to Primary School students in Orissa and in Tamil Nadu on a per day per student basis is given below in the Table-3.1.

TABLE-3.1

OFFICIAL PROVISION OF FOOD MATERIALS PER STUDENT AND PER DAY BASIS BOTH IN ORISSA AND TAMIL NADU

STATE	*RICE*	*DAL*	*OIL*	*VEGETABLE*	*SALT*	*FIRE WOOD*	*SPICES*	*EGG*
ORISSA	100 gms	15gms Green gram	1 ml	9 Paisa /day/student	2 gm	Rs.1.30 per month	----	-----
TAMIL NADU	100 gms	15gms Red gram	1 ml	9 Paisa /day/student	1 gm	Rs.1.30 (5.5 p/day)	0.3 paisa per day	1 egg per week

The above table shows the quantity of items given only to students in the primary level (class I to V).

Both the states provide boiled rice to students. Rice, being the staple food of more than half of the population, is qualitatively the most important of the cereal. Although the protein content of rice is lower (6.4 gams). than that of many other cereals, yet the protein content of rice is useful for the development of the body. In dal, Tamil Nadu provides red gram, whereas, in Orissa, green gram is usually served to the students. Both green gram and red gram have the same nutritive value but red gram when mixed with tamarind does create additional folic acid, which is not good for health when one takes the diet round the year. In Tamil Nadu, money is given separately for spices while in Orissa money given for this purpose also includes the cost of vegetables. In Orissa 2 grams of salt is given, while in Tamil Nadu, it is only 1gram. They major differences in food structure between the states is that, in Tamil Nadu, one egg is given to each student once in a week, while in Orissa, there is no provision of providing eggs to the students, which is a major disadvantage of the Mid-day Meals structure in Orissa. For fuel charges Rs.1.30 per student per month is given to schools in both the states.

To sum up, the present type of Mid-day Meals Scheme has been successful in achieving the objectives that were set while launching the scheme in 1995. Practical experience proves that the scheme is a success in Tamil Nadu, while in Orissa, it is partially successful. The chief merits of the scheme, as it exists in the states Orissa and Tamil Nadu, are given below:

1. The scheme has made people more aware about the nutritional requirements.

2. The scheme has helped to provide one square meal a day to those poor students, who were earlier not getting this benefit.

3. The scheme has created interest and encouraged students to attend classes regularly.

4. It has helped those poor students who dropout from school, to continue their studies. Mid-day Meals thus act as an incentive.

5. The Tami Nadu Government has created several new jobs exclusively for the management of the scheme, which is a major plus point in the administration of the scheme. In Orissa, the scheme is being looked after by routine officials to consider this as an additional burden and hence they pay less attention and devote inadequate time for the success of the scheme.

6. In Tamil Nadu, along with other food material, egg is given once, a week which is important from nutrition point of view. It is also an added attraction to students to come to school regularly. In Orissa, on the other hand, no egg is distributed. From that point of view, the protein intake of children in Orissa is less compared to Tamil Nadu.

7. In Tamil Nadu, there are two departments handling the scheme both in urban and in rural areas of the State, which ensures smooth operation of the scheme. But in Orissa, a single department handles the scheme, both in rural and urban areas, which is burdensome and creates organisational difficulties.

8. InTamil Nadu, there is separate budgetary provision for nu trition, a part of which is allotted for Mid-day Meals Scheme. In Orissa, on the other hand, there is no separate budgetary provision either for nutrition or for Mid-day Meals. The expenditure is normally met out of the allocation meant for school education. For this, the scheme is not as vibrant in Orissa as compared to Tamil Nadu.

CHART- 3.1

ORGANISATIONAL STRUCTURE OF ANGANWADI SCHEME, ORISSA

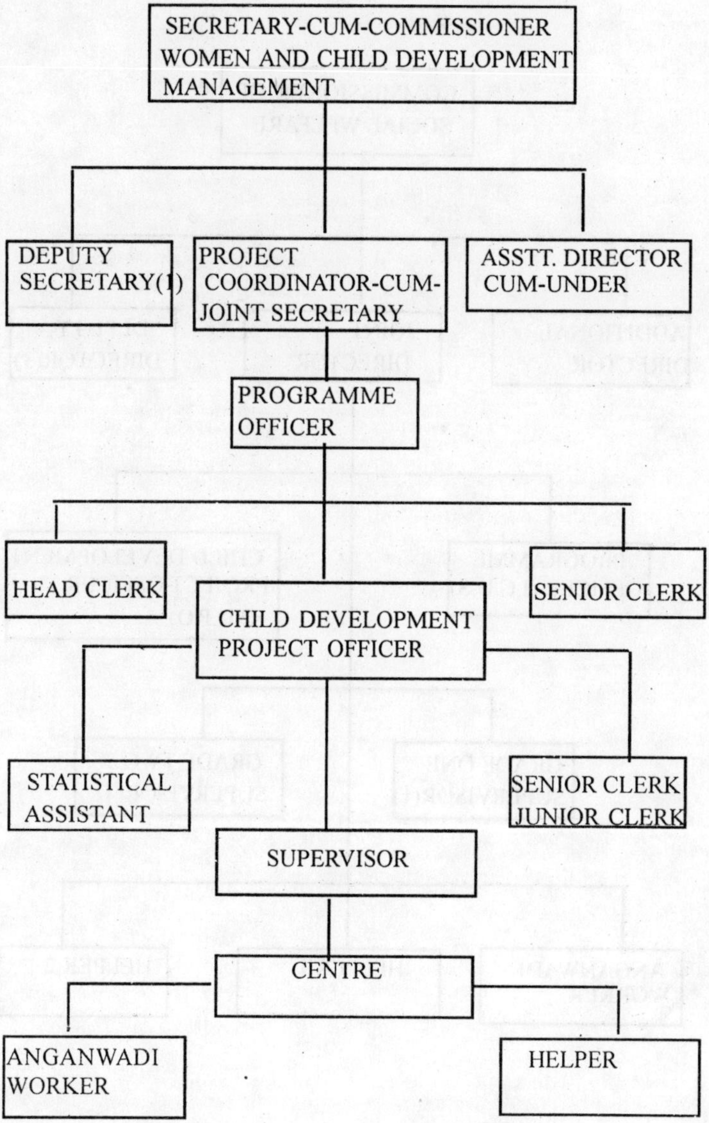

CHART - 3.2

ORGANISATION STRUCTURE OF ANGANWADI SCHEME, TAMIL NADU

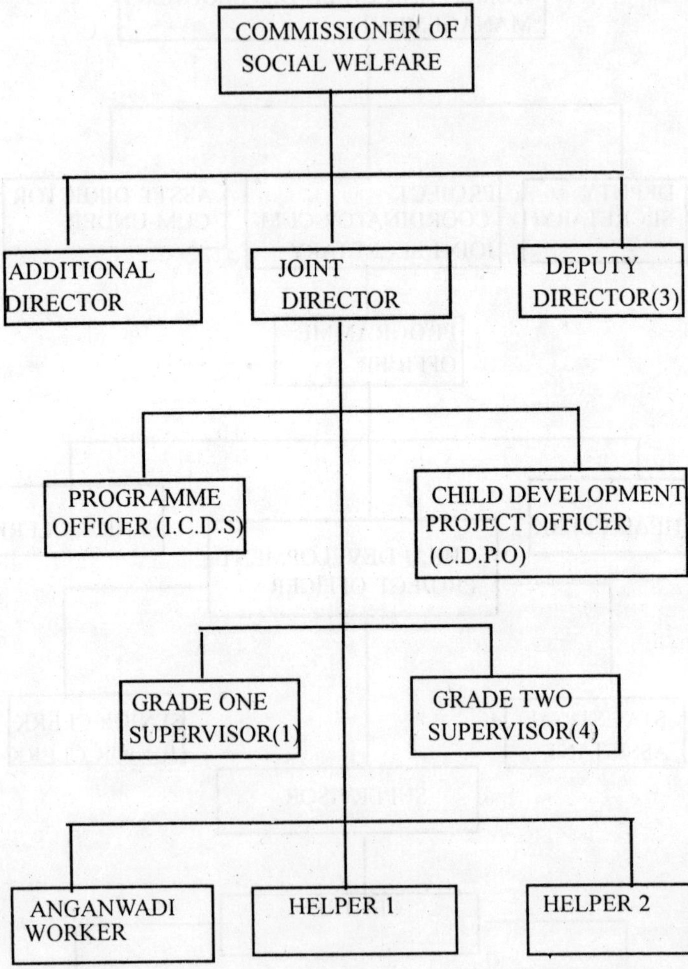

CHART - 3.3

ORGANISATIONAL STRUCTURE OF BALWADI SCHEME, ORISSA

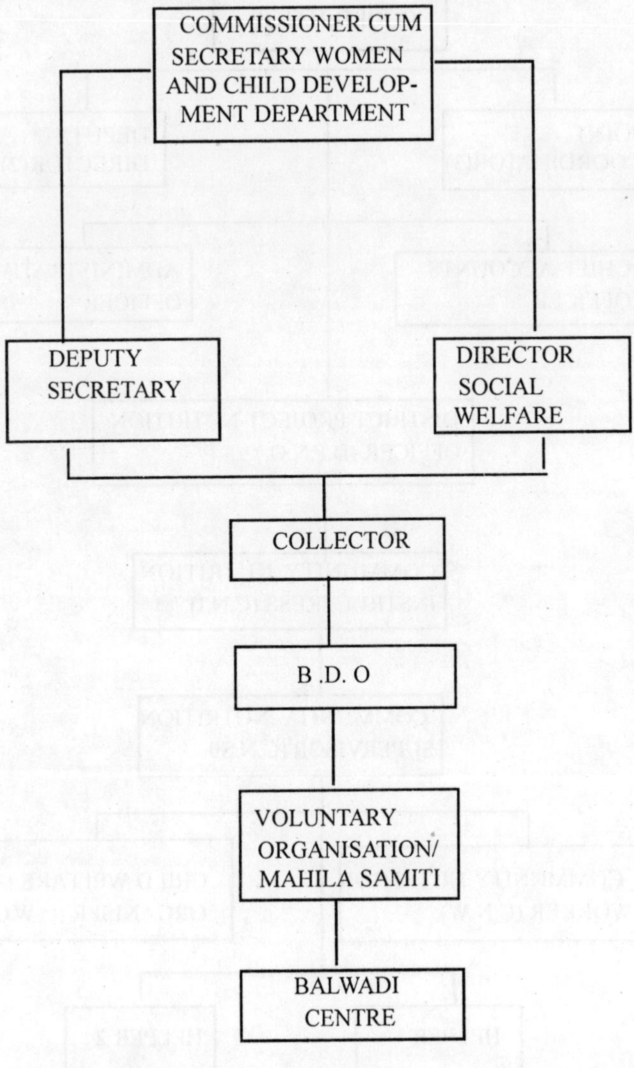

CHART - 3.4

ORGANISATION STRUCTURE OF
BALWADI SCHEME, TAMIL NADU

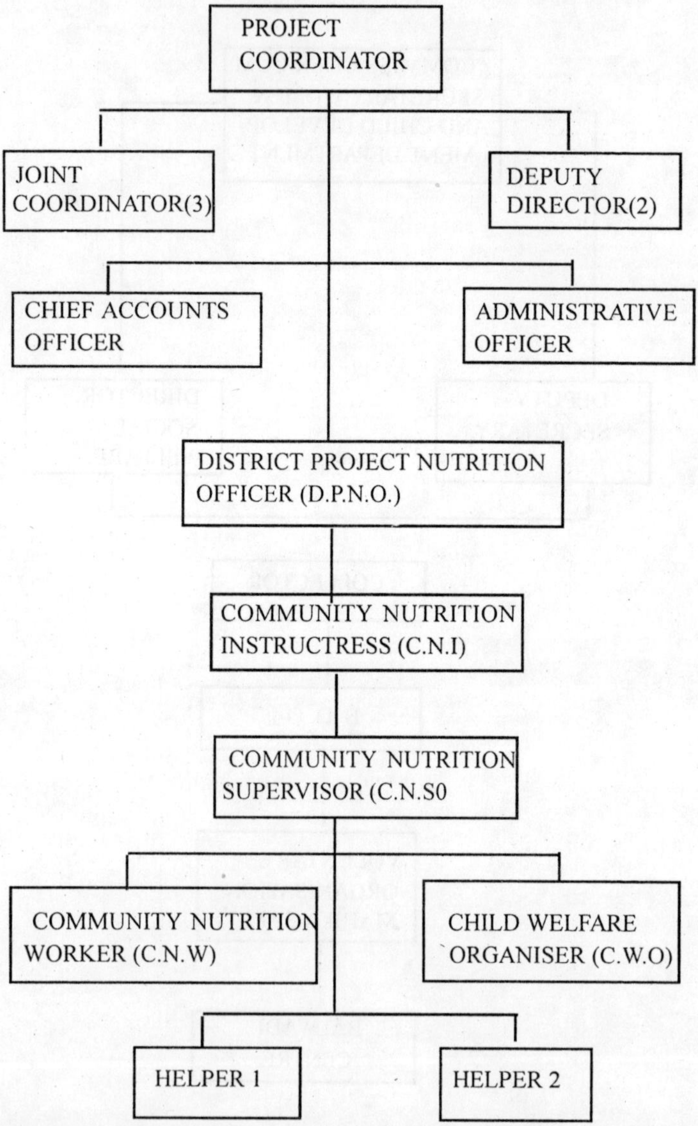

CHART - 3.5

ORGANISATIONAL STRUCTURE OF
MIK-DAY MEALS SCHEME, ORISSA

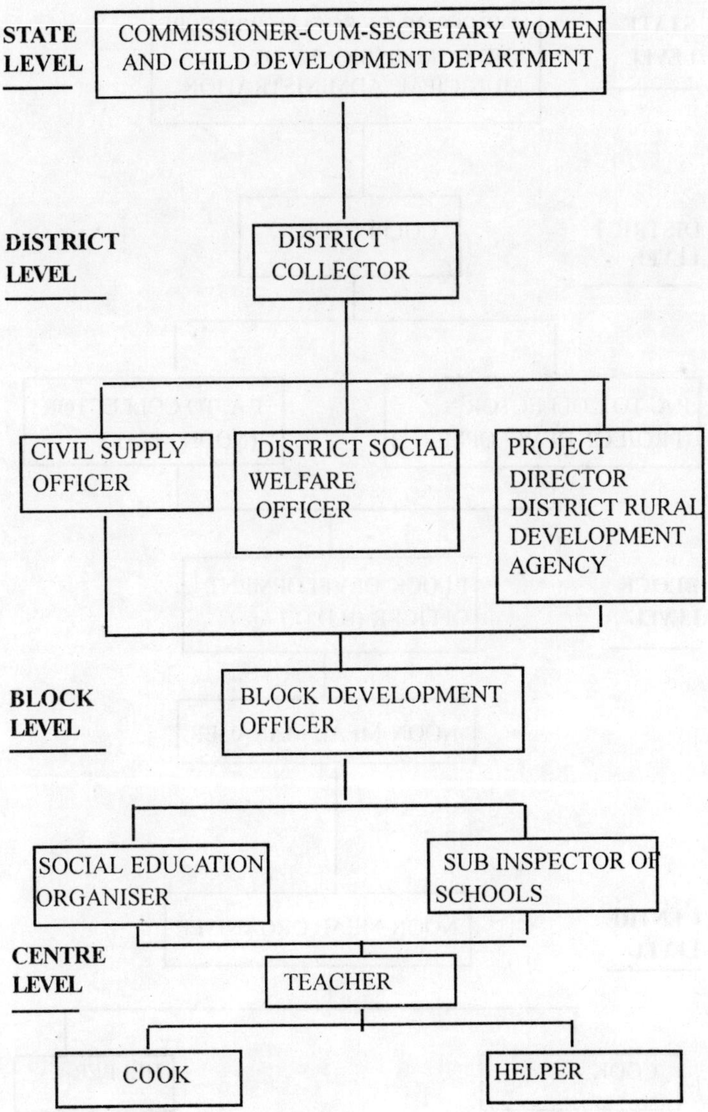

CHART - 3.6

ORGANISATIONAL STRUCTURE OF NOON MEAL SCHEME IN TAMIL NADU

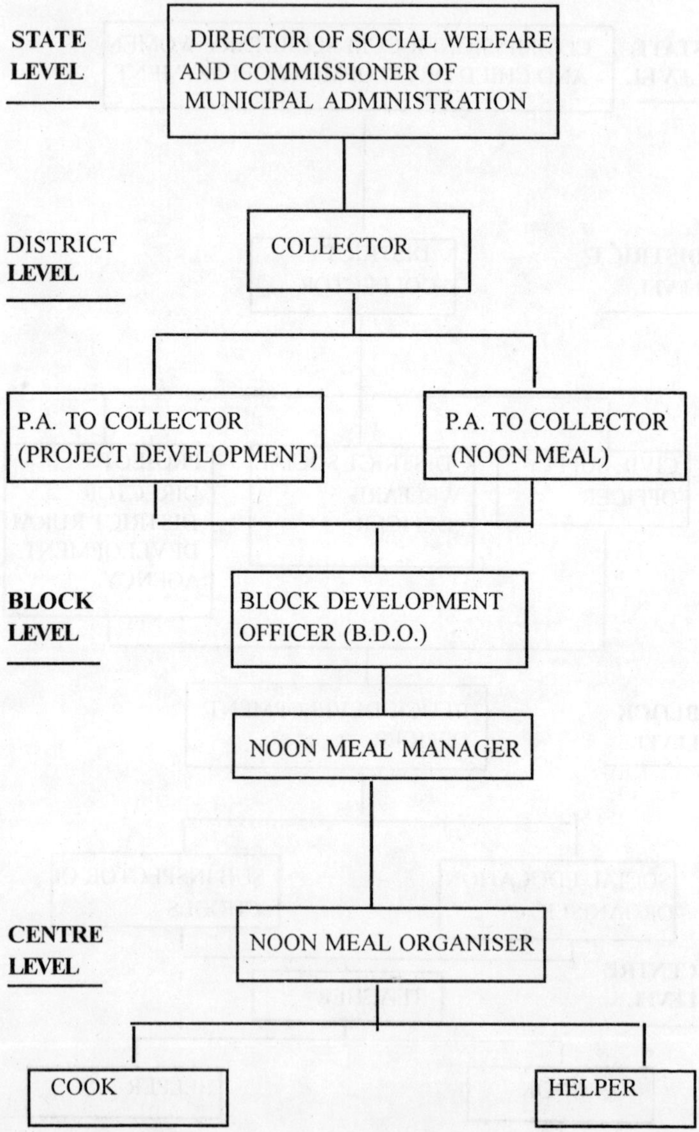

CHAPTER-4

IMPACT OF MID-DAY MEALS SCHEME ON ENROLMENT, ATTENDANCE, RETENTION AND DROPOUT OF STUDENT: A COMPARATIVE PICTURE

In order to give a boost to universal elementary education in terms of increasing enrolment, attendance and retention in primary classes by supplementing nutritional requirement of children attending primary schools, the National programme on Nutritional Support to Primary Education or Mid-day Meals Scheme was launched at the national level. Since the study is confined to Orissa and Tamil Nadu, it is plausible in this context to analyse as to what extent the scheme is successful in achieving the objectives of increased enrolment, attendance and retention, and bringing down dropouts in both the states. For this, time series data covering a period of 10 years from 1989-90 to 1998-99 on aspects like enrolment, attendance, retention and dropouts have been taken into consideration. To study the impact of Mid-day Meals (Mid-day Meals) programme on the above variables in the sample areas of Orissa and Tamil Nadu, the time series data covering the period of a decade have been classified into two periods, viz., the periods-Mid-day Meals period (1989-90 to 1994-95) and the post-Mid-day Meals period (1995-96 to 1998-99). The detail analysis of the study is given below.

ENROLMENT

This section deals with the growth rates of enrolment of students of different castes and sexes of the sample schools in the selected districts and blocks of Orissa and Tamil Nadu during pre-Mid-day Meals period and post-Mid-day Meals period, and the reasons responsible for the change in the growth rates of enrolment of students in the sample areas of both the states. Table-4.1 and Table-4.2 presents the growth rates of enrolment of students of the pre-Mid-day Meals, post-Mid-day Meals and over the entire 10 year period in the sample areas of Orissa and Tamil Nadu respectively.

1. Orissa

In Orissa, the growth rate of enrolment of students over the period 1989-90 to 1998-99 is 0.89 per cent per annum. But, when the growth rates of pre-Mid-day Meals and post-Mid-day Meals are taken to consideration, it is 1.39 per cent in the pre-Mid-day Meals period as against 0.63 per cent in the post-Mid-day Meals period. This indicates that in the post-Mid-day Meals period growth rate of enrolment has declined compared to pre-Mid-day Meals period. However, there has been a slight increase in the enrolment growth rate of girls, i.e. from 0.96 per cent in the pre-Mid-day Meals period to 0.97 per cent in the post-Mid-day Meals period. Further more, the growth rates of enrolment of SC boys and girls have declined in the post-Mid-day Meals period as compared to the Pre-Mid-day Meals period. In the above cases, though the growth rates have declined in the post-Mid-day Meals period, but are still positive. This implies that there has been an increase in the number of students enrolled in the post-Mid-day Meals period as compared to the pre-mid-day Meals period (Annexure 4.1). On the other hand, in case of general students, the growth rate of boys and girls are found to be negative in the post-Mid-day Meals period, whereas, the same are positive in the pre-Mid-day meals period. Regarding ST students, an impressive change in the growth rates of enrolment of students are found between pre-Mid-day Meals and post-Mid-day Meals period. In the pre-Mid-day Meals period, the enrolment growth rate of ST students is - 4.55 per cent as against 8.39 per cent in the post-Mid-day Meals period. This shows that Mid-day Meals have greater impact on the enrolment of ST students as compared to SC students.

In Puri district, the enrolment of students in absolute number, during the entire 10 years period (1989-90 to 1998-99), moves through a lot of ups and downs (Annexure 4.2). There is no year - wise systematic increase or decrease in enrolment. However, it can be seen from Table-4.1 that, during the post-Mid-day Meals period, the average annual growth rate of enrolment is - 1.06 per cent. This implies that on an average enrolment has declined in the post-Mid-day Meals period. But during the pre-Mid-day Meals period, this growth rate is positive, i.e. 1.21 per cent. This indicates that there is annual average increase in the enrolment of students in the pre-Mid-day Meals period. The overall growth rate is positive, which is 0.45 per cent per annum. The caste and sex-wise analysis also shows the same trend except in the case of SC boys. In other words, the average annual growth rate of enrolment is positive in the pre-Mid-day Meals and negative in the post-Mid-day Meals period.

The two blocks, which are taken under the study in Puri district, are Satyabadi block (educationally backward). The average annual growth rate of enrolment of students in Satyabadi block over the period 1989-90 to 1998-99 is negative, i.e. -0.99 per cent. The negative growth rate is also found both in pre and post-Mid-day Meals period. But the decline is more in the post-Mid-day Meals period as compared to the pre-Mid-day meals period. The pre-Mid-day Meals period growth rate is -0.43 per cent, while the post-Mid-day Meals period growth rate is -2.27 per cent. In case of SC students, the pre-Mid-day Meals period growth rate is 1.78 per cent. On the other hand, in the post-Mid-day Meals period, the enrolment of SC students registers a negative growth rate of 5.31 percent. The enrolment growth rate of other caste girls during the post-Mid-day Meals period is 1.15 per cent as against 0.76 per cent in the pre-Mid-day Meals period. In the case of boys the enrolment growth rates both in pre and post-Mid-day Meals period remained negative. The enrolment growth rate in the block indicates that, except for other caste girls, the enrolment growth rates of all other castes and sexes are moving on a declining path.

Unlike Satyabadi block, in Puri Sadar block, the pre-Mid-day Meals period growth rate of enrolment is positive, i.e 4.00 per cent annum. On the other hand, the post-Mid-day Meals period growth rate is negative, i.e., -0.36 per cent per annum. This shows that, after the introduction of Mid-day Meals, the enrolment of students has declined in the block. But the caste-wise growth rate indicates a different but encouraging picture. It shows that, in case of SC students, the post-Mid-day Meals period growth rate (7.70 per cent) is higher than the pre-Mid-day Meals period growth rate (6.14 per cent). The same is true in case of both SC boys and SC girls. There is no enrolment of ST students in the block in both the pre-Mid-day Meals and post-Mid-day Meals period.

From the above analysis, it is found that, in Puri district as well in the two sample blocks, enrolment growth rate in the post-Mid-day Meals period is negative. But, in the educationally advanced block of Satyabadi, the growth rate is negative both in pre and post-Mid-day Meals period and the rate of decline is faster in the post-Mid-day Meals period as compared to pre-Mid-day Meals period.

The average annual growth rate of enrolment of students in Rayagada district depicts a completely different picture. Unlike the advance district of Puri where the enrolment growth rate during the post-Mid-day Meals period is negative, here the growth rate during the same period is positive at 5.94 per cent per annum. This implies that the enrolment of students in the district has gone up after the scheme was introduced. This growth rate was on a declining path during the pre-Mid-day Meals period. i.e., -2.15 per cent. As revealed from Annexure 4.2 maximum increase in the enrolment of students is found in case of ST students. The rate of growth of enrolment of students in the post-Mid-day Meals period is 8.39 per cent as against -4.55 per cent in the pre-Mid-day Meals period. Similar situation is also found in case of ST boys and girls. The average annual growth rate of the enrolment of SC students has reduced in the post-Mid-day Meals period, but it is still positive. In case of other caste students, both the pre and post-Mid-day Meals growth rates are negative but the declining growth rate is found to be more in the post-Mid-day Meals period. From the enrolment growth rates, it can be said that the scheme has definitely made good impact on the enrolment of the students in the district and more particularly on the ST students.

The block-wise analysis of the enrolment figures also indicates the same picture as that of the district of Rayagada. In the educationally advanced block Kolnara, the post-Mid-day Meals period growth rate (5.82 per cent) is higher than the pre-Mid-day Meals period growth rate (4.58 per cent). The enrolment of girls has increased considerably, whereas, for boys, it has decreased in the post-Mid-day Meals period. Like the district figures, the growth rate of enrolment of ST students has gone up from 3.60 per cent in the pre-Mid-day Meals period to 10.16 per cent in the post-Mid-day Meals period, and that of SC students has come down from 8.76 per cent to 4.55 per cent. In case of other caste students, though the decrease in the enrolment growth rate is found in the post-Mid-day Meals period (1.93 per cent) as compared to the pre-Mid-day Meals period (4.15 per cent) but still it is positive. This is due to the increase in the enrolment growth rate of girl students (i.e. 9.04 per cent in the post-Mid-day Meals period as against -1.12 per cent in the pre-Mid-day Meals period).

Compared to Kolnara block, in Rayagada block (educationally backward), the picture is much more encouraging. During the post-Mid-day Meals period, the enrolment growth rate is 6.13 per cent, which is negative (-8.54 per cent) in the pre-Mid-day Meals period. Similarly, the enrolment growth rates of both boys and girls have gone up considerably, which can be seen from Table-4.1 Similar to Kolnara block, more increase in the enrolment of students is found among ST students.

From the above discussion, it is clear that, in Orissa, the educationally backward district Rayagada shows a positive and healthy growth rate in enrolment in the post-Mid-day Meals period. On the other hand, a negative growth rate in enrolment during the post-Mid-day Meals period is found in the educationally advanced district Puri. Further, more increase in the enrolment growth rate of ST students is observed in Rayagada district in the post-Mid-day Meals period.

2. Tamil Nadu

The enrolment scenario in Tamil Nadu is quite different from that in Orissa. The enrolment growth rates of the state are given in Table-4.2. The table indicates that enrolment in the state grows at the rate of -0.96 per cent per annum over the entire 10 year period (1989-90 to 1998-99), which means enrolment in the state is declining over the period. In the pre-Mid-day Meals period, enrolment decreases at the rate of -0.03 per cent per annum, while in the post-

Mid-day meals period, it declines at a faster rate of -1.61 per cent per annum. The caste-wise analysis shows that, in case of ST students the growth rate has drastically dropped down from 9.27 per cent in the pre-Mid-day Meals period to -16.47 per cent in the post-Mid-day Meals period, whereas, in case of SC students, it has marginally dropped to 1.39 per cent in the post-Mid-day Meals period from 3.12 per cent in the pre-Mid-day Meals period. This implies that the enrolment of ST students is decreasing at an increasing rate, while that of SC students it is increasing but at a decreasing rate. When the case of other caste students are taken into consideration, the growth rate is negative in both the pre-Mid-day Meals period (-0.96 per cent) and post-Mid-day Meals period (-2.67 per cent), but the rate of decline is more in the post-Mid-day Meals period as compared to the pre-Mid-day Meals period.

In the educationally advanced district of Madurai, the enrolment growth rate is negative, i.e., -1.50 per cent in the post-Mid-day Meals period, whereas, it is positive, i.e. 0.83 per cent in the pre-Mid-day Meals period. In case of SC students, the same situation on the growth rate enrolment of students is found between the pre-Mid-day Meals (5.14 per cent) and post-Mid-day Meals (-0.47 per cent) period, but the declining gap between the enrolment growth rates of students is more. Similar to the state, in other caste students, negative growth rate in the enrolment of students is found both in the pre-Mid-day Meals and post-Mid-day Meals period.

The two blocks of Madurai district, which are taken under the study, are Madurai East (educationally advanced) and Alanganuller (educationally backward) block. In Madurai East block, though the overall growth rate of enrolment is positive at 1.26 per cent per annum during the entire 10 year period, but the post-Mid-day Meals period registers a negative growth rate of -0.97 per cent as compared to positive growth rate of 3.00 per cent in the pre-Mid-day Meals period. The enrolment of SC students has declined significantly during the post-Mid-day Meals period, i.e., -1.35 per cent as against 9.47 per cent in the pre-Mid-day Meals period. However, the growth rate of SC students during the entire 10 year period is 3.41 per cent. In case of other caste students, the growth rate is 0.94 per cent in the pre-Mid-day Meals period and -0.83 per cent in the post-

Mid-day Meals period.

In Alanganuller block, the enrolment growth rate was negative, i.e -1.26 per cent even before the scheme was launched, and it continued to fall rapidly in the post-Mid-day Meals period (-2.20 per cent). The caste-wise total enrolment growth rates indicate that, during the post-Mid-day Meals period, enrolment growth rate has fallen. But it is positive as far as SC students are concerned, while it is negative for other caste students.

The enrolment growth rate in Villupuram district is negative both in the pre and post-Mid-day Meals period, it is -1.50 per cent in the pre-Mid-day Meals period and 1.44 per cent in the post-Mid-day Meals period. The overall growth rate during the entire 10 year period is -1.12 per cent. The caste-wise analysis indicates that, in case of other caste and ST students, the growth rates in the post-Mid-Meals period are negative and have fallen sharply as compared to the pre-Mid-day Meals period. On the other hand, the growth rate of SC students in the post-Mid-day Meals period is positive, i.e. 6.02 per cent, but in the pre-Mid-day Meals period, the rate is negative, i.e., -3.07 per cent.

The block-wise analysis of Villupuram district shows that, in the Koliyanur block (educationally advanced), enrolment has declined sharply in the post-Mid-day Meals period (-4.84 per cent per annum) than the pre-Mid-day Meals period (-0.65 per cent per annum). This is due to the decline in the enrolment of ST and other caste students.

On the other hand, the growth rate of enrolment of Thirunavalur block (educationally backward) indicates a different story altogether. Here the total enrolment has gone up by 2.65 per cent per annum during the post-Mid-day Meals period, which was -2.45 per cent per annum during the pre-Mid-day Meals period. This could be possible because the enrolment of SC students has gone up by a staggering 10.23 per cent per annum during the post-Mid-day meals period. The enrolment of other caste students, though has gone up marginally, yet it is still negative at -0.21 per cent.

Thus, the growth rate of the enrolment of students is negative in Tamil Nadu, and other sample blocks and districts except Thirunavalur block (educationally backward) of Villupuram district in the post-Mid-day Meals period. The positive growth rate of enrolment of students in Thirunavalur block is because of the large increase in the enrolment of SC students in the post-Mid-day Meals period.

3 Orissa And Tamil Nadu—A Comparison

A comparison of the enrolment of students in the two states indicates that, during the post-Mid-day Meals period, Orissa has a growth rate of 0.673 per cent, whereas, Tamil Nadu has a growth rate of -1.61 per cent. This indicates that enrolment in Orissa is increasing at a decreasing rate, while in Tamil Nadu, enrolment is decreasing at an increasing rate in the post-Mid-day Meals period, which can be observed from the graph given in the next page. Further, negative growth rate in the enrolment of students is found both in the pre and post-Mid-day Meals period in Tamil Nadu and the rate of decline is more in the post-Mid-day Meals period as compared to the pre-Mid-day Meals period. On the other hand, in Orissa, the enrolment growth rate is positive in the two periods, but the rate of increase in the post-Mid-day Meals period is less than the pre-Mid-day Meals period.

The caste-wise analysis indicates that, in Orissa, the enrolment of ST students has gone up in the post-Mid-day Meals period, while that of SC and other caste students have declined. In Tamil Nadu, the enrolment of students of all castes (SC, ST and others) has declined in the post-Mid-day Meals period.

When district-wise comparison is made, it is found that, in the educationally backward district of Orissa (Rayagada), the growth rate of enrolment of students has increased in the post-Mid-day Meals period, and this is possible because of the increase in the enrolment of SC and ST students. But in the educationally advanced district of Puri, there is a decrease in the enrolment of students in the post-Mid-day Meals period, and the growth rate is negative. On the other hand, in Tamil Nadu, negative growth rate in the enrolment of students is found in the pre-Mid-day Meals period both in the educa-

GROWTH OF ENROLMENT OF STUDENTS IN ORISSA AND TAMIL NADU FROM 1989-90 TO 1989-99

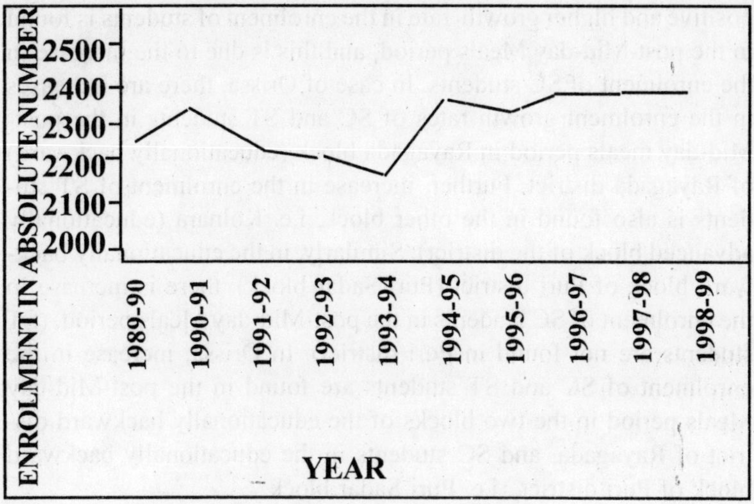

ENROLMENT IN ORISSA

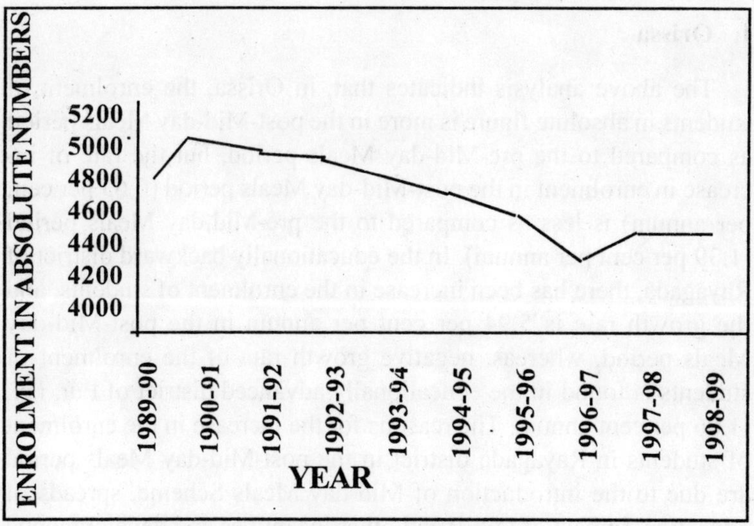

ENROLMENT IN TAMILNADU

tionally advanced and educationally backward districts. But, in Thirunavalur block (educationally backward) of Villupuram district, positive and higher growth rate in the enrolment of students is found in the post-Mid-day Meals period, and this is due to the increase in the enrolment of SC students. In case of Orissa, there are increases in the enrolment growth rates of SC and ST students in the post-Mid-day meals period in Rayagada block (educationally backward) of Rayagada district. Further, increase in the enrolment of ST students is also found in the other block, i.e. Kolnara (educationally advanced block of the district). Similarly, in the educationally backward block of Puri district (Puri Sadar block), there is increase in the enrolment of SC students in the post-Mid-day Meals period. (ST students are not found in Puri district). In Orissa, increase in the enrolment of SC and ST students are found in the post-Mid-day Meals period in the two blocks of the educationally backward district of Rayagada, and SC students in the educationally backward block of Puri district,. i.e. Puri Sadar block.

REASONS FOR THE INCREASE OR DECREASE IN ENROLMENT

1. Orissa

The above analysis indicates that, in Orissa, the enrolment of students in absolute figure is more in the post-Mid-day Meals period as compared to the pre-Mid-day Meals period, but the rate of increase in enrolment in the post-Mid-day Meals period (0.63 per cent per annum) is less as compared to the pre-Mid-day Meals period (1.39 per cent per annum). In the educationally backward district of Rayagada, there has been increase in the enrolment of students, and the growth rate is 5.94 per cent per annum in the post-Mid-day Meals period, whereas, negative growth rate of the enrolment of students is found in the educationally advanced district of Pur, i.e., -1.06 per cent annum. The reasons for the increase in the enrolment of students in Rayagada district in the post-Mid-day Meals period are due to the introduction of Mid-day Meals Scheme, spreads of education, impact of DPEP and other incentives and developmental progammes of the government. The negative growth rate in the enrolment of students in the educationally advanced district Puri does not necessarily mean that the scheme has no impact on the enrolment of students. The reasons responsible for the negative growth rate might be: (1) decline in the number of children in the age-group 6-11; (2) increase in the interest of parents to send their children to study in English Medium Schools and Public Schools, which are being opened largely in different areas, and (3) already higher percentage of enrolment of students has been made by schools in the district. Further, the enrolment growth rates indicate that the scheme has greater impact on the SC and ST students in the educationally backward district of Rayagada.

Regarding the impact of Mid-day Meal on enrolment of students, opinions of the teachers of the sample schools have been taken. In Puri district, 50 per cent of teachers said that Mid-day meals has definite impact in increasing the enrolment of students in the schools and, in Rayagada district, 85 per cent. teachers gave the same opinion.

In spite of the increase in the enrolment of students in schools in the post-Mid-day Meals period in Rayagada district, the enrolment rate in the district is not so good as said by the teachers. As per the opinion of teachers, educated villages, panchayat representatives, and NGO/social worker, the reasons for poor enrolment of students are poor financial background, illiteracy among parents, lack of interest among children to study, the burden of domestic work, taking care of siblings, etc. In Puri district also, some students are not going to school because of the above reasons.

2. Tamil Nadu

In Tamil Nadu, the growth rate of the enrolment of students is negative both in the pre and post-Mid-day Meals period, but the rate of decline is more in the post-Mid-day Meals period as compared to the pre-Mid-day Meals period. In both the educationally advanced and educationally backward districts, negative growth rate of enrolment is found in the post-Mid-day Meals period. The negative growth rate does not necessarily mean that Mid-day Meals has no impact on the enrolment of students. The reasons for negative growth rate are as follows first Tamil Nadu, being an educationally advanced state, has reached a saturation point with regard to enrolment of students and, during the field survey, it was known from the school teachers that there were almost 100 per cent enrolment of children in the schools in the sample areas; secondly there might be yearly decline in the number of children in the age-group 6-11; thirdly, the noon-meals scheme is operating in Tamil Nadu for the last 18 years (from 1982) i.e. much earlier than 1995, and the scheme might have achieved its objective of increased enrolment, and fourthly, preference of some children for studying in English Medium or other Public Schools, Moreover, as per the opinions of the sample teachers, educated villagers, and panchayat representatives, Mid-day Meal Scheme has no role on the enrolment of students. Even if Mid-day Meals were stopped, students would still comet to school for reading, as parents are very much aware about the education of their children. But the scheme is much useful for poor students, who are unable to attend schools for want of food. The Mid-day Meals meet the hunger need of the children in the noontime and, thereby, provides zeal and energy for pursuing study in the school.

In spite of greater enrolment rate in the state of Tamil Nadu, there are some children, who are not going to school, because of poverty and engagement of the children in domestic work. But the number is very less as said by the teacher during the field survey.

ATTENDANCE

Enrolling name in the school is not sufficient for learning. For better learning, regular attendance in the class is necessary. This section enquires about the extent Mid-day Meals has influenced in increasing the attendance of students in the schools. For this, comparison of the average attendance rates of students is made between the pre-Mid-day Meals period (1989-90 to 1994-95) and the post-Mid-day Meals period (1995-96 to 1998-99).

1. Orissa

Table-4.3 shows that in Orissa, the average attendance rate of students has gone up from 80.29 per cent in the pre-Mid-day Meals period to 86.09 per cent in the post-Mid-day Meals period. This indicates that attendance rate has increased by 5.80 percentage point in the post-Mid-day Meals period over the pre-Mid-day Meals period. The sex and caste-wise analysis indicate that average attendance rate in the post-Mid-day Meals period has gone up as compared to the pre-Mid-day Meals period. But, in case of SC students, there has been in increase of 7.24 percentage point in attendance rate, i.e., from 78.38 per cent in the pre-Mid-day Meals period to 85.62 per cent in the post-Mid-day Meals period Further, if we look at Annexure 4.6, we find that total attendance rate during pre-Mid-day Meals period was varying between 77 to 84 per cent, but after 1995 it started to vary between 85 to 88 per cent. This proves that attendance rate has gone up in the post-Mid-day Meals period in the state.

In Puri district, the average attendance rate has gone up from 80.75 per cent in the pre-Mid-day Meals period to 85.84 per cent in the post-Mid-day Meals period. The caste and sex-wise analysis also indicate the increasing trend in the attendance rate. In Satybadi block of Puri district, the scenario is almost the same as that of the district, and the average attendance rate has increased from 82.89 per cent in the pre-Mid-day Meals period to 88.50 per cent in the post-Mid-day Meals period. In the pre-Mid-day Meals period, the average attendance rate is 82.89 per cent, while in the Post-Mid-day Meals period, it is 88.50 per cent in the block. Similarly, in the educationally backward block Puri Sadar, the average attendance rate has gone up to 84.60 per cent as compared to 79.69 per cent in the pre-Mid-day Meals period.

Just like Puri district, in Rayagada district also the average attendance rate has increased in the post-Mid-day Meals period. In the pre-Mid-day Meals period, the average attendance rate was 78.81 per cent, while in the post-Mid-day Meals period , it has gone up to 86.89 per cent indicating an increase of 8.08 percentage point, which can be attributed to the Mid-day Meals scheme. The caste and sex-wise analysis indicate that the average attendance rates of all castes and sexes have increased in the post-Mid-day Meals period. In Kolnara block of the district, the average attendance rate has gone up considerably from 80.09 per cent in the pre-Mid-day Meals period to 89.57 per cent in the post-Mid-day Meals period. The cast and sex-wise figures also indicate the same picture. Similarly, in Rayagada block, the average attendance rate has increased from 77.56 per cent in the pre-Mid-day Meals period to 83.39 per cent in the post-Mid-day Meals period.

A comparison of the two districts of Orissa indicates that attendance rate has gone up in the post-Mid-day Meals period as compared to the pre-Mid-day Meals period. But the increase in average attendance rate of the backward district (8.08 percentage point) is more than that of the advanced district (5.09 percentage point). This shows that Mid-day Meals have resulted in increasing the attendance rate in both the districts of the state.

2. Tamil Nadu

In Tamil Nadu, the average attendance rate in the post-Mid-day Meals period has gone up to 91.88 per cent, which was 87.44 per cent in the pre-Mid-day Meals period. The most significant, thing is that the average attendance rates of SC and ST students have gone up significantly, whereas, that of other caste students, though the average attendance rate has increased, yet the increase is much lesser than that of SC and ST students. In case of SC and ST students, the average attendance rates have increased by 9.63 and 18.49 percentage points respectively in the post-Mid-day Meals period over the pre-Mid-day Meals period. On the other hand, in case of other caste students, the increase is only 3.16 percentage point. Thus, the state figures indicate that there is a positive impact of Mid-day Meals on the attendance rate of students in the schools.

Madurai district of Tamil Nadu also depicts the same picture on the attendance rate of students. Here, the average attendance rate of SC students has shown a healthy increase, i.e., 11.20 percentage point as compared to 2.13 percentage point increase in case of other caste students. Madurai East block (educationally advanced) and Alanganuller block (educationally backward) of the district also shows the same thing. But the increase in average attendance rate of SC students of Madurai East block is not as significant as that of the Alanganuller block.

The other district under study is Villupuram (educationally backward) district. The average attendance rate in this district has increased from 87.74 per cent in the pre Mid-day Meals period to 92.18 per cent in the post-Mid-day Meals. The average attendance rate of all castes and sexes have also gone up in the district. However, the average attendance rate of ST students has increased more significantly during the post-Mid-day Meals period as compared to that of SC and other cast students. In the pre-Mid-day Meals period, the average attendance rate of ST students was 75.16 per cent, which has increased to 96.43 per cent in the post-Mid-day Meals period, and the increase is 21.27 percentage point. The same is the case in Koliyanur as well as Thirunavalur block of the district. Here also the average attendance rates of all castes and sexes have increased in the post-Mid-day Meals period. In Koliyanur block, the increase in the average attendance rate of SC and other caste students is less as compared to that of Thirunavalur block. In Koliyanur block, the average attendance rate of ST students in the post-Mid-day Meals period is 100 per cent, which is very significant and encouraging. However, there was no enrolment of ST students in this block during the pre-Mid-day Meals period. On the other hand, in Thirunavalur block, the average attendance rate of ST students has gone up considerably in the post-Mid-day Meals, i.e., by 15.75 percentage point.

A comparison of the two districts of Tamil Nadu indicate that the average attendance rate in the post-Mid-day Meals period has increased as compared to that of the pre-Mid-day Meals period in both the districts irrespective of caste and sex. However, a careful analysis of Table-4.4 indicates that, in Madurai district, the average attendance rate of SC students has gone up significantly (There is no ST students in the district), whereas, in the educationally backward district of Villupuram, the average attendance rate of ST students has increased significantly during the post-Mid-day-Meals period.

3. Orissa And Tamil Nadu — A Comparision

In Orissa and Tamil Nadu, the average attendance rate of students is more in the post-Mid-day Meals period as compared to that in the pre-Mid-day Meals period irrespective of caste and sex. But the average attendance rate of Tamil Nadu is found to be higher than that of Orissa both in the pre and post-Mid-day Meals period. Further, in both the states, there have been more increases in the average attendance rates of SC and ST students. The increase in the average attendance rates of SC and ST students is more in Tamil Nadu than that in Orissa.

The district-wise comparison shows that, in Orissa, the increase in the average attendance rate is more in the educationally backward district as compared to educationally advanced district, whereas, in Tamil Nadu, the increase in the average attendance rate is more or less same both in the educationally advanced and backward district.

4. Reasons for the Increase in Attendance Rate

The above analysis shows that the average attendance rate of students has increased in the post-Mid-day Meals period as compared to the pre-Mid-day Meals period irrespective of caste and sex in all the sample districts and blocks of Orissa and Tamil Nadu. Greater increase in the attendance rate is found among the Scheduled Caste and Scheduled Tribe students both in Orissa and Tamil Nadu. As per the opinions of teachers, educated villagers, panchayat representatives and NGO/social workers, such increase in the attendance rate is partly due to the impact of Mid-day Meals and partly due to the spread of education.

However, in spite of the increase in average attendance rate in the post-Mid-day Meals period, there is still more scope for increase in the attendance rate of students both in Orissa and Tamil Nadu. The scope is more in Orissa as compared to Tamil Nadu, because, the attendance rate is comparatively less in Orissa than that in Tamil Nadu, In Orissa, as per the opinion of sample teachers, the reasons for poor attendance of students are: (1) engagement in the field during the harvesting season, (2) taking care of siblings at home, (3) taking domestic animals like cows, goats, etc. for grazing, (4) lack of interest in study and (5) helping parents to earn money. In Tamil Nadu, though the attendance rate is not poor and the average attendance rate is 91.88 per cent in the post-Mid-day Meals period, but still there is possibility of increase in attendance rate. The reasons, which obstructs increase in the attendance rate in the state, are: (1) engagement in field in the harvesting season, (2) absence of students during the festival seasons, (3) health related problems and (4) engagement in domestic work.

DROPOUT AND RETENTION

The analysis below gives a clear picture of how dropout and retention have behaved between the pre-Mid-day Meals period and the post-Mid-day Meals period in the states of Orissa and Tamil Nadu.

1. Orissa

The Table-4.5 and 4.6 show the average dropout and retention rates of the pre-Mid-day Meals, the post-Mid-day Meals period and over the entire period in the sample blocks and districts of Orissa respectively. The average dropout rate in the pre-Mid-day Meals period was as high as 41.01%, which has reduced to 25.58% during the post-Mid-day Meals period. Indicating the fact that average dropout rate in the state has declined by 15.43 percentage point after the scheme was introduced. The caste-wise average dropout rate indicates that the dropout rates of SC and other caste students have reduced drastically from 37.30 per cent and 35.28 per cent in the pre-Mid-day Meals period to 22.53 per cent and 20.45 per cent in the post-Mid-day Meals period respectively. The extent of decrease is 14.77 percentage point for SC students and 14.83 percentage points for other caste students. But the average dropout rate of ST students, though has reduced by 8.36 percentage point in the post-Mid-day Meals period over the pre-Mid-day Meals period, still it is very high, i.e., 50.70 per cent in the post-Mid-day Meals period. This indicates that the scheme is successful in reducing the dropout rates of students of all castes, but still the dropout rate of ST students is very high as compared to other students.

The reduction in the average dropout rate implies there is increase in the average retention rate. The state figure shows that average retention rate in the pre-Mid-day Meals period was 58.99 per cent, which has increased to 74.42 per cent in the post-Mid-day Meals period.

The Puri district figures indicate almost the same picture. Here also, the average dropout rates have declined for all castes and sexes, which means retention rates in schools have increased. The dropout rate has reduced from 32.56 per cent in the pre-Mid-day Meals period to 18.24 per cent in the post-Mid-day Meals period, and the decrease is by 14.32 percentage point.

Puri being an educationally advanced district, the dropout rate here is much less than that of the state figure. In the educationally advanced block of Satyabadi, the average dropout rate has declined from 28.07 per cent to 15.04 per cent, which means that the average retention rate has increased from 71.93 per cent to 84.96 per cent in the post-Mid-day Meals period. In the block, the average dropout rates of boys and girls of SC and other castes have reduced in the post-Mid-day Meals period (There is no ST students in the block), but the reduction is more in case of other caste students. Similarly, in the educationally backward Puri Sadar block, the average dropout rates of all castes and sexes have declined during the post-Mid-day Meals period. In this block, the declined rate is a little bit more, i.e., 15.13 percentage point as compared to that of educationally advanced block Satyabadi, i.e., 13.03 percentage point.

The district and block figures show that the average dropout rates in the two sample blocks have fallen during the post-mid-day Meals period. But the decline in the dropout rates among other caste students is much faster than that of SC students. Puri being an educationally advanced district, the awareness about education is more here. Therefore more number of children, instead of dropping out, continue their studies. It would be wrong to say that the reduction in dropout rates is basically due to Mid-day Meals. Of course, there is some impact of the scheme on the dropout rates, but that is restricted only to very poor students.

Enrolment in Class 1 preceding 4 years-Enrolment in Class V during the year Dropout Rate at Primary stage during the Year = --x 100

Enrolment in Class 1 preceding 4 years.

In Rayagada district, the average dropout rate in the post-Mid-day Meals period have declined by 13.50 percentage point, but it is still as high as 42.59 per cent. This implies that the average retention rate during the post-Mid-day Meals period is as low as 57.41 per cent. But the caste-wise analysis indicates that the average dropout rate among SC students has fallen drastically from 53.81 per cent in the pre-Mid-day Meals period to 22.89 per cent in the post-Mid-day Meals period, and the extent of decline is 30.92 percentage point. This shows that the scheme is a great success among SC students.The average dropout rate of ST students is still high at 50.70 per cent in the post-Mid-day Meals period. In other words, the retention rate of ST students in the post-Mid-day Meals period is very less i.e., 49.30 per cent. In the pre-Mid-day Meals period, the average dropout of ST students in the district was 59.06 per cent and the rate has declined by 8.36 percentage point in the post-Mid-day Meals period.

In the educationally advanced block Kolnara, the average drop-out rate in the pre-Mid-day Meals period has declined from 46.08 per cent to 38.69 per cent in the post-Mid-day Meals period indicating a decline of 7.39 percentage point. The average dropout rate among SC students is quite satisfactory. Here the average dropout rate during the post-Mid-day Meals period is -4.20 per cent, indicating the fact that the enrolment in class V is more than the enrolment in class I preceding four years. This is also possible because of the lesser number of enrolment of SC students in the block (Annexure 4.3). As a result of negative dropout rate, the retention rate of SC students becomes 104.20 per cent in the post-Mid-day Meals period. In the educationally backward block Rayagada, the average dropout rate has declined from 64.74 per cent to 55.12 per cent, but it is still very high as compared to Kolnara block. Here the dropout rates of all castes and sexes have fallen during the post-Mid-day Meals period.

A comparison of two districts indicates that the dropout rate in both the districts have reduced in the post-Mid-day Meals period, and the extent of decline in the two districts are more or less same. But the dropout rate is comparatively more in Rayagada district as compared to Puri district both in the pre and post-Mid-day Meals period. The opposite happens in case of retention rate of students in the two districts.

2. Tamil Nadu

The average dropout rate and retention rate of the sample blocks and districts of Tamil Nadu can be seen from Table-4.7 and Table-4.8 respectively.

The state figure shows that average dropout rate has declined by 2.94 percentage point in the post-Mid-day Meals period over the pre-Mid-day Meals period, which is a marginal decline. It has reduced from 26.11 per cent in the pre-Mid-day Meals period to 23.17 per cent in the post-Mid-day Meals period. The average dropout rates of SC and ST students have declined, while that of other caste students has increased. The average dropout rate of SC student has declined significantly from 27.59 per cent to 8.97 per cent. In other words, retention rate has increased from 72.41 per cent to 91.03 per cent, which is a very good positive sign.The average dropout rate of other caste students has increased marginally from 25.58 per cent to 27.79 per cent. In case of ST students, the dropout rate has decreased from 36.11 per cent to 29.17 per cent and the extent of decline is 6.94 percentage point.

In the educationally advanced district Madurai, the average dropout rate has declined from 19.33 per cent to 18.88 per cent in the post-Mid-day Meals period indicating the marginal decline of 0.45 percentage point. The average dropout rate has increased marginally by 1.17 percentage point in case of other caste students, whereas, it has decreased by 4.70 percentage point in case of SC student.

The average dropout rate of the educationally advanced block of the district in the post-Mid-day Meals period is as low as 11.47 per cent as against 19.73 per cent in the pre-Mid-day Meals period. In this block, the average dropout rates of all castes and sexes have declined during post-Mid-day Meals period. In the backward block of Alanganuller, the average dropout rate has declined from 25.08 per cent to 17.19 per cent, but it is still higher than the Madurai East block. The dropout rates based on caste and sec have declined in the post-Mid-day meals period in Alanganuller block.

In Villupuram district (educationally backward), though the average dropout rate has declined, it is still as high as 30.83 per cent in the post-Mid-day Meals period, which means the average retention rate is 69.17 per cent in the same period. In the district, the average dropout rate has declined for all castes except other caste students, which has increased from 34.40 per cent to 40.38 per cent. The dropout rate of SC students is negative in the post-Mid-day Meals period, which means the dropout of students is zero and there have been more enrolments of SC students in class V as compared to enrolment in class I, four years back, In Koliyanur block of the district, average dropout rate has increased marginally from 22.63 per cent to 22.79 per cent. But the caste-wise analysis is same as that of the district. In the educationally backward block Thirunavalur, the opposite is the case, here the average dropout rate has declined by 8.82 percentage point, but it is still high at 38.77 per cent in the post-Mid-day Meals period. The dropout rate of ST students during the post-Mid-day Meals period is a staggering 100 per cent, which means retention of student is zero. This is due to the lesser number of ST students in the sample schools in different years (see Annexure 4.5). But the average dropout rate of SC students has declined from 44.06 per cent in the pre-Mid-day Meals period to 17.25 per cent in the post-Mid-day Meals period registering a decline of 26.81 percentage point.

A comparison of the two districts in Tamil Nadu indicates that, the average dropout rate of SC students have decreased in the post-Mid-day Meals period in both the districts. In case of other caste students, the dropout rates have increased both in Madurai district and Villupuram district.

3. Orissa And Tamil Nadu — A Comparison

The analysis of the dropout rates of Orissa and Tamil Nadu indicate that there is a reduction in the average dropout rates in both the states in the post-Mid-day Meals period as compared to the pre-Mid-day Meals period. In Orissa, the reduction is significant (by 15.43 percentage point), whereas, in Tamil Nadu, it is marginal (by 2.94 percentage point). Further, reduction in dropout rate in the post-Mid-day Meals period is found to be more in both the states. In case of ST students also, there is reduction in dropout rates in the two states. On the other hand, in the case of caste students, there is reduction of 14.83 percentage point in Orissa, whereas, in Tamil Nadu, the dropout rate has increased marginally by 2.21 percentage point. Another observation is that, Orissa being an educationally backward state, the overall dropout rates are more as compared to Tamil Nadu, which is an educationally advanced state.

The district-wise analysis shows that, in Orissa there is reduction in the dropout rates of students irrespective of caste and sex in both the sample districts. In Tamil Nadu, reduction in dropout rate is found in the sample districts in the aggregate. While making the caste-wise analysis, there is increase in the average dropout rate of other caste students in the post-Mid-day Meals period in both the districts of the Tamil Nadu. In case of SC and ST students the dropout rate exhibited a significant decline.

The decline in the dropout rates means an increase in the retention rates. Therefore, in both the states, the retention rates have increased during the post-Mid-day Meals period. But the increase is more in Orissa than in Tamil Nadu. In, Orissa, the retention rate has increased from 58.99 per cent in the pre-Mid-day Meals period to 74.42 per cent in post-Mid-day Meals period, which is a positive and healthy increase. This indicates that Mid-day-Meals have definitely helped the students to continue studies in Orissa. However, the increase in retention rate in the post-Mid-day Meals period over the pre-Mid-day Meals period is marginal in Tamil Nadu i.e. 2.94 percentage point. The district and block-wise analysis on retention rate is also the reverse of the analysis of dropout rates.

Reasons For Dropout

1. Orissa

In Orissa, the state, district and block figures indicate that the dropout rate in the post-Mid-day Meals period has gone down significantly, which is possible due to the impact of Mid-day Meals Scheme and spread of the importance of education. However, a close look at the data shows that the dropout rate in the backward district of Rayagada is still very high at 42.59 per cent in the post-

Mid-day Meals period. During the field study, we found that the basic reasons responsible for the higher dropout rates in both the districts of Orissa, as stated by the teacher respondents, are lack of finance to continue studies, lack of interest to study, preference and compulsion to work as child labour. Apart from these reasons in Puri district, it is found that some children dropout from schools, as they prefer to go to towns for better education. Further, the opening up of English Medium Schools and N.F.E. Centres also causes dropouts in formal primary schools run by the government. Students get more facilities in N.F.E. Centres than primary schools and, therefore, there is a diversion of students to these schools. But in the strict sense, these are not actually dropout cases. Similarly in Rayagada district, the field study suggests that children dropout from schools,because, they do not understand the value of education, and they have to take care of siblings at home. In some cases, it is observed that parents do not allow the girl child to continue studies as they feel that she can be engaged in work and earn money for the family. This is the important reason for higher dropout rates among girl students in Rayagada district.

2. Tamil Nadu

In Tamil Nadu, the average dropout rate has reduced from 26.11 per cent to 23.17 per cent in the post-Mid-day Meals period. However, in Villupuram district this rate is at 30.83 per cent in the post-Mid-day Meals period, which is a cause for concern. As per the discussion with the teachers, educated villagers, NGÓ/social workers, it is found that the important reasons that are responsible for higher dropout rates are (1) the poor financial background of students, (2) compulsion to work as child labour, and (3) the heavy nature of domestic work. All these problems prohibit the students to continue studies. Apart from the above mentioned reasons, other important reason responsible is the opening up of English Medium and Public Schools. These schools attract more students from primary schools, which increase dropouts in primary schools. All these problems are found both in the educationally advanced and backward district of Tamil Nadu.

Another important thing, which is observed during the analysis of dropout rate of other caste students is that in the post-Mid-day Meals period, the dropout rate has increased as compared to pre-Mid-day Meals period in both the districts of Tamil Nadu. As per the information given by the teachers, the reason is migration of labour class families, having children reading in primary schools, to town areas.

From the above discussion, we can conclude that there has been increase in the attendance rate and retention rate, decrease in the dropout rate of students in the post-Mid-day Meals period as compared to the pre-Mid-day Meals period both in Orissa and Tamil Nadu. Regarding the enrolment of the students, the rate of increase is less in the post-Mid-day Meals period as compared to the pre-Mid-day Meals period in Orissa, but still in absolute figures, the number is increasing in the post-day-Mid Meals period. In Tamil Nadu, the rate of growth of enrolment is negative in both the pre and post-Mid-day Meals period, which could be attributed to the decline in population in the age group of 6-11 years. From this, it can be said that the scheme has some definite impact on these variables. However, other reasons like spread of education, general awareness about education, the impact of other development schemes by Government cannot be negated.

TABLE-4.1

GROWTH RATES (IN PER CENT) OF ENROLMENT OF STUDENTS IN DIFFERENT PERIODS IN THE SAMPLE AREAS OF ORISSA

Area	*Period*	*SC*			*ST*			*Others*			*Total*		
		B	*G*	*T*	*B*	*G*	*T*	*B*	*G*	*T*	*B*	*G*	*T*
PURI	1989-90 to 1994-95	3.71	4.91	4.03	--	--	--	0.07	1.30	0.61	0.75	1.84	1.21
DISTRICT	1995-96 to 1998-99	0.82	-0.58	-0.05	--	--	--	-1.40	-0.99	-1.27	-1.17	-0.89	-1.06
	1989-90 to 1998-99	2.75	3.08	2.67	--	--	--	-0.42	0.54	-0.02	0.11	0.93	0.45
SATYA-	1989-90 to 1994-95	4.31	-0.56	1.78	--	--	--	-1.65	0.76	-0.63	-0.09	-0.72	-0.43
BADI	1995-96 to 1998-99	-4.74	-5.91	-5.31	--	--	--	-1.60	1.15	-0.37	-2.78	-1.65	-2.27
BLOCK	1989-90 to 1998-99	1.59	1.01	1.11	--	--	--	-1.88	-0.73	-1.44	-0.98	-0.95	-0.99
PURI	1989-90 to 1994-95	6.25	6.69	6.14	--	--	--	3.83	3.80	3.72	4.10	4.12	4.00
SADAR	1995-96 to 1998-99	10.11	7.39	7.70	--	--	--	-1.24	-1.64	-1.51	-0.28	-0.38	-0.36
BLOCK	1989-90 to 1998-99	5.48	7.08	5.59	--	--	--	0.32	1.30	0.68	0.79	2.05	1.29
RAYA-	1989-90 to 1994-95	11.01	14.53	11.47	-2.61	-6.71	-4.55	3.52	-2.80	-0.62	-0.77	-3.79	-2.15
GADA	1995-96 to 1998-99	3.46	10.94	6.55	7.66	10.13	8.39	-3.89	3.28	-0.62	4.51	8.03	5.94
DISTRICT	1989-90 to 1998-99	8.72	13.35	10.08	3.34	1.60	2.39	1.65	0.60	0.68	2.89	2.23	2.54

(Cont...)

TABLE-4.1 (Cont...)

GROWTH RATES (IN PER CENT) OF ENROLMENT OF STUDENTS IN DIFFERENT PERIODS IN THE SAMPLE AREAS OF ORISSA

Area	*Period*	*SC*			*ST*			*Others*			*Total*		
		B	*G*	*T*	*B*	*G*	*T*	*B*	*G*	*T*	*B*	*G*	*T*
KOLNARA	1989-90 to 1994-95	7.02	12.13	8.76	4.07	4.92	3.60	11.91	-1.12	4.15	6.20	3.03	4.58
BLOCK	1995-96 to 1998-99	3.05	7.33	4.55	8.44	13.27	10.16	-3.12	9.04	1.93	3.81	8.48	5.82
	1989-90 to 1998-99	6.15	11.32	7.99	8.34	6.99	6.97	5.58	3.53	3.43	6.41	5.19	5.73
RAYA--	1989-90 to 1994-95	-27.87	101.88	53.15	-5.29	-13.60	-8.54	-10.06	-5.17	-8.34	-6.56	-11.35	-8.54
GADA	1995-96 to 1998-99	5.81	25.78	13.29	7.08	7.36	7.00	-4.58	5.74	-1.41	5.40	7.67	6.13
BLOCK	1989-90 to 1998-99	-9.26	65.19	35.20	0.96	-0.34	0.18	-2.35	-0.11	-2.23	0.11	-0.26	-0.19
ORISSA	1989-90 to 1994-95	5.34	3.39	4.31	-2.61	-6.71	-4.55	2.06	2.05	2.02	1.80	0.96	1.39
STATE	1995-96 to 1998-99	0.96	1.49	1.15	7.66	10.13	8.39	-1.68	-0.67	-1.27	0.35	0.97	0.63
	1989-90 to 1998-99	3.37	4.50	3.75	3.34	1.60	2.39	-0.41	0.42	-0.06	0.75	1.11	0.89

Source: Compiled from the date collected from the Sample Schools.

TABLE-4.2

GROWTH RATES (IN PER CENT) OF ENROLMENT OF STUDENTS IN DIFFERENT PERIODS IN THE SAMPLE AREAS OF TAMIL NADU

Area	*Period*	*SC*			*ST*			*Others*			*Total*		
		B	*G*	*T*	*B*	*G*	*T*	*B*	*G*	*T*	*B*	*G*	*T*
MADURAI	1989-90 to 1994-95	4.17	6.36	5.14	--	--	--	0.72	-2.39	-0.76	1.66	-0.07	0.83
DISTRICT	1995-96 to 1998-99	1.15	-2.33	-0.47	--	--	--	-1.66	-2.18	-1.93	-0.87	-2.21	-1.50
	1989-90 to 1998-99	1.54	1.23	1.37	--	--	--	-0.74	-2.31	-1.50	-0.12	-1.44	-0.75
MADURAI	1989-90 to 1994-95	8.35	11.23	9.47	--	--	--	2.02	-0.24	0.94	3.61	2.37	3.00
EAST	1995-96 to 1998-99	0.92	-3.85	-1.35	--	--	--	-0.33	-1.29	-0.83	-0.03	-1.97	-0.97
BLOCK	1989-90 to 1998-99	3.24	3.93	3.41	--	--	--	1.46	-0.07	0.72	1.82	0.70	1.26
ALANGA-	1989-90 to 1994-95	0.50	3.27	1.79	--	--	--	-0.58	-4.36	-2.41	-0.30	-2.27	-1.26
NULLER	1995-96 to 1998-99	1.48	-0.71	0.45	--	--	--	-3.69	-3.44	-3.58	-1.94	-2.48	-2.20
BLOCK	1989-90 to 1998-99	0.25	-0.41	-0.12	--	--	--	-3.40	-4.74	-4.08	-2.26	-3.55	-2.89
VILLUPU-	1989-90 to 1994-95	-1.49	-4.89	-3.07	12.81	13.33	9.27	-2.90	0.61	-1.21	-2.70	-0.19	-1.50
RAM	1995-96 to 1998-99	4.02	9.01	6.02	-16.52	-14.44	-20.17	-1.85	-5.38	-3.66	-0.38	-2.49	-1.44
DISTRICT	1989-90 to 1998-99	9.00	7.99	8.44	10.87	19.26	10.65	-3.58	-2.56	-3.12	-1.31	-0.87	-1.12

(Cont...)

TABLE-4.2 (Cont...)

GROWTH RATES (IN PER CENT) OF ENROLMENT OF STUDENTS IN DIFFERENT PERIODS IN THE SAMPLE AREAS OF TAMIL NADU

Area	*Period*	*SC*			*ST*			*Others*			*Total*		
		B	*G*	*T*	*B*	*G*	*T*	*B*	*G*	*T*	*B*	*G*	*T*
KOLIYA-	1989-90 to 1994-95	-4.35	-8.12	-6.59	--	--	--	-3.08	3.11	-0.05	-3.30	2.09	-0.65
NNUR	1995-96 to 1998-99	1.99	-0.59	0.70	-5.00	-7.78	-15.00	-3.97	-8.10	-6.18	-2.69	-6.76	-4.84
BLOCK	1989-90 to 1998-99	21.95	19.57	20.55	-5.00	-7.78	-15.00	-4.50	-2.78	-3.74	-2.28	-1.30	-1.87
THIRUN-	1989-90 to 1994-95	--0.03	-2.55	-1.21	8.76	13.33	8.88	-2.56	-2.87	-2.78	-2.02	-2.78	-2.45
VALLUR	1995-96 to 1998-99	5.53	18.35	10.23	0.00	-100.00	0.00	1.16	-1.59	-0.21	2.47	2.91	2.65
BLOCK	1989-90 to 1998-99	5.78	6.35	5.72	5.48	-11.90	2.42	-2.23	-2.00	-2.18	-0.16	-0.18	-0.22
TAMIL	1989-90 to 1994-95	2.68	3.65	3.12	12.81	13.33	9.27	-0.69	-1.22	-0.96	0.10	-0.15	-0.03
NADU	1995-96 to 1998-99	1.98	0.70	1.39	-16.52	-7.78	-16.47	-1.84	-3.54	-2.67	-0.81	-2.47	-1.61
STATE	1989-90 to 1998-99	2.96	2.38	2.68	10.87	21.48	11.88	-1.85	-2.47	-2.17	-0.62	-1.31	-0.96

Source: Compiled from the date collected from the Sample Schools.

TABLE-4.3

AVERAGE ATTENDANCE RATE OF STUDENTS (IN PER CENT) IN DIFFERENT PERIODS IN THE SAMPLE AREAS OF ORISSA

Area	*Period*	*SC*			*ST*			*Others*			*Total*		
		B	*G*	*T*	*B*	*G*	*T*	*B*	*G*	*T*	*B*	*G*	*T*
PURI	1989-90 to 1994-95	79.01	77.34	78.29	--	--	--	82.54	80.17	81.43	81.78	79.57	80.75
DISTRICT	1995-96 to 1998-99	86.60	82.90	84.74	--	--	--	86.73	85.59	86.18	86.65	84.97	85.84
	1989-90 to 1998-99	82.05	79.57	80.87	--	--	--	84.22	82.34	83.33	83.73	81.73	82.79
		(7.59)	(5.56)	(6.45)				(4.19)	(5.42)	(4.75)	(4.87)	(5.40)	(5.09)
SATYA-	1989-90 to 1994-95	79.01	76.37	77.79	--	--	--	86.94	84.69	85.90	84.03	81.62	82.89
BADI	1995-96 to 1998-99	88.76	85.96	87.40	--	--	--	90.70	87.62	89.24	89.95	86.91	88.50
BLOCK	1989-90 to 1998-99	82.91	80.20	81.63	--	--	--	88.44	85.86	87.24	86.40	83.73	85.13
		(9.75)	(9.59)	(9.61)				(3.76)	(2.93)	(3.34)	(5.92)	(5.29)	(5.61)
PURI	1989-90 to 1994-95	78.95	78.99	79.02	--	--	--	80.88	78.60	79.80	80.63	78.65	79.69
SADAR	1995-96 to 1998-99	83.97	79.62	81.70	--	--	--	85.37	84.93	85.15	85.10	84.07	84.60
BLOCK	1989-90 to 1998-99	80.96	79.24	80.09	--	--	--	82.67	81.13	81.94	82.42	80.82	81.66
		(5.02)	(0.63)	(2.68)				(4.49)	(6.63)	(5.35)	(4.47)	(5.52)	(4.91)
RAYAGA-	1989-90 to 1994-95	79.12	78.89	78.84	81.44	78.20	80.08	77.68	73.57	75.59	80.34	76.78	78.81
DA	1995-96 to 1998-99	88.79	89.74	89.30	87.48	83.93	86.11	86.81	87.62	87.18	87.55	85.93	86.89
DISTRICT	1989-90 to 1998-99	82.99	83.23	83.02	83.85	80.49	82.49	81.33	79.19	80.23	83.22	80.44	82.04
		(9.67)	(10.85)	(10.46)	(6.04)	(5.73)	(6.03)	(9.13)	(14.05)	(11.59)	(7.21)	(9.15)	(8.08)

(Cont...)

TABLE-4.3 (Cont...)

AVERAGE ATTENDANCE RATE OF STUDENTS (IN PER CENT) IN DIFFERENT PERIODS IN THE SAMPLE AREAS OF ORISSA

Area	Period	SC			ST			Others			Total		
		B	G	T	B	G	T	B	G	T	B	G	T
KOLNA	1989-90 to 1994-95	79.57	80.45	79.76	80.65	79.12	80.03	83.25	77.74	80.24	81.19	78.69	80.09
RA	1995-96 to 1998-99	89.52	92.06	90.69	91.20	87.65	89.69	88.13	87.90	88.11	90.10	88.89	89.57
BLOCK	1989-90 to 1998-99	83.55	85.09	84.13	84.87	87.53	83.89	85.20	81.80	83.39	84.75	82.77	83.88
		(9.95)	(11.61)	(10.93)	(10.55)	(8.53)	(9.66)	(4.88)	(10.16)	(7.87)	(8.91)	(10.20)	(9.48)
RAYA-	1989-90 to 1994-95	75.22	70.92	72.08	81.74	77.26	79.97	71.36	66.28	68.95	79.55	74.65	77.56
GADA	1995-96 to 1998-99	86.27	83.50	84.94	84.51	80.23	82.98	83.05	85.57	84.23	84.49	81.54	83.39
BLOCK	1989-90 to 1998-99	79.64	75.95	77.22	82.85	78.45	81.17	76.04	74.00	75.06	81.52	77.40	79.90
		(11.05)	(12.58)	(12.86)	(2.77)	(2.97)	(3.01)	(11.69)	(19.29)	(15.28)	(4.94)	(6.89)	(5.83)
ORISSA	1989-90 to 1994-95	78.99	77.57	78.38	81.44	78.20	80.08	82.14	79.49	80.90	81.44	78.91	80.29
	1995-96 to 1998-99	87.01	84.18	85.62	87.48	83.93	86.11	86.73	85.75	86.26	86.89	85.19	86.09
STATE	1989-90 to 1998-99	82.20	80.22	81.28	83.85	80.49	82.49	83.97	82.00	/83.04	83.62	81.42	82.61
		(8.02)	(6.61)	(7.24)	(6.04)	(5.73)	(6.03)	(4.59)	(6.26)	(5.36)	(5.45)	(6.28)	(5.80)

Note : Bracketed figures indicate increase by percentage point in the post Mid-day Meals period over the pre-MDM period.

Source: Compiled from the data collected from the Sample Schools.

TABLE -4.4

AVERAGE ATTENDANCE RATE OF STUDENTS (IN PER CENT) IN DIFFERENT PERIODS IN THE SAMPLE AREAS OF TAMIL NADU

AREA	*Period*	*SC*			*ST*			*Others*			*Total*		
		B	*G*	*T*	*B*	*G*	*T*	*B*	*G*	*T*	*B*	*G*	*T*
MADURAI	1989-90 to 1994-95	78.99	76.61	77.83	-	-	-	90.29	91.28	90.76	87.24	87.29	87.26
DISTRICT	1995-96 to 1998-99	89.15	88.92	89.03	-	--	--	91.84	94.22	92.89	91.05	92.60	91.73
	1989-90 to 1998-99	83.05	81.53	82.31	--	--	--	90.91	92.46	91.61	88.76	89.41	89.05
		(10.16)	(12.31)	(11.20)				(1.55)	(2.94)	(2.13)	(3.81)	(5.31)	(4.47)
MADURAI	1989-90 to 1994-95	89.08	88.54	88.79	--	--	--	93.39	92.91	93.17	92.29	91.85	92.07
EAST	1995-96 to 1998-99	93.07	93.61	93.32	--	--	--	93.23	95.16	94.03	93.19	94.76	93.85
BLOCK	1989-90 to 1998-99	90.68	90.57	90.60	--	--	--	93.32	93.81	93.51	92.65	93.01	92.78
		(3.99)	(5.07)	(4.53)				(0.16)	(2.25)	(0.86)	(0.90)	(2.91)	(1.78)
ALANGAN-	1989-90 to 1994-95	69.75	67.05	68.42	--	--	--	86.70	89.48	88.02	81.77	82.76	82.23
ULLER	1995-96 to 1998-99	85.00	84.37	84.67	--	--	--	89.48	92.82	91.03	87.92	89.34	88.81
BLOCK	1989-90 to 1998-99	75.85	73.98	74.92	--	--	--	87.82	90.81	89.22	84.23	85.59	84.86
		(15.25)	(17.32)	(16.25)				(2.78)	(3.34)	(3.01)	(6.15)	(7.08)	(6.58)
VILLUPU-	1989-90 to 1994-95	83.37	84.89	84.04	72.46	79.86	75.16	88.80	88.27	88.53	97.80	87.69	87.74
RAM	1995-96 to 1998-99	89.81	88.24	89.09	95.45	97.50	96.43	93.51	93.30	93.42	92.38	91.95	92.18
DISTRICT	1989-90 to 1998-99	85.94	86.23	86.06	81.66	86.92	83.67	90.69	90.28	90.49	89.63	89.39	89.52
		(6.44)	(3.35)	(5.04)	(22.99)	(17.64)	(21.27)	(4.71)	(5.03)	(4.89)	(4.58)	(4.26)	(4.44)

(Cont...)

TABLE 4.4 (Cont...)

AGERAGE ATTENDANCE RATE OF STUDENTS (IN PER CENT) IN DIFFERENT PERIODDS IN THE SAMPLE AREAS OF TAMIL NADU

Area	Period	SC			ST			Others			Total		
		B	G	T	B	G	T	B	G	T	B	G	T
KOLIYA-	1989-90 to 1994-95	89.18	87.15	88.12	--	-	--	89.78	89.50	89.63	89.73	89.29	89.50
NNUR	1995-96 to 1998-99	9140	89.77	90.65	100.00	100.00	100.00	92.79	92.89	92.86	92.52	92.32	92.44
BLOCK	1989-90 to 1998-99	90.07	88.20	89.14	100.00	100.00	100.00	90.98	90.86	90.93	90.85	90.50	90.68
		(2.22)	(2.62)	(2.53)	--	--	--	(3.01)	(3.39)	(3.23)	(2.79)	(3.03)	(2.94)
THIRUNA-	1989-90 to 1994-95	81.81	83.84	82.66	72.46	79.86	75.16	87.51	86.31	86.94	85.78	85.62	85.71
VALLUR	1995-96 to 1998-99	88.74	87.32	88.02	90.48	75.00	90.91	94.59	93.78	94.17	92.31	91.49	91.90
BLOCK	1989-90 to 1998-99	84.58	85.23	84.81	78.47	79.17	80.41	90.34	89.30	89.83	88.39	87.97	88.19
		(6.93)	(3.48)	(5.36)	(18.02)	(4.86)	(15.75)	(7.08)	(7.47)	(7.23)	(6.53)	(5.87)	(6.19)
TAMIL	1989-90 to 1994-95	80.04	78.61	79.36	72.46	79.86	75.16	89.73	90.08	89.89	87.45	87.44	87.44
NADU	1995-96 to 1998-99	89.36	88.54	88.99	95.45	91.25	93.65	92.35	93.87	93.05	91.46	92.37	91.88
STATE	1989-90 to 1998-99	83.77	82.58	83.21	81.66	84.42	82.46	90.78	91.59	91.15	89.05	89.41	89.21
		(9.32)	(9.93)	(9.63)	(22.99)	(11.39)	(18.49)	(2.62)	(3.79)	(3.16)	(4.01)	(4..93)	(4.44)

Note : Bracketed figures indicate increase by percentage point in the post-MDM period over the pre-MDM period.

Source :Compiled from the data collected from the Sample Schools.

TABLE 4.5

AVERAGE DROPOUT RATE (IN PER CENT) OF STUDENTS IN DIFFERENT PERIODS IN THE SAMPLE AREAS OF ORISSA

Area	Period	SC				ST			Others			Total	
		B	G	T		B	G	T	B	G	T	B	G
PURI	1989-90 to 1994-95	30.61	32.34	31.38	--	--	--	32.26	33.49	32.83	31.94	33.29	32.56
DISTRICT	1995-96 to 1998-99	21.46	21.96	21.68	--	--	--	18.07	16.37	17.20	18.87	17.66	18.24
	1989-90 to 1998-99	26.95	28.19	27.50	--	-	--	26.59	26.64	26.58	26.71	27.03	26.83
		(9.15)	(10.38)	(9.70)				(14.19)	(17.12)	(15.63)	(13.07)	(15.63)	(14.32)
SATYABA	1989-90 to 1994-95	26.32	30.18	28.05	-	--	--	27.99	28/.47	28.15	27.13	29.12	28.07
-DI	1995-96 to 1998-99	20.47	20.44	20.45	--	--	--	14.22	9.74	12.09	16.32	13.70	15.04
BLOCK	1989-90 to 1998-99	23.98	26.28	25.01	--	--	--	22.48	20.98	21.73	22.81	22.95	22.86
		(5.85)	(9.74)	(7.60)				(13.77)	(18.73)	(16.06)	(10.81)	(15.42)	(13.03)
PURI	1989-90 to 1994-95	36.08	35.67	35.93	--	--	--	33.84	35.57	34.64	34.13	35.62	34.79
SADAR	1995-96 to 1998-99	22.75	23.87	23.37	--	--	--	19.28	18.50	18.90	19.94	19.39	19.66
BLOCK	1989-90 to 1998-99	30.75	30.95	30.91	--	--	--	28.02	28.75	28.34	28.45	29.13	28.74\
		(13.33)	(11.80)	(12.56)				(14.56)	(17.07)	(15.74)	(14.19)	(16.23)	(15.13)
RAYAGA-	1989-90 to 1994-95	28.29	78.06	53.81	63.34	53.72	59.06	43.57	46.07	45.83	57.79	54.26	56.09
DA	1995-96 to 1998-99	8.08	39.19	22.89	49.68	52.62	50.70	38.84	35.27	35.45	41.15	44.56	42.59
DISTRICT	1989-90 to 1998-99	20.21	62.51	41.44	57.88	53.28	55.72	41.68	41.75	41.68	51.14	50.38	50.69
		(20.21)	(38.87)	(30.92)	(13.66)	(1.10)	(8.36)	(4.73)	(10.80)	(10.38)	(16.64)	(9.70)	(13.50)

(Cont...)

TABLE 4.5 (Cont...)

AVERAGE DROPOUT RATE (IN PER CENT) OF STUDENTS IN DIFFERENT PERIODS IN THE SAMPLE AREAS OF ORISSA

Area	Period	SC			ST			Others			Total		
		B	G	T	B	G	T	B	G	T	B	G	T
KOLNARA	1989-90 to 1994-95	.-8.33	79.17	43.12	55.30	58.62	57.23	46.80	55.26	52.96	48.48	42.67	46.08
BLOCK	1995-96 to 1998-99	-12.43	1.79	-4.20	36.21	41.36	39.41	38.82	37.26	40.09	29.61	41.50	38.69
	1989-90 to 1998-99	.-9.97	48.21	24.19	47.67	45.22	47.27	42.01	46.32	48.06	40.93	43.20	43.12
		(4.10)	(77.38)	(47.32)	(19.09)	(17.26)	(17.82)	(7.98)	(18.00)	(12.87)	(18.87)	(1.17)	(7.39)
RAYAGA-	1989-90 to 1994-95	87.50	66.67	83.33	65.12	68.22	66.54	51.51	58.55	55.05	62.95	67.01	64.74
-DA	1995-96 to 1998-99	52.50	52.59	52.54	56.81	48.17	53.45	40.92	43.10	41.47	56.14	54.11	55.12
BLOCK	1989-90 to 1998-99	75.83	57.67	74.23	61.80	60.20	61.30	47.27	52.37	49.62	60.23	61.85	60.89
		(35.00)	(14.08)	(30.79)	(8.31)	(20.05)	(13.09)	(10.59)	(15.45)	(13.58)	(6.81)	(12.90)	(9.62)
ORISSA	1989-90 to 1994-95	33.78	41.72	37.30	63.34	53.72	59.06	35.83	34.50	35.28	41.90	39.89	41.01
	1995-96 to 1998-99	19.34	25.87	22.53	49.68	52.62	50.70	21.39	19.52	20.45	26.26	24.85	25.58
STATE	1989-90 to 1998-99	28.00	35.38	31.39	57.88	53.28	55.72	30.05	28.51	29.34	35.65	33.87	34.84
		(14.44)	(15.85)	(14.77)	(13.66)	(1.10)	(8.36)	(14.44)	(14.98)	(14.83)	(15.64)	(15.04)	(15.43)

Note : Bracketed figures indicate increase by percentage point in the post MDM period over the pre-MDM period.

Source: Compiled from the data collected from the Sample Schools.

TABLE 4.6

AVERAGE RETENTION RATE (IN PER CNET) OF STUDENTS IN DIFFERENT PERIOD IN THE SAMPLE AREAS OF ORISSA

AREA	*Period*	*SC*			*ST*			*Others*			*Total*		
		B	*G*	*T*	*B*	*G*	*T*	*B*	*G*	*T*	*B*	*G*	*T*
PURI	1989-90 to 1994-95	69.39	67.66	68.62	--	--	--	67.74	66.51	67.17	68.06	66.71	67.44
DISTRICT	1995-96 to 1998-99	78.54	78.04	78.32	--	--	--	81.93	83.63	82.80	81.13	82.34	81.76
	1989-90 to 1989-99	73.05	71.81	72.50	--	--	--	73.41	73.36	73.42	73.29	72.97	73.17
SATYABA-	1989-90 to 1994-95	73.68	69.82	71.95	--	--	--	72.01	71.53	71.85	72.87	70.88	71.93
DI	1995-96 to 1998-99	79.53	79.57	79.55	--	--	--	85.78	90.26	87.91	83.68	86.30	84.96
BLOCK	1989-90 to 1998-99	76.02	73.72	74.99	--	--	--	77.52	79.02	78.27	77.19	77.05	77.14
PURI	1989-90 to 1994-95	63.92	64.33	64.07	--	--	--	66.16	64.43	65.36	65.87	64.38	65.21
SADAR	1995-96 to 1998-99	77.25	76.13	76.63	--	--	--	80.72	81.50	81.10	80.06	80.61	80.34
BLOCK	1989-90 to 1998-99	69.25	69.05	69.09	--	-	--	71.98	71.25	71.66	71.55	70.87	71.26
RAYAG-	1989-90 to 1994-95	71.71	21.94	46.19	36.66	46.28	40.94	56.43	53.93	54.17	42.21	45.74	43.91
ADA	1995-96 to 1998.-99	91.92	60.81	77.11	50.32	47.38	49.30	61.16	64.73	64.55	58.85	55.44	57.41
DISTRICT	1995-96 to 1998-99	79.79	37.49	58.56	42.12	46.72	44.28	58.32	58.25	58.32	48.86	49.62	49.31

(Cont...)

TABLE 4.6 (Cont...)

AVERAGE RETENTION RATE (IN PER CENT) OF STUDENTS IN DIFFERENT PERIOD IN THE SAMPLE AREAS OF ORISSA

Area	*Period*	*SC*			*ST*			*Others*			*Total*		
		B	*G*	*T*	*B*	*G*	*T*	*B*	*G*	*T*	*B*	*G*	*T*
KOLNARA	1989-90 to 1994-95	108.33	20.83	56.88	44.70	41.38	42.77	53.20	44.74	47.04	51.52	57.33	53.92
BLOCK	1995-96 to 1998-99	112.43	98.21	104.20	63.79	58.64	60.59	61.18	62.74	59.91	70.39	58.50	61.31
	1989-90 to 1989-99	109.97	51.79	75.81	52.33	54.78	55.73	57.99	53.68	51.94	59..07	53.80	56.88
RAYAGA-	1989-90 to 1994-95	12.50	33.33	16.67	34.88	31.78	33.46	48.49	41.45	44.95	37.05	32.99	35.26
DA	1995-96 to 1998-99	47.50	47.41	47.46	43.19	51.83	46.55	59.08	56.90	58.53	43.86	45.89	44.88
BLOCK	1989-90 to 1998-99	24.17	42.33	25.77	38.20	39.80	38.70	52.73	47.63	50.38	39.77	38.15	39.11
ORISSA	1989-90 to 1994-95	66.22	58.28	62.70	36.66	46.28	40.94	64.17	65.50	64.72	58.10	60.11	58.99
STATE	1995-96 to 1998-99	80.66	74.13	77.47	50.32	47.38	49.30	78.61	80.48	79.55	73.74	75.15	74.42
	1989-90 to 1998-99	72.00	64.62	68.61	42.12	46.72	44.28	69.95	71.49	70.66	64.35	66.13	65.16

Source: Compiled from the data collected from the Sample School.

TABLE-4.7

AVERAGE DROPOUT RATE OF STUDENTS (IN PER CENT) IN DIFFERENT PERIODS IN THE SAMPLE AERAS OF TAMIL NADU

Area	Period	SC			ST			Others			Total		
		B	G	T	B	G	T	B	G	T	B	G	T
MADURAI	1989-90 to 1994-95	23.76	19.84	21.87	--	--	--	20.50	15.97	18.38	21.41	17.04	19.33
DISTRICT	1995-96 to 1998-99	20.36	14.16	17.17	--	--	--	21.63	16.88	19.55	21.31	15.99	18.88
	1989-90 to 1989-99	22.40	17.57	19.99	--	--	--	20.95	16.34	18.85	21.37	16.62	19.15
		(13.40)	(5.68)	(4.70)				(-1.13)	(-0.91)	(-1.17)	(0.10)	(1.05)	(0.45)
MADURAI	1989-90 to 1994-95	19.96	13.20	16.71	--	--	--	21.81	19.11	20.60	21.48	17.60	19.73
EAST	1995-96 to 1998-99	14.51	7.44	11.02	--	--	--	13.55	9.02	11.64	13.76	8.57	11.47
BLOCK	1989-90 to 1998-99	17.78	10.90	14.43	--	--	--	18.51	15.07	17.01	18.39	13.99	16.43
		(5.45)	(5.76)	(5.69)				(8.26)	(10.09)	(8.96)	(7.72)	(9.03)	(8.26)
ALANGA -	1989-90 to 1994-95	28.89	26.05	27.60	--	--	--	27.27	20.49	23.93	27.80	22.28	25.08
NULLER	1995-96 to 1998-99	21.55	15.20	18.16	--	--	--	19.19	13.60	16.71	19.97	14.16	17.19
BLOCK	1989-90 to 1998-99	25.96	21.71	23.82	--	--	--	24.04	17.74	21.04	24.67	19.03	21.92
		(7.34)	(10.85)	(9.44)				(8.08)	(6.89)	(7.22)	(7.83)	(8.12)	(7.89)
VILLUPU-	1989-90 to 1994-95	37.88	43.63	40.66	50.00	62.50	36.11	29.37	39.49	34.40	31.16	40.17	35.61
RAM	1995-96 to 1998-99	-20.12	-36.50	-25.12	50.00	100.00	29.17	37.99	42.44	40.38	28.25	33.25	30.00
DISTRICT	1995-96 to 1998-99	14.68	11.58	14.35	50.00	81.25	33.33	32.82	40.67	36.79	30.00	37.40	33.70
		(58.00)	(80.13)	(65.78)	(0.00)	(-37.50)	(6.94)	(-8.62)	(-0.98)	(-5.98)	(2.91)	(6.92)	(4.78)

(Cont..)

TABLE-4.7 (Cont..)

AVERAGE DROPOUT RATE OF STUDENTS (IN PER CENT) IN DIFFERENT PERIODS IN THE SAMPLE AERAS OF TAMIL NADU

Area	Period	SC			ST			Others			Total		
		B	G	T	B	G	T	B	G	T	B	G	T
KOLIYAN-	1989-90 to 1994-95	23.06	34.76	31.06	NE	NE	NE	14.80	28.65	21.76	16.08	29.08	22.63
NUR	1995-96 to 1998-99	-377.27	-231.67	-277.16	NC	NC	NC	35.16	39.04	37.27	19.79	25.33	22.79
BLOCK	1989-90 to 1989-99	-137.08	-71.81	-92.23	NC	NC	NC	22.94	32.80	27.96	17.56	27.58	22.69
		(400.33)	(266.43)	(308.22)				(-20.36)	(-10.39)	(-15.51)	(-3.71)	(3.75)	(-0.16)
THIRUN-	1989-90 to 1994-95.	41.81	46.48	44.06	50.00	62.50	36.11	44.15	52.76	48.37	43.99	51.50	47.59
AVALLUR	1995-96 to 1998-99	16.24	15.36	17.25	100.00	100.00	100.00	41.65	46.90	44.34	35.87	41.85	38.77
BLOCK	1989-90 to 1998-99	31.58	34.03	33.34	72.22	81.25	61.67	43.15	50.41	46.76	40.74	47.64	44.06
		(25.57)	(31.12)	(26.81)	(-50.00)	(-37.50)	(-63.89)	(2.50)	(5.86)	(4.03)	(8.12)	(9.65)	(8.82)
TAMIL	1989-90 to 1994-95	28.32	26.81	27.59	50.00	62.50	36.11	24.49	26.79	25.58	25.45	26.86	26.11
NADU	1995-96 to 1998-99	11.56	6.39	8.97	50.00	100.00	29.17	27.60	27.98	27.79	23.75	22.49	23.17
STATE	1989-90 to 1998-99	21.61	18.64	20.15	50.00	81.25	33.33	25.74	27.27	26.46	24.77	25.11	24.93
		(16.76)	(20.42)	(18.62)	(0.00)	(-37.50)	(6.94)	(-3.11)	(-1.19)	(-2.21)	(1.70)	(4.37)	(2.94)

Note : 1. No Enrolment
2. Not calculated because of the very negligible number of students.
3. Bracketed figures indicate decrease by percentage point in the post -MDM period over the pre-MDM period.

Source: Compiled from the data collected from the Sample Schools.

TABLE 4.8

AVERAGE RETENTION RATE (IN PER CENT) OF STUDENTS IN DIFFERENT PERIODS IN THE SAMPLE AREAS OF TAMIL NADU

Area	Period	SC			ST			Others			Total		
		B	G	T	B	G	T	B	G	T	B	G	T
MADURAI	1989-90 to 1994-95	76.24	80.16	78.13	--	--	--	79.50	84.03	81.62	78.59	82.96	80.67
DISTRICT	1995-96 to 1998-99	79.64	85.84	82.83	--	--	--	78.37	83.12	80.45	78.69	84.01	81.12
	1989-90 to 1989-99	77.60	82.43	80.01	-	--	--	79.05	83.66	81.15	78.63	83.38	80.85
MADURAI	1989-90 to 1994-95	80.04	86.80	83.29	--	--	--	78.19	80.90	79.40	78.52	82.40	80.27
EAST	1995-96 to 1998-99	85.49	92.56	88.98	--	--	--	86.45	90.98	88.36	86.24	91.43	88.53
BLOCK	1989-90 to 1998-99	82.22	89.11	85.57	--	--	--	81.49	84.93	82.99	81.61	86.01	83.57
ALANGA-	1989-90 to 1994-95	71.11	73.95	72.40	--	--	--	72.73	79.51	76.07	72.20	77.72	74.92
NULLER	1995-96 to 1998-99	78.45	84.80	81.84	--	--	--	80.81	86.40	83.29	80.03	85.84	82.81
BLOCK	1989-90 to 1998-99	74.04	78.29	76.18	--	--	--	75.96	82.27	78.96	75.33	80.97	78.08
VILLUPU-	1989-90 to 1994-95	62.12	56.37	59.34	50.00	37.50	63.89	70.63	60.51	65.60	68.84	59.83	64.39
RAM	1995-96 to 1998-99	120.12	136.50	125.12	50.00	0.00	70.83	62.01	57.56	59.62	71.75	66.75	69.17
DISTRICT	1995-96 to 1998-99	85.32	88.42	85.65	50.00	18.75	66.67	67.18	59.33	63.21	70.00	62.60	66.30

(Cont...)

TABLE-4.8 (Cont...)

AVERAGE RETENTION RATE (IN PER CENT) OF STUDENTS IN DIFFERENT PERIODS IN THE SAMPLE AREAS OF TAMIL NADU

Atrs	Period	SC			ST			Others			Total		
		B	G	T	B	G	T	B	G	T	B	G	T
KOLIYAN	1989-90 to 1994-95	76.94	65.24	68.94	--	--	--	85.20	71.35	78.24	83.92	70.92	77.37
NUR	1995-96 to 1998-99	477.27	331.67	377.16	--	--	--	64.84	60.96	62.73	80.21	74.67	77.21
BLOCK	1989-90 to 1989-99	237.08	171.81	192.23	--	--	--	77.06	67.20	72.04	82.44	72.42	77.31
THIRUNA-	1989-90 to 1994-95	58.19	53.52	55.94	50.00	37.50	63.89	55.85	47.24	51.63	56.01	48.50	52.41
VALLUR	1995-96 to 1998-99	83.76	84.64	82.75	0.00	0.00	0.00	58.35	53.10	55.66	64.13	58.15	61.23
BLOCK	1989-90 to 1998-99	68.42	65.97	66.66	27.78	18.75	38.33	56.85	49.59	53.24	59.26	52.36	55.94
TAMIL	1989-90 to 1994-95	71.68	73.19	72.41	50.00	37.50	63.89	75.51	73.21	74.42	74.55	73.14	73.89
NADU	1995-96 to 1998-99	88.44	93.61	91.03	50.00	0.00	70.83	72.40	72.02	72.21	76.25	77.51	76.83
.STATE	1989-90 to 1998-99	78.39	81.36	79.85	50.00	18.75	66.67	74.26	72.73	73.54	75.23	74.89	75.07

Source: Compiled from the data collected from the Sample School

CHAPTER-5

SOCIO-CULTURAL, ADMINISTRATIVE, MANAGERIAL AND FINANCIAL FACTORS INFLUENCING MID-DAY MEALS SCHEME

The effective implementation of any welfare programme run by the government depends on various factors like socio-cultural, administrative, managerial, financial, political, etc. Mid-day Meals scheme is a welfare programme, which has been introduced by Government of India at the national level on 15th of August 1995. By now, near about four years have passed and, during this time period, the above mentioned factors might have influenced the operation of Mid-day Meals Scheme. Keeping this fact in view, this chapter attempts to find the details of the socio-cultural, administrative, managerial and financial factors, which have influenced the success or failure of Mid-day Meals Scheme in Orissa and Tamil Nadu. While analysing the factors, opinions of teachers, government officials, panchayat representative, educated villagers, NGO/social workers, parents and students of the sample areas are taken into consideration.

SOCIO-CULTURAL FACTORS

During the field survey, a number of socio-cultural problems are found to be influencing the operation of Mid-day Meals Scheme both in Orissa, and in Tamil Nadu. But the influence is more pronounced in the former state than in the latter. The opinions given by the respondents (teachers, officials, panchayat representatives, educated villagers, NGO/social workers, parents and students) with regard to the types of socio-cultural problems are given below.

At first, it is found that general and higher caste students were not eating the food given under Mid-day Meals Scheme in some primary schools in the sample areas of Orissa on account of their social status and prestige. Out of 20 sample schools of Orissa, teachers of 7 schools (35.00 per cent) revealed this fact during the period of survey. Further, this problem was more acute in the educationally backward district of Rayagada as compared to the educationally advanced district of Puri in Orissa. In Rayagada, 40 per cent of the teachers while confirmed this fact, in Puri 30 per cent of teachers reported about this problem. On the other hand, in Tamil Nadu, the teachers coming across this problem was not reported. The opinions of the various government official also suggested the same finding. In Orissa, 40 percent of the official revealed that general and higher caste students were not interested in taking Mid-day meals because of their social prestige and status. This was found to be more in the educationally backward district of Rayagada as 50 per cent of the officials of the district gave similar opinions. In the educationally advanced district of Puri, 30 per cent of the officials confirmed the above statement. The officials in Tamil Nadu, on the other hand, did not reveal anything on this matter. Majority of them believed that this was not a problem in Tamil Nadu.

Secondly, income is also one of the factors influencing students in taking Mid-day Meals. This was more visible in the educationally advanced district than in the educationally backward district. The field data as reported by 30 per cent of the teachers reveal that the problem is seen more in Puri district than in Rayagada district. Students of higher income groups usually abstain from taking Mid-day Meals. In Tamil Nadu, the problem of this type also exists but this is not so pronounced as in the case of Orissa. The problem is rather seen visibly in backward district of Villupuram than in educationally advanced district of Madurai.

Thirdly, on the issue of the students of all caste, creed and income groups taking Mid-day Meals together in the school, the teacher respondents of both the districts in Orissa expressed their opinion in the positive. Only one teacher respondent of Puri district, however, confirmed that the upper caste students of his school usually declined to sit with lower caste students for taking Mid-day Meals together. This is an exceptional case and hence does not carry much weightage. In Tamil Nadu, all the students, whether belonging to upper caste or lower caste are found to be taking Mid-day Meals together in schools.

Fourthly, there is the issue of Mid-day Meals being prepared by lower caste cooks and helpers and students taking such Mid-day Meals. The official and non-official respondents surveyed revealed that there were complaint by students and parents when Mid-day Meals were cooked and served by cooks and helpers belonging to lower castes. There was no such problem in Tamil Nadu.

Finally, the students in primary school are mostly given boiled rice, dal or dalma. The latter is prepared out of mung or arhar dal. In Tamil Nadu, the students also get boiled rice and Sambar. The Sambar is made out of red gram mixed with Tamarind. The field survey confirmed that Sambar made out of red gram and tamarind is not liked by students round the year. There is also a feeling that red gram contains less nutritive value. After discussion with the nutrition experts it is confirmed that from the nutritional point of view both mung/arhar and gram are the same. In order to keep pace with the taste of respondents, the students of Tamil Nadu need to be provided with sambar prepared out of other grams occasionally. Likewise, the students of Orissa be encouraged to take dal prepared out of red gram. This would provide the same nutritive value to the students.

With regard to the socio-cultural factors influencing Mid-day Meals, the general observation during the field survey in Orissa are as follows. Firstly, the higher caste students like Brahmins, Karans, etc., and students from rich families are not taking Mid-day Meals because of their social status and position. Besides, poor quality of food in both the educationally advanced and backward districts of Orissa also discourage them to take Mid-day Meals in schools. But the higher caste students coming from poor families are taking the Mid-day Meals in the schools. Secondly, in Orissa, students of different castes are eating the meals in the schools together and as such there is no caste feeling among the students. Thirdly, though there is no caste-feeling in taking the Mid-day Meals together in the schools, yet the general students will not like to take meals if the same is prepared by lower caste (SC/ST) cooks and helpers. This is particularly seen in Puri district., which has the largest concentration of the high caste population. On the other hand, in the educationally backward district of Rayagada, the ST students would not eat if the meal is prepared by SC cook and helper. It was found from the field survey that 60 per cent cooks and helpers were from ST community and the rest 40 per cent of cooks and helpers were from general community in the district. In most of the schools, the number of ST students were more as compared to general and SC students, as the percentage share of ST and general population to the total in the district were 56.04 and 29.68 respectively.

Compared to Orissa, in Tamil Nadu, the socio-culture problems relating to Mid-day Meals scheme are very less. There is no caste feeling among the students while taking the Mid-day Meals. Sometimes, the students from rich families are not taking Mid-day Meals because of their high social status and affluence. Since in Tamil Nadu, there is no caste feeling among the students, the students take Mid-day Meals together in the schools without complaint. The students have no inhibition if the Mid-day Meals are prepared by lower caste cooks and helpers.

ADMINISTRATIVE FACTORS

The fate of any scheme primarily depends on how good and effective the administration is. By good administratiion, we mean effective and successful decision making and proper co-operation and co-ordination among officials involved in various stages of the operation. During the course of survey in Orissa and Tamil Nadu, a number of administrative loopholes, are identified in the operating of Mid-day Meals scheme. However, the number of leakages are found to be comparatively more in Orissa than in Tamil Nadu.

At first, the organisational structure of Mid-day Meals Scheme in Orissa shows that the officials like District Social Welfare Officer (DSWO), Block Development Officer (BDO), Social Education Organiser (SEO), Sub-Inspector of Schools, etc., are doing the additional work of Mid-day Meals Scheme in addition to their main official routine-based assignments. Nearly 50 per cent out of 20 official surveyed in Orissa replied that they were overburdened with so many official jobs that they were not finding enough time to look into the proper operation of the Mid-day Meals Scheme in the state. On the contrary, in Tamil Nadu, there is separate staff for running Mid-day Meals Scheme both at the district, block and centre level, although Collector and BDO are the administrative heads of the district and block level respectively. On account of the existence of separate staff for looking after the operation Mid-day Meals Scheme, the burden is not so widely felt.

Secondly, out of 20 sample teachers interviewed in Orissa, 70 per cent of them revealed that most of the officials in charge of Mid-day Meal programme did not supervise and monitor the operation of the scheme regularly. In Tamil Nadu also, the same problem was noticed, but the percentage of teachers supporting the above statement was comparatively less. It was 35 per cent at the state level, while at the Madurai and Villupuram districts level it was 30 and 40 per cent respectively of the total teachers.

Thirdly, about 80 per cent of the sample teachers confirmed that there was leakage in the operation of Mid-day Meals Scheme in Orissa. The percentage share of teachers mentioning the above statement in Puri and Rayagada districts were 90 per cent and 70 per cent respectively. For the leakage, poor quality of dal and rice were supplied to the schools. Even the quantity of rice and dal was less than the official allocation of such items. According to the teachers, for each bag of one quintal of rice or dal, there was a shortage of 10 to 15 Kgs per bag. Sometimes, rice supplied by FCI godowns were being replaced by poor quality rice and supplied to the schools. In Tamil Nadu also, such a type of leakage was noticed in the supply of rice and dal.

Fourthly, right quantities of rice (100 gms) and dal (15 gms) as fixed by the government on per student per day basis were not available to the students in primary schools in Orissa. Out of hundred parents interviewed in Orissa, 66 per cent of the total confirmed the view of inadequate supply of rice and dal during Mid-day Meals in schools in Orissa. In Puri district, the percentage share of parents supporting the above point was 78 and, in Rayagada district, it was 54 per cent. As per the opinion of parents in Tamil Nadu, the noon-meal organisers were giving the food items to the students on the basis of the quantities of rice and dal received by them from the government. In Tamil Nadu also, there was a shortage of 10 to 15 kilograms per bag of one quintal rice or dal and this automatically reduced the share of each student consuming rice and dal during Mid-day Meals everyday. The problem thus exists both in Orissa and in Tamil Nadu, but the problem is more acute in the former than in the latter.

Fifthly, it is noticed that all the students of the sample schools were not taking Mid-day Meals, as the percentage of regular attendance of student in the school was less than one hundred per cent. Teachers however, claimed that all students are taking Mid-day Meals in the school, which on verification was found to be incorrect. Teachers by showing inflated percentage of attendance and higher enrolment figure used to receive more quotas of rice, dal and other items and this provided the scope for pilferaging in Orissa. In Puri district, out of 10 schools surveyed, the committee members of 6 schools admitted that the surplus money, if any saved from Mid-day Meals Scheme were utilised for school development in the forms of fencing and repairing of school building etc. Thus, there was an element of diversion of funds from Mid-day Meals account by showing inflated figures of enrolment and attendance of the students in schools. But in Tamil Nadu, this is rarely noticed. There Mid-day Meals items are given on the basis of the feeding strength of students of the schools which is quite less than the total enrolment and attendance. The entire food prepared as per the feeding strength of the school was equally distributed among the students attending the school. As a result, per head share of food items was less than the officially sanctioned quota. Moreover, the feeding strength of school often remained without revision for a number of years and this further created problems for the administration of noon-meals scheme.

In Orissa, the dal is often purchased by the Government from Orissa Consumer Co-operative Federation (OCCF), National Consumer Co-operative Federation (NCCF), and Tribal Development Consumer Co-operatives (TDCC). These organisations undertake to supply dal after purchasing from different agents and agencies handling the product. The supply of dal by agents, however, is considered to be of inferior quality than the dal available in the open market. To gain more profit, the agents supply inferior quality of dal and in inadequate quantity to meet school lunch programme. This creates a problem in the operation of school lunch programme. Hence, the practice of encouraging agents to supply dal be discouraged and the administration need to rely more upon the local market in the event of partial dislocation of supply of dal by the government. Giving scope to agents for the supply of dal for school lunch programme encourages pilferage on several counts. On the other hand, in Tamil Nadu, no such problem is found because of political and administrative alertness. The items like dal, oil and salt are being supplied by Tamil Nadu Civil Supply Corporation directly to the schools.

Seventhly, the quality of rice and dal are not always found to be of good quality. During the field survey, it was noticed that, because of the old stock of rice, the cooking was taking long hours and when cooked it was producing bad smell. The same problem was found in case of dal also. Furthermore, due to poor allocation of money for the purchase of firewood, the problem of boiling rice and dal was more acute. Often students were engaged to collect firewood for the preparation of Mid-day Meals,. Such a practice was interfering with their study habit, as classroom teaching was partially postponed on account of the collection of firewood as instructed by the teachers in schools. In Tamil Nadu also, the quality of ice and dal were not good. But compared to Orissa, the quality of rice and dal were found to be better. Majority of the students and parents during the course of the field survey in Tamil Nadu suggested the improvement in the quality of rice and dal. Thus, the above analysis shows that the administrative factors prevailing in Orissa were not very helpful for the success of the same,. However, this is not so much a critical factor in Tamil Nadu, although the problem exists to some extent in the state.

MANAGERIAL FACTORS

The successful implementation of a scheme depends on proper management of the scheme at different levels. For this, adequate and dedicated staff, and necessary infrastructure facilities are required.

In the first place, for proper management of the scheme, there is no adequate and separate staff in Orissa. Because of this, the existing officials are not able to supervise properly the operation of the scheme. In addition to Mid-day Meals work, the officials have a lot of other routine official responsibilities to perform. On account of this, they find no time to supervise the operation of the scheme effectively. Out of the 20 officials interviewed, 75 per cent of the officials informed about the shortage of staff at the district and block levels to look after the operation of Mid-day Meals Scheme effectively. Besides, on account of the lack of any incentives tagged with the programme, the officials are less encouraged to shoulder the responsibility of Mid-day Meals Scheme.

In Tamil Nadu, there is separate staff for looking after the scheme. There is a separate wing manned by senior and experienced officials to look after the success of the programme. There was regular monitoring and screening of the problems at the district level by the collector who is the chairman of the review committee. In Orissa, on the other hand, Mid-day Meals Scheme is one of the schemes like other welfare schemes. The same officials, who are looking after the various welfare schemes, are also concerned with Mid-day Meals Scheme. Hence, from the effective participation point of view, the staff in Tamil Nadu is more committed and purpose oriented than the staff in Orissa.

Secondly, the teachers (mainly head masters) of the schools are looking after the distribution of Mid-day Meals in Orissa. Very often head masters delegate this responsibility to one of the assistant teachers in the school. As a result of this, study hours in schools are being disturbed as the teacher is mostly engaged in the preparation of Mid-day Meals in the school. Besides, the teacher is required to maintain attendance of the students participating in Mid-day Meals programme. He is also required to maintain the stock of food items received and the expenditure of such items on day to day basis. He is also to properly maintain the records of firewood, oil, salt and spices purchased and consumed in the Mid-day Meals programme for audit and inspection. He is further required to supervise the cooking activities done by the cook and helper in the school. At the same time, he is required to submit the details of the utilisation of Mid-day Meal items to the block authority and to other government officials. All the 10 surveyed teachers of Puri district of Orissa, told that their teaching activities were being disturbed because of their involvement in the Mid-day Meals Scheme. Similarly, 8 out of 10 teachers in Rayagada district also gave the same opinion. But, in Tamil Nadu, this is not happening because, the teachers are not involved in the scheme. In every school centre, there is a noon-meal organiser, who is looking after all the Mid-day Meals activities and also actively helps the cook and the helper in the preparation of the meals for the students.

Thirdly, there are also instances where non-students like beggars, poor and elderly people also share the Mid-day Meals along with the students in schools of Orissa. When this practice is a regular phenomenon, it is objectionable. In Tamil Nadu also, similar problems are witnessed in some selected sample schools. Regular encouragement of this practice reduces the share of food items meant for genuine students. Through proper monitoring, this problem can be reduced.

Fourthly, delayed supply of rice and dal by the government was the cause of the dislocation of Mid-day Meal programme. This was witnessed in Puri and Rayagada districts of the state. Nearly 50 per cent of the teachers in Puri district and 40 per cent of the teachers in Rayagada district confirmed this apprehension. On account of this, the teachers were not able to provide Mid-day Meals in certain working days in the school. This was also a problem in Tamil Nadu, but the matter is more complex in Orissa.

Finally, the Mid-day Meals in Orissa are given in the school only on working days. There is no provision of Mid-day Meals on public holidays and Sundays. On the other hand, Mid-day Meals are given both on working days and on holidays excluding Sundays in Tamil Nadu. The management of Mid-day Meals both on working and holidays is easier because of the presence of separate staff entrusted with the responsibility of supplying Mid-day Meals. Besides, teachers are in no way connected with Mid-day Meals programme in

Tamil Nadu.

In Orissa, in the absence of a separate staff, the teachers look after the whole programme. Since he is a government employee, he avails all public holidays as entitled to him. Besides, in Orissa, the system of giving Mid-day Meals on holidays excluding Sundays is not inbuilt into the programme of Mid-day Meals right from the inception.

FINANCIAL FACTORS

Finance is the prerequisite of the successful operation of any scheme. Without finance, no development can take place in an economy. In order to increase the enrolment, attendance and retention of students in the schools, the Government of India has introduced the Mid-day Meals Scheme at the national level. For this, the Government of India is providing rice and the transport cost of rice from the FCI godown to the schools in Orissa and Tamil Nadu along with other states. In Orissa, the cost of dal, spices, vegetables, firewood, oil and salt is borne by Women and Child Development Department. On the other hand, the cost of the above items in Tamil Nadu is borne by the Director of Social Welfare and Commissioner of Municipal Administration Department. Tamil Nadu government has a separate budgetary provision for nutrition, a major part of which is earmarked for noon meal scheme, whereas, Orissa Government does not have any budgetary provision for Mid-day Meals Scheme. Operation of Mid-day Meals scheme in the two states, i.e., Orissa and Tamil Nadu, encounter a number of financial problems. The details of the types of financial factors influencing the scheme are analysed below.

In the first place, delay in providing money to the schools for the purchase of vegetables, spices and firewood are found both in Orissa and Tamil Nadu. Out of 20 officials interviewed in Orissa, 45 per cent of them reported that money was not being provided timely to the schools. This statement was supported by 50 per cent sample officials in Puri district and 40 per cent sample officials in Rayagada district. The percentage share of officials supporting the above contention in Tamil Nadu was comparatively less, i.e., 20 per cent. In Madurai and Villupuram district of Tamil Nadu, the percentage share of officials supporting the statement was 10 and 30 per cent respectively.

Taking the view of sample teachers, it is noticed that, 40 per cent of the teachers were of the opinion that there is inordinate delay in providing money to the schools in Orissa. In Puri and Rayagada district, the percentage share of teachers having the said opinion was 50 and 30 respectively. In case of Tamil Nadu, the percentage of teachers supporting the statement was also found to be 40 per cent. In the case of the two districts of Tamll Nadu, the percentage share of teachers confirming the viewpoint remained almost the same.

The delay was more pronounced in Orissa than in Taml Nadu. On accounts of the delay in the receipt of money, the teachers of Orissa were often found to be meeting the expenses on this head from their own resources. In Tamil Nadu, the Noon meal organisers occasionally used to spend money from their own to avoid the delay for purchase of firewood, vegetables etc., but they were getting reimbursed later from the block authorities.

The second financial problem is that the money, provided for the purchase of vegetables, spices and firewood etc. by the state governments, is not adequate when current market prices of the above items are taken into consideration. This problem is found both in Orissa and Tamil Nadu. In Orissa, all the 20 sample teachers supported the existence of this problem. In Tamil Nadu, 18 out of 20 teachers confirmed about the delay in the disbursement of money by the government for the purchase of above items. Inadequate provision of money by the governments for purchase of vegetables, firewood and spices is one of the reasons for the poor quality of dalma in Orissa and dal in Tamil Nadu in Mid-day Meals.

Finally, the salary of a cook and a helper of Mid-day Meals Scheme in Orissa is very less. It is found from the field survey that, on an average the cook and helper are working for four hours each per day for preparing the Mid-day Meals both in Orissa and Tamil Nadu, In return, the cook and the helper are getting a consolidated amount of Rs. 200/- and Rs. 100/- per month respectively in Orissa. With this paltry sum, it is very difficult to find a cook and a helper now-a-days for the Mid-day Meals programme. On the other hand in Tamil

Nadu, there is no such problem. There the cook is getting Rs.520/- p.m. with exgratia D.A. and the helper is getting Rs. 450/- p.m. with exgratia D.A. Moreover, they are treated as government employees. Hence, they are more committed to the job.

If these problems are overcome in course of time, the programme is bound to reap quick results. For this, the advantageous factors visible in the case of Tamil Nadu may be imitated by Orissa while restructuring the programme in the near future.

CHAPTER-6

WEAKNESSES OF THE SCHEME AND REMEDIAL MEASURES

This chapter deals with the various weaknesses of the Mid-day Meals Scheme and the efforts undertaken to overcome these. The analysis in this chapter is made with reference to specific issues as discussed in the following sections.

INADEQUACY OF IMPLEMENTATION

Implementation is the most important feature of any scheme. Unless a scheme is properly implemented, the objectives it has set cannot be fulfilled. Therefore, it is absolutely necessary that the scheme be implemented properly. If there are any loopholes then they must be rectified immediately, so as to make the scheme a success.

The basic objectives of all the nutritional support programmes in India are to provide free food to children below 14 years of age. It is the responsibility of the state governments to see that the scheme is implemented properly without any loopholes. The nutrition programme should be a continuous process. It should take care of children right from birth till they attain the age of 14 years.

In Tamil Nadu, the Anganwadi and Balwadi schemes take care of children below 5 years of age and Mid-day Meals Scheme takes care of children from 5 to 14 years of age. In Tamil Nadu, the Mid-day Meals Scheme has been extended to cover children up to X class, which is a major plus point of Tamil Nadu Mid-day Meals Scheme. Whereas, in Orissa, the Mid-day Meals programme covers children in the age group of 6 to 11 years and Anganwadi takes care of children up to 6 years of age. This implies that in Orissa there is no Mid-day Meals Scheme running for children in the age group of

12 to 14 years. It is a major shortcoming on the part of the state government for which children within age group of 12 to 14 years are left to themselves without any provision of nutritional support. The children of this age group are also vulnerable and needy. They also require free lunch from school, so that their zeal to attend classes is not affected. A majority of the poor students get enrolled in schools where they receive free food up to class-V only. But, after that they dropout from school as they are deprived of getting free noon-meals beyond this class. In other words, after class V, there is no provision of extending the programme to students of middle and secondary schools. This is contrary to the situation prevailing in Tamil Nadu, where students of middle and secondary levels also enjoy the facility of getting free food from the schools. Thus, supply of free food in schools acts as an incentive for reduction in dropout rates thus leading to increase in attendance in schools. This is particularly true in case of poor children who fail to get two square meals a day in the home.

The average dropout rate in Orissa during 1989-90 to 1998-99 was 34.84 per cent, whereas, in Tamil Nadu, it was much less at 24.93 per cent. In Orissa, since the scheme covers children only up to class V, it may so happen that when a child takes admission in class I, he knows that he can avail the facility only up to class V. Beyond this class there is no provision of Mid-day Meals by the government in Orissa. This has a big psychological impact on the children particularly among the poor children who consider the importance of the Mid-day Meals as a supportive measure for pursuing their studies in the schools. In the absence of this supportive system between 12 and 14 years of age i.e., after V class most of the children unable to be supported by their parents, dropout from schools and accept low paid jobs as child labourers. It is therefore, necessary that in Orissa the scheme be extended to cover children up to middle school, i.e., up to VII class. Because of the continuity of this scheme to cover all school going children in Tamil Nadu, there is significant reduction in dropout and increased attendance in schools.

During the field study, we found that out of 20 officials interviewed in Orissa, nearly 75 per cent said that the scheme be extended to cover children up to class VII. Similarly, out of 30 social workers, educated villagers and panchayat representatives, 43 per cent were in favour of extending the scheme in Puri while in Rayagada, 86 per cent of the same favoured the scheme be extended to cover all children up to VII class.

Another drawback in the implementation of the scheme in Orissa is that food is not given on holidays, whereas, in Tamil Nadu, the scheme operates both on working days as also on holidays except Sundays. Absence of provision to supply Mid-day Meals in holidays except Sundays reduces the interest of the students to come to the school regularly. Presently this is not possible in Orissa because there is no provision for additional and separate staff to look after the programme. The school teacher is already overburdened with work and he has no time to shoulder additional responsibility of providing cooked food on the holidays. With the provision of additional staff specifically to look into Mid-day Meals can be used to provide the same in holidays. During the field work, it was found that out of the 20 teachers interviewed in Orissa, 65 per cent agreed in favour of giving food on holidays. Whereas, 35 per cent said against it. Their real worry was who will manage the scheme.

Another major drawback in the implementation of the scheme is that all the students enrolled are not getting food. In Orissa, food is given to each and every student who has enrolled in the primary schools. Whereas, in Tamil Nadu, the government has fixed a feeding strength and food is given in the schools on the basis of the feeding strength. In Tamil Nadu, during the beginning of the academic session the block officials, extension officers and noon-meal manager visit each and every school and observe the attendance of the students in the school continuously for 3 days. On the basis of this observation, they fix up the feeding strength. This feeding strength remains valid for 3 years and after the end of three years the feeding strength is again revised. If the actual attendance in a class exceeds the feeding strength determined by the officials then a few students are deprived of getting the food or the existing food is shared amongst all students in the class in which case the proportion of food reaching each and every student in the class taking Midday Meals gets reduced. So this system should be changed. Each and every student should get food according to the objective of the scheme which aims at supplying cooked food to all primary school-going children. Therefore, it is suggested that the feeding strength as determined in Tamil Nadu be introduced in Orissa. Besides, the feeding strength which has remained unchanged even after three years be freshly determined in Tamil Nadu, in the absence of which it has resulted in serious dislocation in the distribution of food.

Furthermore, in Orissa, all the students who are enrolled in primary schools are entitled to get free food. This creates a lot of problems. The teacher in charge of Mid-day Meals Scheme shows false attendance and there by gets more quota of food items. There is a little bit of window dressing by the teachers with regard to enrolment and attendance in schools. This can be avoided once feeding strength is determined for each and every class in the school at the elementary level and food quotas are supplied on the basis of feeding strength. Therefore, it is recommended that in Orissa, feeding strength be fixed at the beginning of the academic session in order to prevent dislocation in the distribution of noon-meals in the school. But, this feeding strength should be revised every year so that each and every student can get a legitimate share of the food. This will also help to prevent manipulations often committed by teachers in charge of Mid-day Meal programme.

These are the few weaknesses that exist in the implementation of the scheme in both the states. These weaknesses can be overcome with proper attention and care taken at the official and school level.

ADMINISTRATIVE FAILURE IN REACHING THE BENEFIT

Proper and efficient administration is the key to the success of any scheme. The administrative set up of the scheme as given in chapter 3 greatly differs in both the states. The differences in administrative structure existing both in Tamil Nadu and Orissa is one of the causes for the benefit of the Mid-day Meals not reaching the ultimate beneficiaries, i.e. the school children. The problem is more pronounced in Orissa than in Tamil Nadu, thereby reducing the impact of the scheme.

The administrative set up given in chapter 3 indicates that the

Tamil Nadu government has created several posts for the management of the scheme. The post of Noon-Meals Manager and Organiser has been created exclusively for the management of the scheme. In Orissa, there are no such posts exclusively for the implementation of the scheme. All the officials involved in the scheme are managing this job in addition to their normal routine official responsibilities. This results in less time spent by these officials on the supervision and monitoring of the scheme. Both higher and lower cadre officials are found to be indifferent and apathetic towards the scheme. This is, however, not the case in Tamil Nadu as the staff engaged in the programme are exclusively meant for the programme and, hence, they are committed. During field study in Orissa, 50 per cent of the officials agreed that they are overburdened and cannot devote maximum time towards the scheme. During further investigation, 70 per cent of the teachers confirmed that the officials like B.D.O, I.C.D.S Superintendent, S.I. etc, have not visited schools for supervision for considerable a long period of time. The same problem more or less is there in Tamil Nadu. About 35 per cent of the teachers agreed that the noon-meals scheme operating in the school is not supervised and monitored regularly. In several cases supervision is done only once in a year instead of every two or three months.

Proper supervision is absolutely necessary to avoid malpractice, delay and other related problems. Therefore, it is necessary that both in Orissa and in Tamil Nadu supervision be undertaken regularly and timely. The Orissa state government should create some posts of supervisors for the supervision of the scheme, in addition to separate staff for looking into the implementation of the scheme. By creating these posts the state government can reduce the burden of officials like B.D.O, Collector and S.I etc, and supervision can be effective.

As already mentioned, in Orissa, the teachers are involved in the scheme. They are the ones who handle the scheme at the centre level. The teachers in Orissa spent a lot of time on making arrangements for cooking, purchasing of firewood, vegetables and other essentials necessary for the preparation of food. Besides, they also maintain day to day accounts for audit and inspection. This largely affects the efficiency of the teacher and his ability of teaching. The teaching hours in schools get disturbed. During the field study, it was noticed that in most of the schools, particularly in interior areas the number of teachers appointed were less than the sanctioned strength. With reduced number of teachers in the school when one of the teachers is engaged for Mid-day Meals programme the study hours in the school get dislocated. Teaching gets seriously hampered. The primary objective of the scheme is not only to provide free meal to the students but also to increase the quality of education in the schools for the benefit of the students. Therefore, it is highly essential that the teachers involvement be reduced as far as possible. This does not mean that the teacher be kept aloof from the programme totally. The success of the programme to a large extent depends upon the involvement of teachers. In Tamil Nadu, the teachers have no role to play in Mid-day Meals programme, as there is separate staff for the purpose. This complete isolation is not desirable. In Tamil Nadu, teachers' participation in Mid-day Meals programme be encouraged. For this necessary arrangements in the existing staffing pattern working for Mid-day Meals be undertaken. The teacher and noon-meal organiser must work together. In Orissa, on the other hand, the teacher is already participating in Mid-day Meals Scheme. He needs to be assisted by the creation of a separate post of noon-meal organiser who would be expected to work with the teacher for the implementation of the scheme. The creation of a new post at the centre level will thus limit the job of the teacher, and will not disturb study hour at all.

One of the major problems of the scheme found during field study was short supply of food materials. During the fieldwork, we found that rice supplied to schools was less in quantity than the prescribed quota. In both the states we found that the rice supplied were 10 to 15 kilograms less per quintal. In that case the teacher or the Noon-meal Organiser has no choice but to give less quantity of food material to the students. In Orissa, this shortage was more acute than in Tamil Nadu. The highhandedness of higher officials at the distribution level very often forced the teachers to receive lesser quantity which later affects distribution of food in the school.

In Orissa, the school administration through which the programme is implemented has not provided kitchen rooms to each and every school. Whereas, in Tamil Nadu, each and every school has kitchen room of their own. In Orissa, cooking is done either in the school veranda or a temporarily built shed, which disturbs study atmosphere and the environment becomes unhygienic and uncongenial for students. The absence of permanent kitchen rooms also poses problems for the teachers to store the food materials. The food materials are stored either in classrooms or are taken by the teacher for storage in his house located near by the school. While the former reduced classroom space for accommodation of students, the latter provides the scope of malpractice by errant teachers. Therefore, it is essential that the administration in Orissa needs to take concrete steps towards building a separate kitchen in each and every school where Mid-day Meals scheme is operating. Because there is a separate kitchen room attached to each and every primary school, the study atmosphere rarely gets disturbed in Tamil Nadu. In some primary schools, the school kitchen room is so large that it provides the scope for children to take their meal in those kitchen-cum-dining rooms. Such kitchen rooms in majority of cases have been built under JRY programmes or out of the sanctions received under D.P.E.P programme.

In Orissa, the cook and the helper are not government officials and are paid salaries as low as Rs. 200/- and Rs. 100/- respectively. With such a low salary sometimes it becomes very difficult to find a cook and helper. This is particularly more acute in educationally advanced district of Puri. Even in backward district like Rayagada the problem is not less acute. On the other hand, in Tamil Nadu, the cook and the helper are government officials and are getting a salary of Rs. 520/- and Rs. 450/- per month respectively. Besides, they also enjoy ex-gratia D.A. as and when sanctioned by the government. Therefore, it is recommended that the salary of cook and helper in Orissa be increased at par with the salary of cook and helper in Tamil Nadu. If the scheme is to cater to the needs of ultimate beneficiaries, the school going children.

SHORTAGE OF FUNDS AND AVAILABLE FUNDS NOT REACHING THE ULTIMATE BENEFICIARIES

Orissa being a backward state and Tamil Nadu being an advanced state, it is quite natural that the financial position of Tamil Nadu is much stronger than Orissa. The Tamil Nadu Government has created a separate budgetary provision for nutrition, out of this, the Mid-day Meals programme forms a formidable part. This provision comes under the Social Services head. In 1995-96, the Tamil Government made an allotment of Rs. 357.34 crore on nutrition, which was 3.11 per cent of the total allotment made on the entire Social Services sector. This money was increased in 1996-97 to Rs. 406.58 crore, which was 2.97 per cent of the total allotment on Social Service sector. Though the absolute amount has increased, the percentage share has gone down. The allotment on nutrition includes all the nutrition projects operating in the state, including Mid-day Meals, However, the share of Mid-day Meal is higher than other nutritional programmes on account of its vast coverage.

However, in Orrisa, there is no separate budgetary provision for Nutrition. The sate Women and Child Development Department makes allotment of funds for the different schemes. running in the state. The total allotment made on Mid-day Meals Scheme in 1995-96 was Rs. 65.71 crore, in 1996-97 it was Rs. 71.21 crore and in 1997-98 this declined to Rs. 42.51 crore respectively. However, there is a gap between the allotment and the actual expenditure on Mid-day Meals Scheme. In 1995-96 the total expenditure was Rs. 65.66 crore, in 1996-97 it was Rs. 67.26 crore and in 1997-98 it was only Rs. 37.94 crore. There is, thus, a mismatch between allocation and expenditure on Mid-day Meals programme. This mismatch is more pronounced in the year 1997-98 than earlier years. Taking into consideration the coverage of the programme both in terms of the schools and the students, the allocation appears to be inadequate for Mid-day Meals. At the same time whatever is allotted, the actual expenditure seems to be lagging considerably. This is one of the reasons for Mid-day Meals programme not taking a rapid stride in Orissa. More specifically, provisions made under different heads appear to be quite low.

Under the Mid-day Meals Scheme, the central government provides rice to the state governments, while the state government only bears the cost of items like dal, oil, salt, vegetables and spices. In addition to this in Tamil Nadu, the Government provides an egg to each and every student in the school.

During investigation, we found that the Tamil Nadu Government provides 9 paisa for vegetable per student per day, 1 gram of salt per day, 0.3 paisa per day for spices and Rs. 1.30 for fuel charges per month per student. Whereas, in Orissa, the state government provides 9 paisa for vegetable and condiments, 2 grams of salt. In Orissa, the government does not give anything for spices separately. This money is included in vegetables head. The interview of different respondents clearly suggests that the money supplied to schools for purchase of these materials is not at all sufficient. In a school having 100 students, the allotment of 9 paisa for vegetables per day per student, makes a total allotment of Rs 9/- per day for vegetables. Taking into consideration the cost of vegetables in the market, the paltry sum of Rs.9/- for vegetables per day seem to be quite insufficient. If the nutritional objective is to be achieved then this money allocated for the purpose, needs to be increased, so that each student can get some vegetables everyday which is essential for their body growth. Similarly, the money given for firewood is also much less than actually required. As a result of this, the school authority in Orissa and the noon-meal organiser in Tamil Nadu are facing a lot of difficulties. To avoid this difficulty they divert money coming for other developmental activities in the school to meet firewood requirements, which result in less developmental activities in the school. To avoid this diversion the government should allot more money for firewood and other items.

Shortage of funds not only affects the quality but also the quantity of items supplied. During the field study, it was noticed that out of the 20 teachers interviewed in both the states, a majority of the teachers, i.e., more than 75 per cent agreed that the quantity of rice and dal distributed to the students was far from satisfactory. The students had actually received lesser quantity than officially prescribed quota. This was confirmed by on the spot verification of the distribution of Mid-day Meals in several schools both in Orissa and Tamil Nadu.

There is also delay in the disbursement of money meant for Mid-day Meals by block officials. In Orissa, 65 per cent of the teachers and in Tamil Nadu, 20 per cent of the teachers confirmed that they had not received money in time. As a result of this, the teachers in charge of the Mid-day Meals Scheme in Orissa and the Noon-Meal Organiser in Tamil Nadu are often forced to cut down the number of days on which Mid-day Meals are to be distributed in the schools. There is urgent need for increasing the amount of funds for the purchase of vegetables, spices and firewood. Besides, the fund so allocated need be available to the schools in time, more particularly at the beginning of the month.

Apart from the shortage of funds, it is seen that money spent is less than the money allocated. Which means that there is a gap between allocation and expenditure. In Orissa, in 1995-96, this gap was Rs. 5.00 lakh, in 1996-97 it was about Rs. 4.0 crore and in 1997-98 it became Rs. 4.6 crore indicating the fact that money allocated is not spent for the purpose for which it is meant.

Moreover, money allocated is also not reaching the ultimate beneficiaries. This means that money sanctioned for Mid-day Meals Scheme is being used for purposes other than Mid-day Meals. There is a diversion of funds from Mid-day Meals head to other heads. This happens mostly at the centre level. The field study reveals that there is no case of diversion of funds in Tamil Nadu. However, in Orissa, 15 per cent of the teachers admit that there is diversion of money from Mid-day Meals to other heads. According to them, when they don't receive money for normal developmental activities in schools like repair of school building, purchase of teaching materials etc., they divert the money coming for Mid-day Meals to meet these expenses. The only way to prevent this diversion seems to be effective and vigorous supervision on the part of the block and district level officials involved in the scheme.

It is observed from the field survey that the Mid-day Meals programme that operates in Tamil Nadu covering students up to X class has become a burden on the state exchequer. The state government has to spend quite a large sum of money towards the payment of salaries of the staff especially those engaged for Mid-day Meals work. Besides, the state government also meets all expenses like the cost of dal, vegetables, species, oil and firewood etc. Central government provides only rice free of cost, but all other expenses become the liability of the state government.

Similar problem is also faced by Orissa government. In Orissa, the Mid-day Meals Scheme is confined only up to class V but all expenses for the programme except rice is borne by the state government. Of course, there is no separate staff to look after Mid-day Meals programme like Tamil Nadu but looking into the coverage of schools and number of beneficiaries touched by state government, the burden of the state government is no less.

The solution to the problem is a complex issue. However, in order to make a harmonious balance between development and welfare, both the state governments must be encouraged to make separate budgetary allocation for Mid-day Meals, if the scheme is to be continued on a long-term basis. There is the proposal that Mid-day Meals now given up to X class with larger staff component (2 cooks and 2 helpers, if the students strength in the school is more than a thousand) be reduced in a phased manner to be confined only up to VII class. Similarly, with separate budgetary allocation for Mid-day Meals in Orissa, the scope of Mid-day Meals be enhanced to cover children up to class VII to bring parity in the scheme in two states and indirectly restricting the flow of child labour.

CONVERGENCE OF THE SCHEMES

There is an important issue relating to the convergence of the schemes. The primary objective of both, Balwadi scheme and Anganwadi scheme is to improve the nutritional and health status of children at the pre-school age (below 5 years), whereas, the main objective of the Mid-day Meals Scheme is to improve the nutritional and health status of school going children (above 5 years) with the primary goal of increasing enrolment and attendance of children in school. After observing the functioning of Balwadi and Anganwadi schemes, it appears that there is a possibility of converging Anganwadi with Balwadi. In Tamil Nadu, Balwadi is more extensively used than Anganwadi. Besides at the operational level, Balwadi performs the same function as that of Anganwadi. In Tamil Nadu, Balwadi covers children up to 6 years of age and Anganwadi covers children up to 3 years of age, which implies that Anganwadi comes under Balwadi.

That means there are two sets of schemes running for the same target group. Moreover, the food structure of the two schemes is similar. To avoid this duplication of activities it is necessary that both the schemes be merged in Tamil Nadu. However this possibility does not arise in Orissa, as Balwadi scheme is not operating in the state.

It is further seen that the adminstrative structure of Anganwadi scheme in Tamil Nadu is vast and cumbersome whereas the administrative structure of Balwadi is easy and simple. In Tamil Nadu, Anganwadi has a vast administrative set up but handles only a few projects in the state. There are only three projects, which are handled by Anganwadi scheme in the state. These three schemes are: (i) pre and post natal care of expectant and nursing mother, (ii) supply of 'food ball' to children below 3 years and (iii) care of old and disabled persons in the state, but Balwadi manages a number of projects in the state. Hence, from the oeprational point of view Anganwadi may be included in the Balwadi. By doing so the government will get maximum operational benefit. The super structure of welfare department, which looks after the Anganwadi scheme will not be there, which will result in less expenditure on the part of the state exchequer.

In Balwadi, supervision and implementation of the programme is easy and simple. In Tamil Nadu, at the district level, there are a number of community Nutrition supervisors working under the District Project Nutrition Officer (D.P.N.O.). These supervisors are efficient and competent enough in undertaking any supervision activities. Hence, if Anganwadi is merged with Balwadi, the supervision will be more effective and time bound, which might deliver better results. The district and block level officials like the Collector, BDO and others are normally so overburdented that they cannot devote reasonable time for the supervision of different schemes. If the number of schemes operating in the district and block levels is small, then the time spent on supervision of these schemes by Collector and BDO, as the case may be, would be much less. So it is absolutely necessary that projects having similar objectives and target groups be merged. So if we merge Anganwadi with Balwadi, then the district level officials can spend maximum time towards the supervision of these schemes, which will ultimately lead to better management and yield better results.

In Tamil Nadu, though both these schemes are operating with the same objective, yet there is a lack of co-operation and co-ordination between the two programmes. Each of the schemes is operating independently without having any linkage with the other. The officials working in these two programmes have no common point of contact, except on special occasions. So if we bring both the schemes under one umbrella, the co-operation and co-ordination among officials will be effective leading to efficient management of the scheme. So it is absolutely necessary that both the schemes be merged together. Similarly, once Anganwadi is merged with Balwadi, there will be only one officer at the district level for looking after the schemes. Hence, duplication of activities can be avoided.

Further if Anganwadi is merged with Balwadi scheme, the government will have the benefit of economising the use of available funds. Now the government is spending quite a considerable amount of funds for the staff engaged in Anganwadi scheme who have very limited functions to perform. Now, when Anganwadi is merged with Balwadi, the funds that are spent on Anganwadi can now be utilised in a better manner by Balwadi. This will strengthen the financial position of Balwadi.

From the above discusison we can summarise that in Tamil Nadu, it is absolutely necessary that Anganwadi scheme be merged with Balwadi scheme. However, this question does not arise in Orissa, as Balwadi is no more in operation in the state. After discussing the convergence of Anganwadi with Balwadi, the question now arises whether Balwadi can be merged with Mid-day Meals Scheme. The Balwadi and the Mid-day Meals Scheme though appears to be operationally the same, yet the two schemes are distinctly separate. The two schemes cannot be merged and should be kept separate from each other.

Firstly, though the primary objective of both the schemes is to give nutritional support to children, yet the target groups covered by them are different. In Balwadi schemes the target group is children below 6 years of age, whereas, in Mid-day Meals scheme it covers children between 6 and 11 years of age. Hence, it is not desirable to merge two schemes having two age groups of children.

Secondly, the nutritional requirement of a child below 6 years of age is different than that of a child above 6 years of age. Though the food structure given under Balwadi Scheme and Mid-day Meals Scheme are somewhat similar, yet the quantity given are different. In Balwadi for children between 3 to 5 years of age the quantity of rice given is 80 gms, while in Mid-day Meals it is 100 gms of rice. The quantity of food distributed in noon-meal scheme is higher on account of the higher age group of children covered under the scheme. Besides, the other composition of food in the two schemes is also different.

Thirdly, the Mid-day Meals Scheme is a part of the education policy of the state. Under this education policy, the state governments, apart from providing free lunch to students, also provides free books, writing materials, free uniforms, free bus service etc. However, this facility differs from state to state. In Orissa only SC and ST students are entitled to some of these facilities, whereas, in Tamil Nadu, all the students are getting these facilities. So we can say that under Mid-day Meals Scheme, the state government provides an education package, which is not available under Balwadi scheme. The basic objective of Mid-day Meals is to increase nutritional status of children as well as to increase the standard of education. But, the aim of Balwadi scheme is only to improve the nutrition and health status of children. Besides, it continues to be assisted by the central government, Hence, merging of these two schemes may lead to enormous financial burden on the part of the state government.

And finally, the merging of the two schemes might lead to mismanagement. If we merge the two schemes together, large number of students will come under one umbrella, having different age groups. It will be difficult to control and manage such a large number of children under one administration and might lead to mismanagement and corruption. Hence, both the schemes need be treated separately. In Orissa, there is no Balwadi scheme. It is winded up long since. The existing Anganwadi scheme is covering children between 0 to 60 months. On the other hand, Mid-day Meals cover the students above 5 years up to 11 years. Hence, the question of convergence of the two schemes does not arise. Both the schemes be treated as separate as they cater to different target groups of beneficiaries.

After discussing the various aspects of convergence of different schemes, we finally come to the conclusion that in Tamil Nadu, Anganwadi scheme be merged with Balwadi scheme. We hope that the convergence will yield better results. But as far as Mid-day Meals is concerned, the scheme should be treated separately and need not be merged with Balwadi scheme. In Orissa, in the absence of Balwadi scheme. Anganwadi and Mid-day Meals Scheme be treated separately. The scope of convergence does not arise in the state.

CHAPTER-7

SUMMARY AND CONCLUSION

The objective of this chapter is to present the summary of the discussions pursued in the preceding chapters, highlight the major findings of the study and to suggest policy recommendations for the overall improvement of the programme at the national level in general and sample states in particular.

Summary of Discussions

The study broadly covers seven chapters. The first chapter is an introductory one. It deals with background, scope, objectives and methodology of the study. Besides, it also points out several limitations, confining the study to more specific issues for the purpose of analysis. The objectives set for the study mainly seek to answer the following issues: (a) to what extent Mid-day Meals programme has helped to increase enrolment, attendance and retention by bringing down dropout rates of children in primary schools both in Orissa and Tamil Nadu, (b) to identify differences if any, in structure organisation and operation of the programme, (c) to analyse what are the factors that have contributed towards the success or failure of the programme and finally, to discuss whether there could be any convergence of the schemes like Anganwadi, Balwadi and Mid-day Meals Scheme dealing with same target group of children into one composite programme to achieve greater administrative efficiency and larger financial discipline.

In the study, multi-stage random sampling method has been used. In the first stage, states (Orissa and Tamil Nadu) have been selected on the basis of literacy rate and as per the suggestion of planning commission. In the second stage, the selection of districts, i.e., Puri and Rayagada in Orissa and Madurai and Villupuram in Tamil Nadu, has been made again on the basis of literacy rate as per 1991 Census. In the third stage, selection of blocks in both the states has been made by the same procedure as was done for the districts. The final stage covers the respondents, viz., students, parents, teachers, panchayat representative, educated literate persons, social activists / NGOs and government officials. The study, therefore, is more comprehensive and analytical.

The second chapter deals with socio-economic background of Orissa and Tamil Nadu, the district and blocks under reference, and the characteristic features of the samples respondents. The discussion in the chapter clearly reveals that, in respect of several parameters of development, Tamil Nadu has an edge over Orissa and hence the former is acknowledged as the advanced state while the latter is considered to be a backward state of the Country. The poverty ratio is much lower in Tamil Nadu as compared to that of Orissa. Similarly, per capita Net National Product in Tamil Nadu is higher than that of Orissa, because of the differences in development existing in the two states. The study of Nutritional Support to Primary Education (Mid-day Meals) programme is considered more desirable in order to understand how the same programme operates in two sets of economic environment one developed and another backward.

The third chapter deals with evolution, structure, organisation and operation of the Mid-day Meals programme in Orissa and Tamil Nadu. The discussion clearly brings out the differences existing in the two states.

In the fourth chapter the impact of Mid-day Meals Scheme on enrolment, attendance, retention and dropout of students in the sample districts and blocks of Orissa and Tamil Nadu have been examined.

The fifth chapter deals with the socio-cultural, administrative, managerial and financial factors influencing Mid-day Meals Scheme in both the states.

In the sixth chapter, various weaknesses of the Mid-day Meals scheme and the efforts undertaken to overcome the weaknesses have been analysed.

In the concluding chapter, major findings of the study have been discussed. On the basis of the findings a number policy recommendations has been suggested for the overall improvement of the Mid-day Meals programme.

Major Findings

The major findings of the study were as follows:

* The Mid-day Meals programme in Tamil Nadu has a long historical background. The scheme was introduced in 1956 by K.Kamraj, the then Chief Minister of Tamil Nadu The pro gramme then was popularly known as "Kamraj experiment". Subsequently it was developed by late M.G. Ramachandran, the then Chief Minister in 1982. His experiment was popularly known as 'MGR Model'. Thus, the programme as it exi--sts today in Tamil Nadu has a long history behind it. In Orissa, the programme was implemented in 1995. The comparison seems to be unequal. But there are several strong points in the programme implemented in Tamil Nadu, which can be adopted in Orissa to strengthen and develop the working of the scheme for the benefit of ultimate users, i.e., the school going children.

* There is separate staff to look after Mid-day Meals programme in Tamil Nadu like Noon Meal Manager, Noon Meal organi ser, cook and helper. They are functioning at different levels of district and block level administration. They are conside--red as government servants and enjoy certain facilities as ap--plicable to government employees. In Orissa, on the other hand, except cook and helper, others who are associated with Mid-day Meals programme are regular government staff, who shoulder the Mid-day Meals programme in addition to other normal activities of the welfare department. For this additional responsibility, they do not have any additional incentives.The cook and helper are very low paid persons in Orissa and are temporarily engaged by the school headmaster in charge of Mid-day Meals programme. Unlike .Tamil Nadu, there is no separate staff to exclusively look after the Mid-day Meals programme in Orissa.

* In Tamil Nadu because of the separate staff for school lunch programme, the teachers are in no way associated with the management and distribution of Mid-day Meals. On account of this, the study time of the teacher, his teaching perform--ance and overall teaching environment in the schools are not affected. On the other hand, in Orissa, the headmaster or his representative, the assistant teacher, shoulders all the responsib--ility of managing and distributing cooked food to children. Besides, the teacher also maintains daily record receipts and expenditure under Mid-day Meals programme. Likewise, regu lar attendance of children taking Mid-day Meals is also main--tained by him. All these affect his study time, his ability as a teacher taking classroom teaching and the general study at--mosphere in the school. This makes the programmes in Orissa and Tamil Nadu, different from each other

* The Mid-day Meals programme operates in Tamil Nadu both on working days and in holidays except Sundays. In Orissa on the other hand, the programme operates only on working days. Distribution of Mid-day Meals in Tamil Nadu is done on the basis of feeding strength determined by the concerned officials (BDO, Noon Meal Manager and Education Exten--sion Officer of the block) at the beginning of academic ses--sion. In Orissa, distribution of Mid-day Meals is done on the basis of the enrolment in primary schools, which is often window dressed by the teacher in charge of the programme. Hence the working of the programme and distribution of food appear to be more rational and practical in Tamil Nadu than in Orissa. Even in the supply of cooked food there is also a dif-ference. In Tamil Nadu, the primary school children are provided with boiled rice, sambar prepared out of red gram. Besides an egg is provided to students once in a week. In Orissa, on the other hand, the children get boiled rice, dal or dalama (dal mixed with vegetables). No egg is given to chil--dren in schools in Orissa under Mid-day Meals programme. So far as quantity is concerned, the cooked food given in Tamil Nadu and Orissa is the same (100 gms of rice and 15 gms of sambar or dal/dalama), but so far as quality is conc-erned, the food given in Tamil Nadu contains more nutritive

value with the addition of an egg per student per week than in Orissa.

* The school lunch programme works in Tamil Nadu from the day of the birth of the Child till he completes X class in sec ondary school. The Anganwadi scheme covers the children from 0-36 months. The Balwadi scheme covers the children from 37 months to 60 months and noon meal scheme covers children from 6 years to 16 years (from Class I to class X). The scheme is thus a continuous one though looked after by different agencies. Hence, the child who is born today knows that he is going to be fed up to class X and for this at no stage his schooling is going to be affected. This is one of the major psychological impacts of the programme over the children making it a success. In Orissa, on the other hand, the school lunch programme is discontinuous. The Anganwadi scheme, like any other states of the country, looks after children from 0 months to 36 months by providing cooked food in the form of food balls. There is no Balwadi scheme operating at present in Orissa. It is discontinued since April 1998. As a result, children belonging to the age group of 37 months to 60 months remain outside of any programme and for their food needs they solely depend upon their parents. The Mid-day Meals Scheme as it operates in the state covers the children belonging to the age group of 6 years to 11 years, i.e. from class I to class V children belonging to class-IV and onwards are not covered by the programme. Thus, there is a discontinuity in the supply of food under the programme. This affects inter-est in reading and attendance in schools. This discontinuity particularly for the children belonging to the age group of 37 months to 60 months is a major drawback of the programme. Similarly, the non-inclusion of children in Mid-day Meals pro-gramme reading in classes VI and VII also has a problem particularly when these classes run side by side with the el-ementary school under the same roof.

* Each and every primary school in Tamil Nadu has a brick built kitchen room with a verandah. Hence, from the distri-bution and storage point of view, the noon-meal organiser

does not face and ifficulty in Tamil Nadu. On the other hand, in Orissa, the preparation of food in school verandahor is one in temporarily built shade. Even children are distributed food in the verandah or in the classroom adjacent to kitchen space. This affects study atmosphere. Teaching in classrooms is af--fected. The environment becomes unhygienic and uncong--erial. From storage and distribution points, this creates a problem.

* The Tamil Nadu government has a separate budgetary prov--ision for nutrition, out of which Mid-day Meals programme forms a major component. In Orissa, on the other hand, there is no separate budgetary allocation for Mid-day Meals pro--gramme. The programme is financed out of the normal allo -cation of funds from Woman and Child Welfare Department of government of Orissa. This puts a great hardship in the operation of the programme.

* In Orissa, the enrolment of students in absolute figures is more in the post-Mid-day Meals period (1995-96 to 1998-99) as compared to the pre-Mid-day Meals period (1989-90 to 1994-95), but the rate of increase in enrolment in the post-Mid-day Meals period is less than that of the pre-Mid-day Meals period. If the picture of two sample districts is taken into consideration, in the educationally advanced district Puri, negative growth rate in enrolment is found in the post-Mid-day Meals period as against positive growth rate in the pre-Mid-day Meals period. On the other hand, in the case of the educationally backward district of Rayagada, there is positive and healthy growth rate in enrolment in the post-Mid-day Meals period and negative growth rate in the pre-Mid-day Meals period. The negative growth rate in enrolment in Puri district in the post- Mid-Meals period does not necessarily mean that the Mid-day Meals scheme has no impact on the enrolment of students. The reasons responsible for the negative growth rate are: (i) decline in the number of children in the age-group 6-11 years: (ii) increased interest among parents to send their children to study in English Medium Schools and Public Schools; and (iii) already higher percentage of enrolment of

students attained in the schools. Regarding the positive increase in the enrolment growth rate of students in Rayagada district, are the introduction of Mid-day Meals Scheme, spread of education, impact of DPEP and, other incentives and developmental programmes of the government. Further, the en -rolment growth rates indicate that the scheme has greater impact on the enrolment of SC and ST student in district of Rayagada. On the contrary, the growth rate of the enrolment of student is negative both in the pre-Mid-day Meals and post -Mid-day Meals periods in Tamil Nadu, but the rate of decline is more in the post-Mid-day Meals period as compared to the pre-Mid-day Meals period. Again, negative growth rate in enrolment is found in the post-Mid-day Meals period both in the educationally advanced district of Madurai and educationally backward district of Villupuram of Tamil Nadu. The reasons for negative growth rate in enrolment in Tamil Nadu are as follows: (i) Tamil Nadu, being an educationally advanced state, has reached a saturation point with regard to enrolment of students (ii) there might be yearly decline in the number of children in the age-group 6 years to 11 years, (iii) the noon-meal scheme is operating in Tamil Nadu for the last 18 years (from 1982).i.e., much earlier to 1995 and has made less impact after several years of its operation and (iv) preference of some children for studying in English Medium or other Public Schools etc.

* With regard to attendance rate of students, it is found that the average attendance rate has increased in the post-Mid-day Meals period as compared to the pre-Mid-day Meals period irrespective of caste and sex in all the sample districts and blocks of Orissa and Tamil Nadu. Further, greater increase in the attendance rate is found among the SC and ST students in both the states. The increase in the attendance rate, as said by the sample respondents like teachers, educated villagers, panchayat representatives and NGO/social workers, is partly due to Mid-day Meals Scheme and partly due to the spread of education.

* The analysis of the dropout rates of students in Orissa and

Tamil Nadu indicates that there is reduction in the average dropout rates in both the states in the post- Mid-day Meals period as compared to pre-Mid-day Meals period, and the reduction is more impressive in Orissa than in Tamil Nadu. The district-wise analysis indicates that, in Orissa, there is reduction in the dropout rates of students irrespective of caste and sex in the districts of Puri and Rayagada. On the other hand, in Tamil Nadu, though there is decrease in the dropout rates of students in the post-Mid-day Meals period in the ag--gregate in the two sample districts, but caste-wise analysis shows that the dropout rate exhibits a significant decline in case of SC and ST students, but in the case of other caste students, there is marginal increase in the dropout rates in the post-Mid-day Meals period in both the sample districts of Tamil Nadu. The opposite is the case regarding retention rate in states of Orissa and Tamil Nadu, because, the decline in drop out rate means increase in retention rate and vice versa.

* The important socio-cultural, administrative, managerial and financial factors influencing Mid-day Meals Scheme in the two states are as follow:

(i) In Orissa, some general and higher caste students were not taking Mid-day Meals on account of their social status and prestige. This problem was found to be more in Puri district as compared to Rayagada district. On the other hand, in Tamil Nadu, such problems were not found. This was also true in case of students belonging to higher income earning parents. There were often complaints by students and parents of higher castes when Mid-day Meals were cooked and served by cooks and helpers belonging to lower castes in Orissa. But in Tamil Nadu, there was no much problem. This shows that the socio-cultural problems influencing Mid-day Meals Scheme are more in Orissa than in Tamil Nadu. In the latter state stu--dents of all castes and creed took the noon meals together.

(ii) There are a number of administrative factors, which have influenced the operation of the scheme in the two states. At first, the organisational structure of Mid-day Meals scheme shows that the officials like DSWO, BDO, SEO, SEO. SI etc. are overburdened with work because they are doing the additional work of Mid-day Meals Scheme in addition to their main official routine based assignments. As a result, they are not finding enough time to look into the proper operation of the scheme in the state. On the other hand, in Tamil Nadu, because of the existence of a separate staff for Mid-day Meals at the district and block levels, the burden is not widely felt. Further more there was leakage of 10-15 kgs of rice and the same quantity of dal per bag were noticed during the supply of the above two items to the schools both in Orissa and Tamil Nadu. Similarly, prescribed quantities of rice (100 gms) and dal (15 gms) per student per day were not given to the students in the two states and the problem was more in Orissa than in Tamil Nadu as in the latter state distribution of food was done on the basis of feeding strength. In some samp- -le schools of Orissa, the teachers were receiving more quo tas of rice, dal and other items by showing inflated figures of enrolment and attendance of student in shcools.

(iii) Moreover, because of the lack of adequate and separate staff disturbance in teaching hours due to the involvement of teachers in Mid-day Meals Scheme and delayed supply of rice and dal, a lot of managerial problems are witnessed in the Mid-day Meals Scheme in Orissa. On the other hand, in Tamil Nadu, only the problem of delayed supply of rice and dal is found. But, this problem is more complex in Orissa than in Tamil Nadu.

(iv) The financial factors influencing the operation of Mid-day Meals scheme are also observed in Orissa and Tamil Nadu. At first, for the purchase of vegetables, spices and firewood, money is not provided timely for the school in Orissa. In Tamil Nadu, the same problem was also found. Besides money provided for the purchase of vegetables, spices and fire wood was not adequate. The salary of cook and helper in Orissa was very less. With this paltry sum, it was difficult to find a cook and helper more particularly in Rayagada district of

Orissa.

* Anganwadi/Balwadi scheme in the two states of Orissa and Tamil Nadu cannot be converged with Mid-day Meals prog--ramme on grounds of differences in age, composition of food, availability of education package and effectiveness of management. On the other hand, in Tamil Nadu, there is scope for the convergence of Anganwadi with Balwadi sch--eme as the target groups in both the schemes are the same. In Orissa, because of the absence of Balwadi scheme, the possibility of convergence of Anganwadi scheme with Balwadi scheme does not arise. It is to be noted that neither Anganwadi nor Balwadi can be merged with Mid-day Meals programme on account of the differences in target group of children and quantity of food given to the children etc.

Policy Recommendations:

The following recommendations are made on the basis of the findings of our study to improve the operation of the programme:

1. The teachers need be associated with the noon-meal progra--mme for supervision and monitoring of the programme. The teachers understand the psychology of the students better than anybody else. They well understand the food habit of children and can persuade them to take food that contains more nutrition. Complete exclusion of the teachers from the programme, as is the case in Tamil Nadu is undesirable. Simil--arly entrusting all responsibilities to teachers for the managem--ent of the programme, as is the case in Orissa is unwarran--ted. It is therefore, suggested that in Tamil Nadu the noon-meal organiser be accountable to the headmaster or a design -ated assistant teacher in the school. Both of them must work in co-operation in order to improve the programme for the benefit of the children. In Orissa, on the other hand, the head master or his representative assistant teacher need not be too much engrossed with Mid-day Meals work. Their burden needs to be reduced by creating a post of non-meal organiser on contract basis, with out being made a government serv--ant, who would work in close collaboration with the

teacher in the implementation of the scheme. He should be answerable and accountable to the headmaster or his nominee teacher on matters relating to Mid-day Meals. The responsibilities of the teachers will be limited to supervision and close surveillance of the programme.

2. There is a need for specific budgetary provision for Mid-day Meals programme both in Orissa and Tamil Nadu, if the programme is to be sustained on a long-term basis. The present practice as prevalent in Orissa, of apportioning some amount of money, out of the normal allocation of Women and Child and Welfare Department, for Mid-day Meals Programme does not serve the purpose. In Tamil Nadu, too, out of the total allocation of fund on nutrition head, a portion is earmarked for Mid-day Meals programme. In any year, if the normal allocation of fund on welfare head, as is the case in Orissa or on nutrition head as is the case in Tamil Nadu, gets reduced the size of the apportionment of fund towards Mid-day Meals gets squeezed. To avert these possibilities, the state government of both Tamil Nadu and Orissa need to make separate and specific budgetary provision for Mid-day Meals programme, if the scheme is to continue on a sustainable basis. In the absence of such a specific budgetary provision, the implementation of the scheme appears to be haphazard and lopsided.

3. The present practice of continuing Mid-day Meals programme up to class Ten, as is the case in Tamil Nadu, be discontinued. Instead, the programme be confined up to class Seven in Tamil Nadu. This has the merit of reducing severe pressure on the budget. There will be a good deal of saving of men and materials once the programme is limited up to 7th class. Once this is achieved, the programme would be very effectively implemented. Similarly, in Orissa, the existing practice of not covering children in the age group of 37 months to 60 months be taken up seriously. Similarly, the middle school children belonging to class VI and VII also remain outside the purview of the scheme although in large number of schools they share the same classroom with children of 5th class. It is to be

noted that students of class VI and VII are qually vulnerable, and they require as much care as the children up to class V. In order to make the programme a continuous one, in Orissa, the Angawadi scheme be encouraged to cover the children in age group of 37 months to 60 months, who are not covered by any programme at present. Besides, with specific provi--sion for Mid-day Meals programme and Central government's assistance to the programme in terms of free supply of rice, the students of class VI and VII be covered under the prog--ramme. There will be greater parity in the programme once the objective set above is realised.

4. The distribution of noon-meal in schools is based on feeding strength determined at the beginning of each academic ses--sion. Feeding strength once determined remains in operation for a period of three years. In Tamil Nadu, it was observed that the feeding strength has not been revised even after the lapse of three years. As a result, with the existing feeding strength, more number of enrolled children are accommod--ated. Hence the per capita food availability per day gets reduced. It is, therefore, necessary to change the feeding strength of school every year so that the eventuality can be avoided. Orissa, on the other hand, can adopt the same pro--cedure with a view to improve the management of the pro--gramme. Likewise, there is necessity for implementing the programme both in working days and holidays except Sund--ays in Orissa. This will create interest for reading and at--tending schools.

5. In Tamil Nadu, boiled rice with sambar prepared out of red gram is served in the noon- meal programme. Besides, an egg is also supplied to each and every student once in a week. The Mid-day Meals programme in Tamil Nadu, thus, con -tains more nutrition than the one in Orissa programme. From the nutrition point of view, both red gram and mung/arhar dal contain the same nutritive value. But giving the same type of food round the year affects the interest of the children. Hence, it is suggested that, in Tamil Nadu giving sambar to children made out of red gram be changed after some time.

During this period, dal made out of arhar or mung or bengal gram be given to the students. Besides, the proportion of tamarind used in sambar be reduced to make it more hygienic and palatable. Similarly in Orissa, the children be occasionally given dalma prepared out of red gram or bengal gram. Such a change through the inclusion of different types of food is essential to generate sustained interest in the food supplied through the programme on the part of the tiny children. For, the children always like variety. In this connnection, it is further suggested that the quality of rice and dal be improved in both the states. It is also suggested that like Tamil Nadu, the Orissa government can introduce an egg per student per week to be included in the Mid-day Meals programmes.

6. To achieve continuity in the programme, the basic infrastructural facilities required for the purpose need to be improved. There must be a well-built spacious kitchen room in each and every school. In Tamil Nadu, the kitchen rooms exist in most of the schools. However, such kitchen rooms have remained unrenovated for the last several years. In Orissa, in none of the schools, there are kitchen rooms. Hence for Orissa, construction of a brick built spacious kitchen room is the most essential requirement. Once kitchen rooms are there, the problem of storage and cooking of food will not arise. In this connection, we suggest that a kitchen-cum-dining room be constructed in each and every school in Orissa to continue the programme on a long-term basis. In Tamil Nadu, existing kitchen rooms be renovated to include a dining space so that storage, cooking and distribution of food to children will be catered in the same space. In order to construct kitchen-cum-dining rooms in school, the fund required for the purpose can be met from JRY scheme operating in the locality through block and panchayat officers.

7. The funds allocated by state government for Mid-day Meals programme is found to be deficient. Both in Orissa and Tamil Nadu, only 9 paisa is given for vegetables and spices per student per day. Similarly, only Rs.1.30 is given by the gove-

rnment per student per month for purchase of firewood. It is necessary that these amounts be increased. Most of the teachers, parents and officials felt that the cost of the vegeta bles and spices be increased from 9 paisa to 15 paisa per student per day and firewood from Rs.1.30/- to Rs.2.00/- per student per month. It is further suggested that the present supply of 15 grams of dal per student per day is not adequate. There is the suggestion that 25 grams of dal per day per stu- -dent be given in school lunch programme. Besides, there is also the suggestion that for effective continuity of the pro- -gramme, the Central government needs to provide both rice and dal freely to state governments. This will reduce the burd- -en of state governments to a considerable extent. At the same time, when both rice and dal in provided by the Central gov -ernment, the state government will have greater accounta- -bility in the manegement of two principal food items. Furt- -her, the state governments will be in a position to allocate more money on other items like vegetables, oil and spices, which they are not in a position to do now.

8. There is a common complaint both in Tamil Nadu and Orissa that the rice provided by Food Corporation of India through Civil Supplies Corporation contains less quantity of rice per bag than prescribed. The general view is that there is shorta- -ge of 10 to 15 kgs of rice per bag. It is agreed that required quantity of rice will be directly supplied to schools by Civil Supply Corporation, after weighing rice bags in the presence of the officials in charge of Mid-day Meals programme. It is further believed that with proper co-operation and co-ordi- -nation among the officials of FCI, Civil Supply Corporation, block officials and teachers in charge of Mid-day Meals programmes this problem may be removed.

9. Mid-day Meals is one of the incentive packages given to pri- -mary school-going children. In Tamil Nadu, apart from Mid-day Meals, the primary school-going children also receive an'education package in the forms of free note books, free writing materials, free uniforms and free bus passes etc. Mid-day Meals when combined with such education package cre-

ates interest among children for attending school regularly and showing greater zeal and enthusiansm for learning and acquiring knowledge. In Orissa, the 'education package' does not contain so many items like Tamil Nadu and what ever is given is mostly confined to tribal localities of the state. Hence, it is suggested that the education package including Mid-day Meals be uniform in its application in all the primary schools of the country.

10. The recent official view in Orissa, however, is against the continuance of the scheme. The discontinuance is supported on the following three grounds.

First, there is large-scale corruption in the programme. The programme has not helped the ultimate beneficiaries due to large-scale pilferage by teachers in charge of Mid-day Meals programme.

Secondly, since there is dearth of funds in the state, the programme be confined to tribal areas only. There is no need of continuing the programme in the coastal areas of the state, where the people are relatively better off compared to tribal people. Protagonists who support this view argue that BPL families in coastal regions are more well off than the BPL families in tribal regions.

Finally, there is also a strong feeling that instead of providing cooked food to children, the government can experiment with the scheme of providing 3 kgs of rice and 1 kg of dal in polythene packs per students per month on the basis of 80 percent of attendance in the school. The argument is that the BPL families now get 20 kgs of subsidised rice from fair price shops per month. Now in addition to this, if they will be given another 3 kgs of rice and one kg of dal they will be much better off. They will encourage their children to attend schools as the parents will be now in a better position to feed the children with increased quota of rice and dal.

The counter arguments are still more suggestive.

(i) The programme cannot be scrapped on the ground of large-scale corruption and pilferage on the part of some officials including the teachers. This is an administrative problem. This can be overcome with proper checks and balances, monitor ing and timely supervision by officials engaged in administer ing the programme.

(ii) The proposal of discontinuing the programme in coastal are- -as and continuing the same in tribal areas does not appear to pragmatic. In the coastal areas, there are many BPL families whose economic condition is much worse compared to the BPL families in tribal areas. The children of such families are equally vulnerable and are in need of a supplementary nutri- -tious food. Hence, if the programme is to continue it must continue throughout the state irrespective of regional or caste considerations.

(iii) The practice of giving 3 kgs of rice and 1 kg of dal to each of the BPL families through public distribution is also untena ble. The poor families are so poor that they may sall the same in the open market to earn some money. Instead of the chil- dren of getting the benefit, the benefit will be reaped by well to do amongst the poor, who will be in possession of the food at a very nominal price Besides, the objective of the programme will not be realised as the real beneficiaries, i.e., the primary school-going children, may not reap the benefit Hence, by all intent and purpose, the present system of cooked food be continued both in Orissa and Tamil Nadu.

However, there is a related problem in the administration of Mid-day Meals programme in Tamil Nadu. As is observed, there is a separate wing both at the district, block and school levels to look after noon-meal programme. The problem of Tamil Nadu is that all the officials involved at the block and the school level for managing Mid-day Meals programme are government officials. Even the cook and helpers are also considered as government servants. Maintaining such a large number of staff out of state exchequer creates a serious financial burden on the government. On account of this, the state government is unable to provide adequate funds for other developmental activities. Thus, in course of time through administrative restructuring in welfare and education department, no further creation of posts under noon-meal programme be created either at the block or at the school level.

The work of Mid-day Meals programme in 3 to 4 contiguous blocks can be monitored and supervised by a Noon-Meal Manager stationed in one of the blocks. At school level either the headmaster or his nominee teacher be given the duty of supervising the programme, may be with some additional incentive. With some realignment of the existing practices and functions and strict vigilance the present burden on the state exchequer can be reduced. It must be clearly borne in mind that Mid-day Meals programme is a massive social welfare programme aiming at attracting children into the educational mainstream as also providing them with the much needed supplementary nutrition to make them the worthy citizens of the country. At this stage any consideration for the reduction of cost would, eventually mean that the social welfare goals have been sacrificed at the alters of growth objectives. However, there are considerable scopes to plug the loopholes observed in the operation of the programme effectively by way of strict vigilance, as a result of which the programme would be cost-effective.

There is also considerable scope to involve the NGOs in the programme. An attempt should be made atleast on a pilot basis, to bring the NGO element into the programme.

The suggestion as mentioned above, if adopted properly would certainly make the working and operation of the Mid-day Meals programme more effective.

ANNEXURES

ANNEXURE-1.1

DISTRICTS, BLOCKS, PANCHAYATS, SCHOOLS AND THE SAMPLE UNITS SURVEYED IN ORISSA

Name Of The District	*Name of The Blockt*	*Name Of The Gram Panchayat*	*Name Of The School*	*Student*	*Parents*	*Teacher*	*Panchayat represent-ative*	*NGO/ Social worker**	*Educated Villagers*	*Official ***
PURI	SATYABADI	BALAPUR	RAICHAKRADHARPUR PRI.SCHOOL	5	5	1	1	1	1	10
EDUCAT-IONALLY ADVANCED	EDUCA-TIONALLY ADVANCED	KADUR	MAHABALAPADA PRI.SCHOOL	5	5	1	1	1	1	
		SRIRAMACHANDRAPUR	NAHALA PRI. SCHOOL	5	5	1	1	1	1	
		BIRARAMACHANDRAPUR	BIRARAMACHANDRA PUR PRI.SCHOOL	5	5	1	1	1	1	
		. DASABIDYADHARPUR	DASABIDYADHARPUR PRI. SCHOOL	5	5	1	1	1	1	
	PURI SADAR EDUCATION ALLY BACKWARD	BALIGUALI	SAMAGARA PRI SCHOOL	5	5	1	1	1	1	
		GOPINATHPUR	KHANDIABANDHA PRI SCHOOL	5	5	1	1	1	1	
		KANHEIBIDYADHARPUR	KANHEIBIDYADHARPUR PRI. SCHOOL	5	5	1	1	1	1	
		BIRAHAREKRISHNAPUR	BATAGAON PRI SCHOOL	5	5	1	1	1	1	
		CHANDANPUR	CHANDANPUR PRI. SCHOOL	5	5	1	1	1	1	

(Cont....)

ANNEXURE- 1.1 (Cont...)

DISTRICTS, BLOCKS, PANCHAYATS, SCHOOLS AND THE SAMPLE UNITS SURVEYED IN ORISSA

Name of the District	Name of the Block	Name of the Gram Panchayat	Name of the School	Student	Parents	Teacher	Panchayat Representative	NGO/ Social Worker	Education Villagers	Official
RAYAGADA	KOLNARA	REKHAPADARA	BELANGAPADARA PRI SCHOOL	5	5	1	1	1	1	10
EDUCATIONALLY BACKWARD	EDUCATIONALLY ADVANCED	BANKILI	MINAJHULA PRI SCHOOL	5	5	1	1	1	1	
		GADISESHKAL	RIVOLKANA PRI. SCHOOL	5	5	1	1	1	1	
		SURI	KHAMASINGH PRI SCHOOL	5	5	1	1	1	1	
		KOLNARA	BHUJABALA PRI. SCHOO L	5	5	1	1	1	1	
	RAYAGADA	MALIGAON	KANDHAMALIGAON PRI SCHOOL	5	5	1	1	1	1	
	EDUCATIONALLY BACKWARD	KAMTOLPENTHA	KARLAKONA PRI. SCHOOL	5	5	1	1	1	1	
		PITAMAHAL	DISARIGUDA PRI SCHOOL	5	5	1	1	1	1	
		PENTA	JINJILIBADI PRI. SCHOOL	5	5	1	1	1	1	
		GUMA	GUMA PRI. SCHOOL	5	5	1	1	1	1	
			Total	100	100	20	20	20	20	20

NOTE:* 1. Social worker includes local political leader, youth club member and the persons doing social work in the area.
** 2. Official includes Districts Social Welfare Officer (D.S.W.) District inspector of Schools (D.I) Sub Inspector of Schools, Block Development officer (B.D. O), I.C..D.S. Superintendent (or C.D.P.O) Social Education Organiser (S.E.O) AND CIVIL SUPPLY OFFICER

ANNEXURE-1.2

DISTRICTS, BLOCKS, PANCHAYATS, SCHOOLS AND THE SAMPLE UNITS SURVEYED IN TAMIL NADU

Name of the District	*Name of the Block*	*Name of the Gram Panchayat*	*Name of the School*	*Student*	*Parents*	*Teacher*	*Panachayat Represent-tative*	*NGO/ Social Worker*	*Education Villagers*	*Official*
MADURAI	MADURAI	ANDARKOTTORAM	ANDARKOTTORAM MADURAI EAST P.U.E.S.	5	5	1	1	1	1	10
EDUCAT-IONALLY	EDUCATIO NALLY	KARUPOOURANI	KARUPOOURANI UPPER PRI. SCHOOL	5	5	1	1	1	1	
ADVANCED	ADVANCED	SAKKIMANGALAM	SAKKIMANGALAM. MADURAI EAST P.U.E.S.	5	5	1	1	1	1	
		MELAMADI	MELAMADI P.U.E.S	5	5	1	1	1	1	
		KARSARI	KARSARI MADURAI EAST P.U.E.S	5	5	1	1	1	1	
	ALANGANU ULLER	ACHAMPATI	ACHAMAPATI ADI DRAVID WELFARE SCHOOL	5	5	1	1	1	1	
	EDUCATION ALLY	ALANGANULLER	ALANGANULLER P.U.E.S	5	5	1	1	1	1	
	BACKWARD	VAVIDAMARUTHUR	VAVIDAMARUTHUR P.U.E.S	5	5	1	1	1	1	
		URSERI	URSERI P.U.E.S	5	5	1	1	1	1	
		PANNAIKUDI	PANNAIKUDI P.U.E.S	5	5	1	1	1	1	

Cont...)

ANNEXURE-1.2 (Cont....)

DISTRICTS, BLOCKS, PANCHAYATS, SCHOOLS AND THE SAMPLE UNITS SURVEYED IN TAMIL NADU

Name of the District	*Name of the Block*	*Name of the Gram Panchayat*	*Name of the School*	*Student*	*Parents*		*Teacher*	*Panachayat Represent-tative*	*NGO/ Social Worker*	*Education Villagers*	*Official*
VILLIPURAM											
RAMASAMY	KOLIYANUR	KUTCHIPALAYAM	KURCHIPALAY YAM	5	5		1	1	1	1	10
EDUCATION	EDUCATION	MELAPATHI	MELAPATHI P.U.E.S	5	5		1	1	1	1	
ALLY	ALLY										
BACKWARD	ADVANCED	SOLAGANUR	SOLANGANUR P.U.E.S.	5	5		1	1	1	1	
		KAPPUR	KAPPUR P.U.E.S	5	5		1	1	1	1	
		KAKUPPAM	KAKUPPAM P.U.E.S	5	5		1	1	1	1	
	THIRUNAV ALLUR	KARUVEPPILL AIPALAYAM	KARUVEPPILLAIPALAYAM P.U.E.S	5	5		1	1	1	1	
	EDUCATION ALLY	DEVIYANANTHAL	DEVIYANTHAL P.U.E.S	5	5		1	1	1	1	
	BACKWARD	ADVANCE	AYANUELLORE P.U.E.S	5	5		5	1	1	1	
		CHEMMANDAL	CHEMMANDAL P.U.E.S	5	5		1	1	1	1	
		METTATHUR	METTATHUR P.U.E.S	5	5		1	1	1	1	
TOTAL				100	100	20	20	20	20	20	20

NOTE: 1. P.U.E.S = Panchayat Union Elementary School

2. Social worker includes local political leader, youth club member and the person doing social work in the area

3. Offical includes, P.A. to Collector (Noon meal), District Elemenary education Officer, Assistant Elementary Education Officer, Block Development Officer, noon Meal Manger and Noon Meal Organiser.

ANNEXURE-2.1

SEX AND CASTE-WISE DISTRIBUTION OF POPULATON IN THE SAMPLE AREAS OF ORISSA

Sl. No.	Areas	SC			ST			Others			Total		
		M	F	T	M	F	T	M	F	T	M	F	T
1.	Satyabadi Block	9426 (20.25)	8984 (19.95)	18410 (20.10)	148 (0.32)	113 (0.25)	261 (0.28)	36968 (79.43)	35941 (79.80)	72909 (79.61)	46542 (100.00	45038 (100.00)	91580 (100.00)
2.	Puri Sadar Block	9873 (16.83)	9576 (16.99)	19449 (16.91)	435 (0.74)	416 (0.74)	851 (0.74)	48343 (82.42)	46355 (82.27)	94698 (82.35)	58651 (100.00)	56347 (100.00)	114998 (100.00)
	Puri District	122806 (18.53)	119483 (18.59)	242289 (18.56)	1879 (0.28)	1602 (0.25)	3481 (0.27)	538079 (81.19)	521516 (81.16)	1059595 (81.17)	662764 (100.00)	642601 (100.00)	1305365 (100.00)
3.	Kolnara Block	2678 (9.12)	2735 (9.13)	5413 (9.13)	19873 (67.69)	20902 (69.78)	40775 (68.75)	6806 (23.18)	6315 (21.08)	13121 (22.12)	29357 (100.00)	29952 (100.00)	59309 (100.00)
4.	Rayagada Block	3813 (9.72)	3839 (9.43)	7652 (9.57)	29350 (74.78)	30941 (76.00)	60291 (75.41)	6083 (15.50)	5930 (14.57)	12013 (15.02)	39246 (100.00)	40710 (100.00)	79956 (100.00)
	Rayagada District	50713 (14.29)	51213 (14.26)	101926 (14.30)	195803 (55.17)	204294 (56.89)	400097 (56.04)	108395 (30.54)	103566 (28.84)	211961 (29.68)	354911 (100.00)	359073 (100.00)	713984 (100.00)

Note: Figures in the parentheses indicates the percentage to the corresponding total

Source : Census of India 1991.

ANNEXURE-2.2

SEX AND CASTE-WISE DISTRIBUTION OF POPULATON IN THE SAMPLE AREAS OF TAMIL NADU

Sl. No.	Areas	SC M	SC F	SC T	ST M	ST F	ST T	Others M	Others F	Others T	Total M	Total F	Total T
1.	Madural East Block	12395	12282	24677	14	15	29	49549	47980	97529	61958	60277	122235
		(20.00)	(20.38)	(20.19)	(0.02)	(0.02)	(0.02)	(79.97)	(79.60)	(79.79)	(100.00)	(100.00)	(100.00)
2.	Alanganuller Block	9713	9621	19334	688	652	1340	38282	36978	75260	48683	47251	95934
		(19.95)	(20.36)	(20.15)	(1.41)	(1.38)	(1.40)	(78.64)	(78.26)	(78.45)	(100.00)	(100.00)	(100.00)
	Madurai District	255596	247974	503570	6588	6149	12737	1494167	1439188	2933355	1756351	1693311	3449662
		(14.55)	(14.64)	(14.60)	(0.38)	(0.36)	(0.37)	(85.07)	(85.00)	(85.03)	(100.00)	(100.00)	(100.00)
3.	Koliyanur Block	16737	16267	33004	238	214	452	47604	46175	93779	64579	62656	127235
		(25.92)	(25.96)	(25.94)	(0.37)	(0.34)	(0.36)	(73.71)	(73.70)	(73.71)	(100.00)	(100.00)	(100.00)
4.	Thirunavalur Block	15482	14869	30351	174	168	342	34645	33797	68442	50301	48834	99135
		(30.78)	(30.45)	(30.62)	(0.35)	(0.34)	(0.34)	(68.88)	(69.21)	(69.04)	(100.00)	(100.00)	(100.00)
	Villupuram District	382502	368889	751391	24739	24014	48753	992615	962915	1955530	1399856	1355818	2755674
		(27.32)	(27.21)	(27.27)	(1.87)	(1.77)	(1.77)	(70.91)	(71.02)	(70.96)	(100.00)	(100.00)	(100.00)

Note: i Figures in the parentheses indicates the percentage to the corresponding total.
ii- For the newly formed Villupuram District, data was computed from the 1991 census results by E & AR Department.

Source: Census of India, 1991.

ANNEXURE-2.3

OCCUPATIONAL CLASSIFICATION OF WORKERS IN THE SAMPLE AREAS OF ORISSA

SL. No.	Areas	Cultivators			Agricultural Labourers			House Hold Industry			Other Workers		
		M	*F*	*T*	*M*	*F*	*T*	*M*	*F*	*T*	*M*	*F*	*T*
1.	Satyabadi Block	12718	75	12793	6264	639	6903	504	147	651	5235	837	6072
		(51.45)	(4.42)	(48.42)	(25.34)	(3.76)	(26.13)	(2.04)	(8.66)	(2.46)	(21.18)	(49.29)	(22.98)
2.	Puri Sadar Block	13572	69	1364	9667	1004	10671	785	239	1024	8305	2431	10736
		(41.98)	(1.84)	(37.82)	(29.90)	(26.82)	(29.58)	(2.43)	(6.38)	(2.84)	(25.69)	(64.95)	(29.76)
	Puri District	166895	1843	168733	69526	15577	85103	6883	1911	8794	101095	19519	120614
		(48.46)	(4.74)	(44.03)	(20.19)	(40.10)	(22.21)	(2.00)	(4.92)	(2.29)	(29.35)	(50.24)	(31.47)
3.	Kolnara Block	7407	1683	9090	5198	6913	12111	162	24	186	5391	3147	8538
		(40.79)	(14.30)	(30.33)	(28.63)	(58.75)	(40.47)	(0.89)	(0.20)	(0.62)	(29.69)	(26.74)	(28.53)
4.	Rayagada Block	12157	2817	14974	8115	7722	15837	217	45	262	420	8299	12500
		(49.24)	(14.92)	(34.37)	(32.87)	(40.89)	(36.35)	(0.88)	(0.24)	(0.60)	(1.70)	(43.95)	(28.69)
	Rayagada District	97693	20702	118395	62805	58342	121147	2984	652	3636	49508	56393	96885
		(45.87)	(15.21)	(33.92)	(29.49)	(42.87)	(34.70)	(1.40)	(0.48)	(1.04)	(23.24)	(41.44)	(27.75)

(Cont...)

ANNEXURE-2.3 (Cont...)

OCCUPATIONAL CLASSIFICATION OF WORKERS IN THE SAMPLE AREAS OF ORISSA

SI. No	Areas	Total Main Workers			Marginal Workers			Total Workers		
		M	F	T	M	F	T	M	F	T
1.	Satyabadi Block	24584	1283	25867	137	415	552	24721	1698	26419
		(99.44)	(75.55)	(97.91)	(0.55)	(24.44)	(2.09)	(100)	(100)	(100)
2.	Puri Sadar Block	31821	1853	33674	508	1890	2398	32329	3743	36072
		(98.43)	(49.51)	(93.35)	(1.57)	(50.50)	(6.65)	(100)	(100)	(100)
	Puri District	340307	27737	368044	4092	11113	15205	344399	38850	383249
		(98.81)	(71.39)	(96.03)	(1.19)	(28.60)	(3.97)	(100)	(100)	(100)
3.	Kolnara Block	17758	7941	25699	400	3826	4226	18158	11767	29925
		(97.80)	(67.49)	(85.88)	(2.20)	(32.51)	(14.12)	(100)	(100)	(100)
4.	Rayagada Block	23996	10856	34852	694	8027	8721	24690	18883	43573
		(97.19)	(67.49)	(79.99)	(2.81)	(42.51)	(20.01)	(100)	(100)	(100)
	Rayagada District	207703	86819	294522	5287	49270	54557	212990	136089	349079
		(97.52)	(63.80)	(84.37)	(2.48)	(36.20)	(15.63)	(100)	(100)	(100

Note: Figures in the parentheses indicate percentage to the corresponding total.

Source: Census of India 1991.

For divided Puri district and Rayagada district Statistical Abstract of Orissa (1996).

Directorate of Economics and Statistics, Orissa, Bhubaneswar.

ANNEXURE - 2.4

OCCUPATIONAL CLASSIFICATION OF WORKERS IN THE SAMPLE AREAS OF TAMIL NADU

SL. No.	Type of Workers/ Areas	Cultivators			Agricultural Labourers			House Hold Industry			Other Workers		
		M	F	T	M	F	T	M	F	T	M	F	T
1.	Madurai East Block	6050	2463	8513	14228	14367	28595	1593	1168	2761	14109	5251	19360
		(16.81)	(10.59)	(14.37)	(39.54)	(61.80)	(48.28)	(4.43)	(5.02)	(4.66)	(39.21)	(22.59)	(32.69)
2.	Alanganuller Block	6781	1732	8513	15960	14203	30163	147	77	224	5931	4629	10560
		(23.53)	(8.39)	(17.21)	(55.38)	(68.81)	(60.98)	(0.51)	(0.37)	(0.45)	(20.58)	(22.43)	(21.35)
	Madurai District	177084	72667	249751	326359	309964	636323	11475	8218	19693	464758	147058	611816
		(18.08)	(13.51)	(16.46)	(33.31)	(57.62)	(41.93)	(1.17)	(1.53)	(1.30)	(47.44)	(27.34)	(40.22)
3	.Koliyanur Block	10620	1439	12059	16606	12068	28674	402	142	544	7447	4352	11799
		(30.28)	(7.99)	(22.72)	(47.34)	(67.04)	(54.02)	(1.15)	(0.79)	(1.02)	(21.23)	(24.18)	(22.23)
4.	Thirunavalur Block	15694	4397	20091	9789	9385	19174	295	107	402	2576	3580	6156
		(55.35)	(25.17)	(43.84)	(34.52)	(53.72)	(41.84)	(1.04)	(0.61)	(0.88)	(9.09)	(20.49)	(13.43)
	Villupuram District	358784	91142	449926	258214	255199	513413	11370	2886	14256	144911	127503	272414
		(46.40)	(19.12)	(36.00)	(33.53)	(53.53)	(41.07)	(1.47)	(0.61)	(1.14)	(18.74)	(26.75)	(21.7)

(Cont...)

ANNEXURE-2.4 (Cont...)

OCCUPATIONAL CLASSIFICATION OF WORKERS IN THE SAMPLE AREAS OF TAMIL NADU

SL. No	Type of Workers/ Areas	Total Main Workers			Marginal Workers			Total Workers		
		M	F	T	M	F	T	M	F	T
1.	Madurai East Block	35817	21106	56923	163	2143	2306	35980	23249	59229
		(99.55)	(90.78)	(96.11)	(0.45)	(9.22)	(3.89)	(100)	(100)	(100)
2.	Alanganuller Block	28773	17091	45864	46	3550	3596	28819	20641	49460
		(99.84)	(82.80)	(92.73)	(0.16)	(17.20)	(7.27)	(100)	(100)	(100)
	Madurai District	976272	478457	IE+06	3404	59450	62854	979676	537907	2E+06
		(99.65)	(88.95)	(95.86)	(0.35)	(11.05)	(4.14)	(100)	(100)	(100)
3 .	Koliyanur Block	34911	14673	49584	164	3328	3492	35075	18001	53076
		(99.53)	(81.51)	(93.42)	(0.47)	(18.49)	(6.58)	(100)	(100)	(100)
4.	Thirunavalur Block	28197	14386	42583	157	3083	3240	28354	17469	45823
		(99.45)	(82.35)	(92.93)	(0.55)	(17.65)	(7.07)	(100)	(100)	(100)
	Villupuram District	769339	373090	1E+06	3940	103640	107580	773279	476730	1E+06
		(99.49)	(78.26)	(91.39)	(0.51)	(21.74)	(8.61)	(100)	(100)	(100)

Note: i. Figure in the parentheses indicate percentage to the corresponding total .
ii. For the newly formed Villupuram District, data was computed from the 1991 census results by E&AR Department.

Source : Census of India 1991.

ANNEXURE-2.5

SEX-WISE WORK PARTICIPATION RATE IN THE SAMPLE AREAS OF ORISSA

Sl. No.	*Areas*	*Male*	*Female*	*Total*
1	Satyabadi Block	53.12	3.77	28.84
2.	Puri Sadar Block	55.12	6.64	31.37
	Puri District	51.96	6.05	29.36
3.	Kolnara Block	61.85	39.29	50.46
4.	Rayagada Block	62.91	46.38	43.24
	Rayagada District	60.01	37.90	48.89

Source: Census of India, 1991.

ANNEXURE-2.6

SEX-WISE WORK PARTICIPATION RATE IN THE SAMPLE AREAS OF TAMIL NADU

Sl.No	*Areas*	*Male*	*Female*	*Total*
1.	Madurai East Block	58.07	38.57	48.46
2.	Alanganuller Block	59.20	43.68	51.56
	Madurai District	55.78	31.77	43.99
3.	Koliyanur Block	54.31	28.73	41.71
	Thirunavalur Block	56.37	35.77	46.23
	Villupuram District	55.24	35.16	45.36

Source: Census of India, 1991.

ANNEXURE-2.7

SEX AND CASTE-WISE LITERACY RATES IN THE SAMPLE AREAS OF ORISSA

SI.No.	*Areas.*	*SC*			*ST*			*Others*		
		M	*F*	*T*	*M*	*F*	*T*	*M*	*F*	*T*
1.	Satyabadi Block	58.67	28.23	43.78	53.72	8.89	34.60	78.41	52.06	65.43
2.	Puri Sadar Block	48.34	17.30	32.98	31.10	7.14	19.50	71.90	41.12	56.80
	Puri District	58.61	26.00	42.51	52.45	22.77	38.94	76.8/3	49.41	63.30
3.	Kolnara Block	43.22	14.02	28.26	22.82	4.87	13.60	37.69	14.62	26.03
4.	Rayagada Block	27.51	8.18	17.81	14.23	2.56	8.23	23.75	8.37	15.90
	Rayagada District	33.63	9.46	21.46	17.73	3.40	10.39	36.53	15.63	26.01

Source: Census of India, 1991.

ANNEXURE-2.8

SEX AND CASTE - WISE LITERACY RATES IN THE SAMPLE AREAS OF TAMIL NADU

Sl.No.	*Areas*	*SC*			*ST*			*Total*		
		M	*F*	*T*	*M*	*F*	*T*	*M*	*F*	*T*
1.	Madurai East Block	54.95	29.92	42.40	54.55	50.00	52.17	74.02	49.86	62.06
2.	Alanganuller Block	57.90	30.28	44.16	68.26	44.21	56.50	69.60	42.73	56.35
	Madurai District	58.19	32.38	45.28	64.54	40.70	52.97	77.74	54.74	66.44
3.	Koliyanur Block	54.25	27.86	41.27	42.35	22.03	32.71	67.56	40.73	54.36
4.	Thirunavalur Block	39.37	16.90	28.37	26.57	15.15	21.09	54.36	25.69	40.23
	Villupuram District	NA	NA	NA	NA	NA	NA	60.92	35.38	48.36

NA = Not Available.

Source: District of Census Operation, Tamil Nadu, Madras-18.

ANNEXURE-2.9

NO. OF PRIMARY SCHOOLS PER 100 SQ. KMS. PER 1000 POPULATION AND TEACHER-PUPIL RATIO IN THE SAMPLE AREAS OF ORISSA, 1998-99

Sl. No.	*Areas*	*No of Primary Schools*	*No of Student in Primary Schools*	*No of Teachers in Primary Schools*	*Teacher -Pupil Ratio in Primary Schools*	*No of Primary Schools per 100sq Kms area*	*No of Primary Schools per1000 Population*
1.	Satyabadi Block	96	11292	263	43	52	1.05
2.	Puri Sadar Block	116	16887	298	57	44	1.009
	Puri District	1443	187569	2701	69.44	47	1.1i
3.	Kolnara Block	117	5847	280	21	33	1.97
4.	Rayagada Block	167	10679	290	36	31	2.09
	Rayagada District	1323	74279	3231	23	17	1.85

Source: Office of the D.I of Schools and Block Office of the respective districts and blocks.

ANNEXURE - 2.10

NO. OF PRIMARY SCHOOLS PER 100 SQ.KMS, PER 1000 POPULATION AND TEACHER-PUPIL RATIO IN THE SAMPLE AREAS OF TAMIL NADU, 1998-99

Sl. No.	Areas	No of Primary Schools	No of Students in Primary Schools	No of Teachers in Primary Schools	Teacher -Pupil Ratio in Primary Schools	No of Primary Schools per 100sq Kms area	No of Primary Schools per1000 Population
1.	Madurai East Block	78	17760	196	91	39	0.64
2.	Alanganuller Block	54	11682	279	42	34	0.56
	Madurai District	1038	175562	NA	NA	16	0.30
3.	Koliyanaur Block	76	12279	333	37	39	0.60
4.	Thirunavalur Block	89	11527	238	48	48	0.90
	Villupuram District	1697	324279	7240	45	22	0.61

Source: Office of the District Elementary Education Officer and Block Office of the respective districts and blocks.

ANNEXURE-4.1

CASTE AND SEX-WISE ENROLMENT OF STUDENTS OF SAMPLE SCHOOLS IN DIFFERENT YEARS

ORISSA

	SC			*ST*			*Others*			*Total*		
Year	*B*	*G*	*T*	*B*	*G*	*T*	*B*	*G*	*T*	*B*	*G*	*T*
1989-90	202	173	375	204	163	367	815	689	1504	1221	1025	2246
1990-91	229	212	441	210	163	373	840	684	1524	1279	1059	2338
1991-92	222	204	426	209	142	351	806	713	1519	1237	1059	2296
1992-93	244	195	439	205	124	329	776	701	1477	1225	1020	2245
1993-94	236	212	448	148	113	261	780	701	1481	1164	1026	2190
1994-95	259	199	458	169	114	283	893	760	1653	1321	1073	2394
1995-96	261	237	498	203	134	337	813	726	1539	1277	1097	2374
1996-97	264	254	518	211	124	335	792	747	1539	1267	1125	2392
1997-98	240	244	484	235	168	403	818	705	1523	1293	1117	2410
1998-99	266	247	513	253	172	425	771	710	1481	1290	1129	2419

TAMIL NADU

Year	SC			ST			Others			Total			
	B	G	T	B	G	T	B	G	T	B	G	T	
1989-90	563	480	1043	4	4	8	1963	1799	3762	2530	2283	4813	-
1990-91	603	541	1144	7	6	13	2030	1870	3900	2640	2417	5057	5.1
1991-92	616	584	1200	6	4	10	2003	1837	3840	2625	2425	5050	(-) 0.1
1992-93	592	548	1140	5	8	13	1960	1891	3851	2557	2447	5004	(-) 8.4
1993-94	598	536	1134	6	4	10	1954	1738	3692	2558	2278	4836	(-) 4.3
1994-95	640	568	1208	6	4	10	1894	1684	3578	2540	2256	4796	(-) 0.8
1995-96	687	574	1261	11	10	21	1748	1591	3339	2446	2175	4621	(-) 3.6
1996-97	698	553	1251	5	3	8	1669	1429	3098	2372	1985	4357	(-) 5.7
1997-98	731	582	1313	4	5	9	1712	1394	3106	2447	1981	4428	(+) 1.6
1998-99	728	585	1313	5	4	9	1651	1422	3073	2384	2011	4395	(-) 0.7

Source: Collected from the Sample Schools of Orissa and Tamil Nadu.

ANNEXURE-4.2

CASTE AND SEX-WISE ENROLMENT OF STUDENTS OF THE SAMPLE SCHOOLS OF PURI DISTRICT AND ITS TWO SAMPLE BLOCKS

SATYABADI BLOCK

	SC			*ST*			*Others*			*Total*		
Year	*B*	*G*	*T*	*B*	*G*	*T*	*B*	*G*	*T*	*B*	*G*	*T*
1989-90	97	101	198	0	0	0	226	198	424	323	299	622
1990-91	126	132	258	0	0	0	198	155	353	324	287	611
1991-92	116	109	225	0	0	0	204	170	374	320	279	599
1992-93	116	98	214	0	0	0	211	166	377	327	264	591
1993-94	108	106	214	0	0	0	204	165	369	312	271	583
1994-95	115	91	206	0	0	0	206	196	402	321	287	608
1995-96	123	118	241	0	0	0	198	169	367	321	287	608
1996-97	110	105	215	0	0	0	182	166	348	292	271	563
1997-98	106	99	205	0	0	0	186	159	345	292	258	550
1998-99	106	98	204	0	0	0	188	174	362	294	272	566

PURI SADAR BLOCK

	SC			*ST*			*Others*			*Total*		
Year	*B*	*G*	*T*	*B*	*G*	*T*	*B*	*G*	*T*	*B*	*G*	*T*
1989-90	75	54	129	0	0	0	524	425	949	599	479	1078
1990-91	74	60	134	0	0	0	548	448	996	622	508	1130
1991-92	77	70	147	0	0	0	533	464	997	610	534	1144
1992-93	84	73	157	0	0	0	507	473	980	591	546	1137
1993-94	76	73	149	0	0	0	509	490	999	585	563	1148
1994-95	98	74	172	0	0	0	620	512	1132	718	586	1304
1995-96	86	80	166	0	0	0	542	500	1042	628	580	1208
1996-97	102	104	206	0	0	0	543	526	1069	645	630	1275
1997-98	74	99	173	0	0	0	573	493	1066	647	592	1239
1998-99	103	96	199	0	0	0	519	474	993	622	570	1192

PURI DISTRICT

Year	SC B	SC G	SC T	ST B	ST G	ST T	Others B	Others G	Others T	Total B	Total G	Total T
1989-90	172	155	327	0	0	0	750	623	1373	922	778	1700
1990-91	200	192	392	0	0	0	746	603	1349	946	795	1741
1991-92	193	179	372	0	0	0	737	634	1371	930	813	1743
1992-93	200	171	371	0	0	0	718	639	1357	918	810	1728
1993-94	184	179	363	0	0	0	713	655	1368	897	834	1731
1994-95	213	165	378	0	0	0	826	708	1534	1039	873	1912
1995-96	209	198	407	0	0	0	740	669	1409	949	867	1816
1996-97	212	209	421	0	0	0	725	692	1417	937	901	1838
1997-98	180	198	378	0	0	0	759	652	1411	939	850	1789
1998-99	209	194	403	0	0	0	707	648	1355	916	842	1758

Source: Collected from the Sample Schools of the respective areas..

ANNEXURE-4.3

CASTE AND SEX-WISE ENROLMENT OF STUDENTS OF THE SAMPLE SCHOOLS OF RAYAGADA DISTRICT AND ITS TWO SAMPLE BLOCKS

KOLNARA BLOCK

Year	SC B	SC G	SC T	ST B	ST G	ST T	Others B	Others G	Others T	Total B	Total G	Total T
1989-90	26	15	41	60	57	117	33	44	77	119	116	235
1990-91	27	19	46	76	74	150	45	47	92	148	140	288
1991-92	29	19	48	71	55	126	42	50	92	142	124	266
1992-93	33	19	52	83	49	132	37	44	81	153	112	265
1993-94	31	22	53	64	62	126	51	33	84	146	117	263
1994-95	36	26	62	68	65	133	53	39	92	157	130	287
1995-96	40	31	71	88	64	152	53	43	96	181	138	319
1996-97	41	32	73	93	62	155	45	37	82	179	131	310
1997-98	48	32	80	106	90	196	41	30	71	195	152	347
1998-99	43	38	81	112	88	200	47	48	95	202	174	376

RAYAGADA BLOCK

YEAR	SC B	SC G	SC T	ST B	ST G	ST T	Others B	Others G	Others T	Total B	Total G	Total T
1989-90	4	3	7	144	106	250	32	22	54	180	131	311
1990-91	2	1	3	134	89	223	49	34	83	185	124	309
1991-92	0	6	6	138	87	225	27	29	56	165	122	287
1992-93	11	5	16	122	75	197	21	18	39	154	98	252
1993-94	21	11	32	84	51	135	16	13	29	121	75	196
1994-95	10	8	18	101	49	150	14	13	27	125	70	195
1995-96	12	8	20	115	70	185	20	14	34	147	92	239
1996-97	11	13	24	118	62	180	22	18	40	151	93	244
1997-98	12	14	26	129	78	207	18	23	41	159	115	274
1998-99	14	15	29	141	84	225	17	14	31	172	113	285

RAYAGADA DISTRICT

Year	SC B	SC G	SC T	ST B	ST G	ST T	Othes B	Othes G	Othes T	Total B	Total G	Total T
1989-90	30	18	48	204	163	367	65	66	131	299	247	546
1990-91	29	20	49	210	163	373	94	81	175	333	264	597
1991-92	29	25	54	209	142	351	69	79	148	307	246	553
1992-93	44	24	68	205	124	329	58	62	120	307	210	517
1993-94	52	33	85	148	113	261	67	46	113	267	192	459
1994-95	46	34	80	169	114	283	67	52	119	282	200	482
1995-96	52	39	91	203	134	337	73	57	130	328	230	558
1996-97	52	45	97	211	124	335	67	55	122	330	224	554
1997-98	60	46	106	235	168	403	59	53	112	354	267	621
1998-99	57	53	110	253	172	425	64	62	126	374	287	661

Source: Collected from the Sample Schools of the respective areas..

ANNEXURE-4.4

CASTE AND SEX-WISE ENROLMENT OF STUDENTS OF THE SAMPLE SCHOOLS IN DIFFERENT YEARS OF MADURAI DISTRICT AND ITS TWO SAMPLE BLOCKS

MADURAI EAST BLOCK

Year	SC			ST			Others			Total		
	B	G	T	B	G	T	B	G	T	B	G	T
1989-90	186	138	324	0	0	0	615	547	1162	801	685	1486
1990-91	217	188	405	0	0	0	670	605	1275	887	793	1680
1991-92	210	192	402	0	0	0	665	562	1227	875	754	1629
1992-93	206	200	406	0	0	0	607	551	1158	813	751	1564
1993-94	237	198	435	0	0	0	667	576	1243	904	774	1678
1994-95	273	227	500	0	0	0	672	534	1206	945	761	1706
1995-96	231	206	437	0	0	0	699	558	1257	930	764	1694
1996-97	251	196	447	0	0	0	716	529	1245	967	725	1692
1997-98	254	185	439	0	0	0	756	530	1286	1010	715	1725
1998-99	236	183	419	0	0	0	688	536	1224	924	719	1643

ALLANGANULLER BLOCK

Years	SC			ST			Othes			Total		
	B	G	T	B	G	T	B	G	T	B	G	T
1989-90	231	210	441	0	0	0	564	554	1118	795	764	1559
1990-91	227	218	445	0	0	0	573	551	1124	800	769	1569
1991-92	241	257	498	0	0	0	568	536	1104	809	793	1602
1992-93	230	219	449	0	0	0	581	544	1125	811	763	1574
1993-94	238	234	472	0	0	0	555	446	1001	793	680	1473
1994-95	236	240	476	0	0	0	547	437	984	783	677	1460
1995-96	225	197	422	0	0	0	456	391	847	681	588	1269
1996-97	233	210	443	0	0	0	430	378	808	663	588	1251
1997-98	231	197	428	0	0	0	428	363	791	659	560	1219
1998-99	235	192	427	0	1	1	407	352	759	642	545	1187

MADURAI DISTRICT

	SC			*ST*			*Others*			*Total*		
Year	*B*	*G*	*T*	*B*	*G*	*T*	*B*	*G*	*T*	*B*	*G*	*T*
1989-90	417	348	765	0	0	0	1179	1101	2280	1596	1449	3045
1990-91	444	406	850	0	0	0	1243	1156	2399	1687	1562	3249
1991-92	451	449	900	0	0	0	1233	1098	2331	1684	1547	3231
1992-93	436	419	855	0	0	0	1188	1095	2283	1624	1514	3138
1993-94	475	432	907	0	0	0	1222	1022	2244	1697	1454	3151
1994-95	509	467	976	0	0	0	1219	971	2190	1728	1438	3166
1995-96	456	403	859	0	0	0	1155	949	2104	1611	1352	2963
1996-97	484	406	890	0	0	0	1146	907	2053	1630	1313	2943
1997-98	485	382	867	0	0	0	1184	893	2077	1669	1275	2944
1998-99	471	375	846	0	1	1	1095	888	1983	1566	1264	2830

Source: Collected from the Sample Schools of the respective areas.

ANNEXURE-4.5

CASTE AND SEX-WISE ENROLMENT OF STUDENTS OF THE SAMPLE SCHOOLS IN DIFFERENT YEARS OF VILLUPURAM DISTRICT AND ITS TWO SAMPLE BLOCKS

KOLIYANNUR BLOCK

	SC			*ST*			*Others*			*Total*		
Year	*B*	*G*	*T*	*B*	*G*	*T*	*B*	*G*	*T*	*B*	*G*	*T*
1989-90	40	44	84	0	0	0	454	393	847	494	437	931
1990-91	38	45	83	0	0	0	456	423	879	494	468	962
1991-92	34	44	78	0	0	0	426	442	868	460	486	946
1992-93	26	29	55	0	0	0	430	463	893	456	492	948
1993-94	24	30	54	0	0	0	417	441	858	441	471	912
1994-95	30	27	57	0	0	0	387	456	843	417	483	900
1995-96	94	86	180	4	6	10	336	382	718	434	474	908
1996-97	91	73	164	5	3	8	299	298	597	395	374	769
1997-98	102	80	182	3	5	8	307	287	594	412	372	784
1998-99	99	83	182	3	3	6	296	291	587	398	377	775

THIRUVANALLUR BLOCK

Year	SC B	SC G	SC T	ST B	ST G	ST T	Others B	Others G	Others T	Total B	Total G	Total T
1989-90	106	88	194	4	4	8	330	305	635	440	397	837
1990-91	121	90	211	7	6	13	331	291	622	459	387	846
1991-92	131	91	222	6	4	10	344	297	641	481	392	873
1992-93	130	100	230	5	8	13	342	333	675	477	441	918
1993-94	99	74	173	6	4	10	315	275	590	420	353	773
1994-95	101	74	175	6	4	10	288	257	545	395	335	730
1995-96	137	85	222	7	4	11	257	260	517	401	349	750
1996-97	123	74	197	0	0	0	224	224	448	347	298	645
1997-98	144	120	264	1	0	1	221	214	435	366	334	700
1998-99	158	127	285	2	0	2	260	243	503	420	370	790

VILLUPURAM DISTRICT

Year	SC B	SC G	SC T	ST B	ST G	ST T	Others B	Others G	Others T	Total B	Total G	Total T
1989-90	146	132	278	4	4	8	784	698	1482	934	834	1768
1990-91	159	135	294	7	6	13	787	714	1501	953	855	1808
1991-92	165	135	300	6	4	10	770	739	1509	941	878	1819
1992-93	156	129	285	5	8	13	772	796	1568	933	933	1866
1993-94	123	104	227	6	4	10	732	716	1448	861	824	1685
1994-95	131	101	232	6	4	10	675	713	1388	812	818	1630
1995-96	231	171	402	11	10	21	593	642	1235	835	823	1658
1996-97	214	147	361	5	3	8	523	522	1045	742	672	1414
1997-98	246	200	446	4	5	9	528	501	1029	778	706	1484
1998-99	257	210	467	5	3	8	556	534	1090	818	747	1565

Source : Collected from the Sample Schools of the respective areas.

ANNEXURE-4.6

CASTE AND SEX-WISE ATTENDANCE RATE OF STUDENTS OF THE SAMPLE SCHOOLS IN DIFFERENT YEARS.

ORISSA

	SC		*ST*			*Others*			*Total-*			
Year	*B*	*G*	*T*	*B*	*G*	*T*	*B*	*G*	*T*	*B*	*G*	*T*
1989-90	81.43	81.85	81.63	80.99	75.84	78.70	77.82	78.99	78.35	78.94	78.97	78.96
1990-91	78.43	79.93	79.15	85.40	82.14	83.98	81.04	83.16	81.99	81.29	82.36	81.77
1991-92	77.82	77.31	77.58	85.21	78.24	82.39	87.26	83.53	85.51	85.22	81.62	83.56
1992-93	77.53	81.55	79.31	78.34	74.91	77.05	83.75	82.02	82.92	81.60	81.06	81.36
1993-94	79.17	77.21	78.24	79.65	77.32	78.64	78.23	74.09	76.27	78.60	75.09	76.96
1994-95	79.58	67.58	74.36	79.04	80.75	79.73	84.72	75.19	80.34	82.98	74.37	79.12
1995-96	84.89	81.75	83.39	88.28	82.70	86.06	86.35	84.45	85.45	86.36	83.66	85.11
1996-97	85.59	82.58	84.11	86.80	81.26	84.75	87.54	85.99	86.79	87.01	84.70	85.92
1997-98	90.15	85.67	87.89	86.09	89.36	87.45	84.54	84.55	84.54	85.86	85.52	85.70
1998-99	87.42	86.72	87.08	88.74	82.40	86.18	88.49	88.02	88.26	88.32	86.88	87.65

TAMIL NADU

Year	SC			ST			Others			Total		
	B	G	T	B	G	T	B	G	T	B	G	T
1989-90	77.54	74.64	76.21	50.00	75.00	62.50	88.84	90.58	89.68	86.27	87.21	86.71
1990-91	76.51	73.87	75.26	71.43	66.67	69.23	90.29	91.02	90.64	87.09	87.12	87.11
1991-92	79.38	75.34	77.42	83.33	75.00	80.00	90.26	91.15	90.68	87.69	87.32	87.51
1992-93	79.77	77.65	78.75	80.00	62.50	69.23	89.24	87.21	88.24	87.03	84.99	86.03
1993-94	81.60	83.36	82.43	83.33	100.00	90.00	88.54	89.13	88.81	86.90	87.79	87.32
1994-95	85.47	86.80	86.09	66.67	100.00	80.00	91.20	91.36	91.28	89.70	90.23	89.95
1995-96	89.96	88.50	89.29	81.82	90.00	85.71	92.88	93.60	93.22	92.01	92.24	92.11
1996-97	88.72	87.78	88.31	100.00	100.00	100.00	92.34	95.06	93.59	91.29	93.04	92.09
1997-98	90.42	86.60	88.73	100.00	100.00	100.00	91.61	93.39	92.41	91.27	91.41	91.33
1998-99	88.32	91.28	89.64	100.00	75.00	88.89	92.57	93.44	92.97	91.29	92.78	91.97

Source: Collected from the Sample Schools of Orissa and Tamil Nadu.

ANNEXURE-4.7

CASET AND SEX-WISE ATTENDANCE RATE OF STUDENTS OF THE SAMPLE SCHOOLS IN DIFFERENT YEARS OF PURI DISTRICT AND ITS TWO SAMPLE BLOCKS

SATYABADI BLOCK

Year	SC			ST			Others			Total		
	B	G	T	B	G	T	B	G	T	B	G	T
1989-90	82.33	80.20	81.24	--	--	--	79.65	76.26	78.07	80.45	77.59	79.08
1990-91	78.57	78.03	78.29	--	--	--	88.38	82.33	85.73	84.57	80.35	82.59
1991-92	78.45	76.15	77.33	--	--	--	88.24	89.41	88.77	84.69	84.23	84.47
1992-93	75.00	79.59	77.10	--	--	--	86.33	86.75	86.51	82.31	84.09	83.11
1993-94	80.56	78.30	79.44	--	--	--	88.73	87.88	88.35	85.90	84.13	85.08
1994-95	79.13	65.93	73.30	--	--	--	90.29	85.52	87.96	86.29	79.31	83.00
1995-96	85.52	82.33	83.96	--	--	--	91.22	89.01	90.20	89.04	86.26	87.73
1996-97	87.35	83.25	85.35	--	--	--	92.22	88.35	90.37	90.39	86.37	88.45
1997-98	92.11	88.22	90.23	--	--	--	89.22	86.32	87.88	90.27	87.05	88.76
1998-99	90.06	90.03	90.05	--	--	--	90.12	86.78	88.52	90.10	87.95	89.07

PURI SADAR BLOCK

Year	SC			ST			Others			Total		
	B	G	T	B	G	T	B	G	T	B	G	T
1989-90	84.00	85.19	84.50	--	--	--	76.91	80.24	78.40	77.80	80.79	79.13
1990-91	77.03	81.67	79.10	--	--	--	79.01	84.60	81.53	78.78	84.25	81.24
1991-92	74.03	79.25	76.51	--	--	--	87.80	82.97	85.56	86.07	82.49	84.39
1992-93	84.52	86.30	85.35	--	--	--	84.02	83.51	83.78	84.09	83.88	83.99
1993-94	76.53	75.32	75.94	--	--	--	74.46	69.18	71.87	74.73	69.98	72.40
1994-95	77.62	66.22	72.71	--	--	--	83.06	71.09	77.65	82.32	70.48	77.00
1995-96	80.23	78.33	79.32	--	--	--	84.50	82.40	83.49	83.92	81.84	82.92
1996-97	82.35	78.67	80.49	--	--	--	86.19	85.17	85.69	85.58	84.10	84.85
1997-98	88.36	81.82	84.62	--	--	--	82.72	83.98	83.30	83.37	83.61	83.49
1998-99	84.92	79.65	82.38	--	--	--	88.05	88.19	88.12	87.53	86.75	87.16

PURI DISTRICT

Year	SC			ST			Others			Total		
	B	*G*	*T*	*B*	*G*	*T*	*B*	*G*	*T*	*B*	*G*	*T*
1989-90	83.06	81.94	82.53	--	--	--	77.73	78.97	78.30	78.73	79.56	79.11
1990-91	78.00	79.17	78.57	--	--	--	81.50	84.02	82.63	80.76	82.84	81.71
1991-92	76.68	77.36	77.01	--	--	--	87.92	84.70	86.43	85.59	83.08	84.42
1992-93	79.00	82.46	80.59	--	--	--	84.70	84.35	84.54	83.46	83.95	83.69
1993-94	78.89	77.09	78.00	--	--	--	78.54	73.89	76.32	78.61	74.58	76.67
1994-95	78.44	66.06	73.03	--	--	--	84.87	75.09	80.35	83.55	73.38	78.91
1995-96	83.34	80.71	82.06	--	--	--	86.30	84.07	85.24	85.65	83.30	84.53
1996-97	84.95	80.97	82.97	--	--	--	87.70	85.93	86.84	87.08	84.78	85.95
1997-98	90.57	85.02	87.66	--	--	--	84.31	84.55	84.42	85.51	84.66	85.11
1998-99	87.53	84.89	86.26	--	--	--	88.60	87.81	88.22	88.36	87.14	87.77

Source: Collected from the Sample Schools of the respective areas.

ANNEXURE-4.8

CASTE AND SEX-WISE ATTENDANCE RATE OF STUDENTS OF THE SAMPLE SCHOOLS IN DIFFERENT YEARS OF RAYAGADA DISTRICT AND ITS TWO SAMPLE BLOCKS

KOLNARA BLOCK

Year	SC			ST			Othres			Total		
	B	G	T	B	G	T	B	G	T	B	G	T
1989-90	72.22	82.34	75.92	77.23	73.02	75.18	88.68	84.62	86.36	79.31	78.62	78.97
1990-91	82.50	88.26	84.88	82.03	86.33	84.15	91.62	87.63	89.58	85.03	87.03	86.00
1991-92	85.37	83.21	84.51	86.04	78.36	82.69	86.67	81.08	83.63	86.09	80.20	83.34
1992-93	66.67	77.32	70.56	80.23	77.33	79.15	75.61	56.67	65.32	76.19	69.21	73.24
1993-94	86.05	78.22	82.80	81.06	78.02	79.56	72.34	77.08	74.20	79.07	77.79	78.50
1994-95	84.62	73.33	79.88	77.33	81.63	79.43	84.56	79.34	82.35	81.44	79.28	80.46
1995-96	92.59	88.56	90.83	90.02	86.05	88.35	91.11	91.49	91.28	90.91	88.31	89.78
1996-97	89.66	94.74	91.88	91.55	88.32	90.26	83.33	85.62	84.37	89.05	89.12	89.08
1997-98	88.73	89.47	89.03	89.92	89.02	89.51	89.19	82.82	86.50	89.47	87.89	88.78
1998-99	87.10	95.45	91.02	93.32	87.22	90.64	88.88	91.66	90.28	90.96	90.24	90.63

RAYAGADA BLOCK

YEAR	SC			ST			Others			Total		
	B	G	T	B	G	T	B	G	T	B	G	T.
1989-90	71.43	75.00	72.96	82.55	77.36	80.35	68.56	68.18	68.41	79.82	75.76	78.11
1990-91	66.67	69.23	67.52	87.31	78.65	83.86	64.29	61.76	63.25	80.99	73.95	78.16
1991-92	72.73	57.14	57.14	84.78	78.16	82.22	70.13	62.07	65.96	82.38	73.30	78.52
1992-93	83.33	66.67	78.13	77.05	73.33	75.63	65.39	61.11	63.42	75.91	70.75	73.90
1993-94	71.43	77.23	73.42	78.57	76.47	77.78	83.33	76.33	80.19	77.96	76.56	77.42
1994-95	85.71	80.25	83.28	80.20	79.59	80.00	76.47	68.23	72.50	80.22	77.56	79.27
1995-96	86.03	81.12	84.07	86.96	79.63	84.18	75.42	81.22	77.81	85.31	80.00	83.27
1996-97	82.79	78.53	80.48	83.05	74.19	80.00	90.91	88.89	90.00	84.18	77.64	81.69
1997-98	89.52	86.12	87.69	82.95	89.74	85.51	83.33	86.96	85.37	83.49	88.75	85.69
1998-99	86.73	88.23	87.51	85.11	77.36	82.21	82.53	85.22	83.74	84.98	79.78	82.92

RAYAGADA DISTRICT

Year	SC			ST			Others			Total		
	B	G	T	B	G	T	B	G	T	B	G	T
1989-90	72.12	81.12	75.49	80.99	75.84	78.70	78.77	79.14	78.96	79.61	77.11	78.48
1990-91	81.41	87.31	83.82	85.40	82.14	83.98	77.37	76.77	77.09	82.79	80.88	81.95
1991-92	85.37	76.95	81.47	85.21	78.24	82.39	80.20	74.10	76.94	84.10	76.78	80.84
1992-93	70.83	75.10	72.34	78.34	74.91	77.05	71.91	57.96	64.70	76.05	69.93	73.56
1993-94	80.14	77.89	79.27	79.65	77.32	78.64	74.97	76.87	75.74	78.57	77.31	78.04
1994-95	84.85	74.96	80.65	79.04	80.75	79.73	82.87	76.56	80.11	80.90	78.68	79.98
1995-96	91.08	87.03	89.34	88.28	82.70	86.06	86.81	88.97	87.76	88.40	84.99	86.99
1996-97	88.20	90.05	89.06	86.80	81.26	84.75	85.82	86.69	86.21	86.82	84.36	85.82
1997-98	88.89	88.45	88.70	86.09	89.36	87.45	87.40	84.62	86.08	86.78	88.26	87.42
1998-99	87.01	93.41	90.09	88.74	82.40	86.18	87.19	90.21	88.68	88.21	86.12	87.31

ANNEXURE-4.9

CASTE AND SEX-WISE ATTENDANCE RATE OF STUDENTS OF THE SAMPLE SCHOOLS IN DIFFERENT YEARS OF MADURAI DISTRICT AND ITS TWO SAMMPLE BLOCKS

MADURAI EAST BLOCK

Year	SC			ST			Others			Total		
	B	G	T	B	G	T	B	G	T	B	G	T
1989-90	86.02	87.68	86.73	--	--	--	92.86	96.06	94.36	91.27	94.37	92.70
1990-91	91.24	86.70	89.14	--	--	--	92.99	92.11	92.57	92.56	90.83	91.75
1991-92	88.57	89.06	88.81	--	--	--	93.99	95.09	94.49	92.69	93.55	93.09
1992-93	92.23	88.00	90.15	--	--	--	91.93	88.49	90.29	92.01	88.36	90.26
1993-94	87.76	89.90	88.74	--	--	--	92.73	91.60	92.21	91.43	91.17	91.31
1994-95	88.64	89.87	89.20	--	--	--	95.84	94.09	95.07	93.76	92.83	93.35
1995-96	93.07	93.69	93.36	-	--	--	94.03	93.22	93.67	93.79	93.35	93.59
1996-97	93.23	94.90	93.96	--	--	--	91.58	96.26	93.57	92.01	95.89	96.67
1997-98	94.88	94.05	94.53	--	--	--	92.09	95.83	93.63	92.79	95.37	93.86
1998-99	91.10	91.80	91.41	--	--	--	95.20	95.31	95.25	94.16	94.42	94.27

ALANGANULLER BLOCK

Year	SC			ST			Others			Total		
	B	G	T	B	G	T	B	G	T	B	G	T
1989-90	64.73	60.56	62.74	--	--	--	87.93	89.02	88.47	81.19	81.19	81.19
1990-91	64.32	58.72	61.57	--	--	--	87.06	92.33	89.64	80.61	82.80	81.68
1991-92	68.88	61.09	64.86	--	--	--	89.04	91.06	90.02	83.03	81.35	82.20
1992-93	87.39	62.10	64.81	--	--	--	85.05	87.60	86.28	80.04	80.28	80.16
1993-94	71.85	76.07	73.94	--	--	--	82.06	85.51	83.60	79.00	82.26	80.50
1994-95	81.36	83.75	82.56	--	--	--	89.07	91.34	90.08	86.74	88.65	87.63
1995-96	86.67	81.22	84.12	--	--	--	92.15	95.64	93.76	90.34	90.81	90.56
1996-97	82.09	78.30	80.29	--	--	--	91.73	96.08	93.76	88.34	89.73	88.99
1997-98	86.58	86.29	86.45	--	--	--	85.54	89.52	87.37	85.91	88.39	87.05

MADURAI DISTRICT

Year	SC			ST			Others			Total		
	B	G	T	B	G	T	B	G	T	B	G	T
1989-90	74.23	71.31	72.90	--	--	--	90.50	92.52	91.47	86.25	87.42	86.81
1990-91	77.48	71.67	74.71	--	--	--	90.26	92.22	91.20	86.89	86.88	86.89
1991-92	78.05	73.05	75.56	--	--	--	91.71	93.12	92.38	88.05	87.30	87.69
1992-93	79.13	74.46	76.84	--	--	--	88.56	88.05	88.32	86.03	84.29	85.19
1993-94	79.79	82.41	81.04	--	--	--	87.89	88.95	88.37	85.62	87.00	86.26
1994-95	85.27	86.72	85.96	--	--	--	92.80	92.85	92.82	90.58	90.86	90.71
1995-96	89.91	87.59	88.82	--	--	--	93.29	94.22	93.71	92.33	92.25	92.29
1996-97	87.87	86.31	87.16	--	--	--	91.63	96.19	93.65	90.51	93.13	91.68
1997-98	90.93	90.05	90.54	--	--	--	89.72	93.26	91.25	90.07	92.30	91.04
1998-99	87.90	91.73	89.60	--	--	--	92.72	93.21	92.94	91.27	92.70	91.91

Source : Collected from the Sample Schools of the respective areas.

ANNEXURE-4.10

CASTE AND SEX-WISE ATTENDANCE RATE OF STUDENTS OF THE SAMPLE SCHOOLS IN KOLIYANNUR BLOCK

Year	SC			ST			Others			Total		
	B	G	T	B	G	T	B	G	T	B	G	T
1989-90	85.00	84.36	84.66	--	--	--	88.99	88.80	88.90	88.66	88.36	88.52
1990-91	87.74	85.89	86.74	--	--	--	88.16	88.65	88.40	88.13	88.39	88.25
1991-92	88.24	86.36	87.18	--	--	--	89.67	90.72	90.21	89.57	90.33	89.96
1992-93	89.31	88.02	88.63	--	--	--	89.07	85.31	87.12	89.08	85.47	87.21
1993-94	91.46	89.37	90.30	--	-	--	92.09	92.06	92.07	92.05	91.89	91.97
1994-95	93.33	88.89	91.23	--	--	--	90.70	91.45	91.10	90.89	91.30	91.11
1995-96	92.55	90.70	91.67	100.00	100.00	100.00	90.77	93.46	92.20	91.24	93.04	92.18
1996-97	89.01	90.41	89.63	100.00	100.00	100.00	93.65	91.95	92.80	92.66	91.71	92.20
1997-98	93.14	90.00	91.76	100.00	100.00	100.00	92.83	93.73	93.27	92.96	93.01	92.98
1998-99	90.91	87.95	89.56	100.00	100.00	100.00	93.92	92.44	93.19	93.22	91.51	92.39

THIRUNAVALUR BLOCK

Year	*SC*			*ST*			*Others*			*Total*		
	B	*G*	*T*	*B*	*G*	*T*	*B*	*G*	*T*	*B*	*G*	*T*
1989-90	87.74	82..95	85.57	50.00	75.00	62.50	82.73	85.90	84.25	83.64	85.14	84.35
1990-91	69.42	77.78	72.99	71.43	66.67	69.23	93.35	89.69	91.64	86.71	56.56	86.64
1991-92	81.68	81.32	81.53	83.33	75.00	80.00	85.76	84.51	85.18	84.62	83.67	84.19
1992-93	80.00	88.00	83.48	80.00	62.50	69.23	91.81	87.09	89.48	88.47	86.85	87.69
1993-94	87.88	86.49	87.28	83.33	100.00	90.00	86.35	85.09	85.76	86.67	85.55	86.16
1994-95	84.16	86.49	85.14	66.67	100.00	80.00	85.07	85.60	85.32	84.56	85.97	85.21
1995-96	88.32	90.59	89.19	71.43	75.00	72.73	93.77	91.54	92.65	91.52	91.12	91.33
1996-97	91.87	93.24	92.39	--	--	--	94.20	94.64	94.42	93.37	94.30	93.80
1997-98	86.81	73.33	80.68	100.00	--	100.00	100.00	93..46	96.78	94.81	86.23	90.71
1998-99	87.97	92.13	89.82	100.00	--	100.00	90.38	95.47	92.84	89.52	94.32	91.77

VILLUPURAM DISTRICT

Year	SC			ST			Others			Total		
	B	G	T	B	G	T	B	G	T	B	G	T
1989-90	86.99	83.42	85.29	50.00	75.00	62.50	86.35	87.54	86.91	86.30	86.82	86.55
1990-91	73.80	80.48	76.87	71.43	66.67	69.23	90.34	89.08	89.74	87.44	87.56	87.50
1991-92	83.03	82.96	83.00	83.33	75.00	80.00	87.92	88.23	88.07	87.04	87.36	87.19
1992-93	81.55	88.00	84.47	80.00	62.50	69.23	90.28	86.06	88.14	88.77	86.12	87.45
1993-94	88.58	87.32	88.00	83.33	100.00	90.00	89.62	89.39	89.50	89.43	89.18	89.30
1994-95	86.26	87.13	86.64	66.67	100.00	80.00	88.30	89.34	88.83	87.81	89.12	88.47
1995-96	90.04	90.64	90.30	81.82	90.00	85.71	92.07	92.68	92.39	91.38	92.22	91.80
1996-97	90.65	91.84	91.14	100.00	100.00	100.00	93.88	93.10	93.49	92.99	92.86	92.93
1997-98	89.43	80.00	85.20	100.00	100.00	100.00	95.83	93.61	94.75	93.83	89.80	91.91
1998-99	89.11	90.48	89.72	100.00	100.00	100.00	92.27	93.82	93.03	91.32	92.90	92.08

Source : Colected from the Sample Schools of the respective areas.

ANNEXURE - 4.11

CASTE AND SEX-WISE DROPOUT RATE OF STUDENTS OF THE SAMPLE SCHOOLS IN DIFFERENT YEARS ORISSA

Year	SC			ST			Others			Total		
	B	G	T	B	G	T	B	G	T	B	G	T
1989-90	42.42	40.59	41.62	64.71	54.00	59.41	37.61	37.99	37.79	44.53	42.33	43.49
1990-91	34.81	40.20	36.86	51.28	35.14	43.42	29.67	33.17	31.36	34.43	34.60	34.51
1991-92	31.47	47.82	39.13	60.56	50.94	56.45	41.11	30.81	36.39	45.13	39.29	42.49
1992-93	43.30	49.77	45.86	64.52	71.74	67.59	34.45	38.42	36.34	43.03	47.04	44.83
1993-94	18.27	37.96	27.27	76.47	63.16	71.70	35.58	39.56	37.32	43.56	43.92	43.71
1994-95	32.38	33.96	33.09	62.50	47.37	55.81	36.52	27.07	32.46	40.75	32.17	37.01
1995-96	17.61	30.02	23.68	51.92	56.25	53.57	19.63	21.87	20.72	25.54	28.06	26.72
1996-97	21.56	27.35	24.40	63.16	53.57	60.00	18.80	19.45	19.09	28.71	25.86	27.46
1997-98	27.49	32.76	30.21	37.50	37.50	37.50	30.08	18.80	24.48	30.62	24.34	27.53
1998-99	10.70	13.37	11.82	46.15	63.16	51.72	17.07	17.95	17.50	20.16	21.13	20.60

TAMIL NADU

Year	SC			ST			Others			Total		
	B	G	T	B	G	T	B	G	T	B	G	T
1989-90	29.19	27.08	28.15	100.00	100.00	100.00	20.84	29.25	24.68	22.96	28.87	25.70
1990-91	32.29	28.87	30.63	0.00	--	-100.00	20.64	27.65	24.14	23.53	27.75	25.62
1991-92	24.72	29.40	26.94	100.00	--	100.00	28.26	32.27	30.18	27.57	31.61	29.49
1992-93	38.23	25.57	32.21	0.00	100.00	66.67	29.49	29.08	29.29	31.38	28.57	30.02
1993-94	20.45	23.76	22.05	--	0.00	0.00	20.60	18.40	19.57	20.56	19.70	20.16
1994-95	25.03	26.17	25.57	50.00	50.00	50.00	27.12	24.09	25.62	26.69	24.66	25.70
1995-96	13.21	-0.04	6.54	0.00	100.00	50.00	27.18	30.01	28.50	23.89	22.34	23.15
1996-97	16.50	11.71	14.20	0.00	100.00	66.67	26.84	30.35	28.50	24.45	26.30	25.33
1997-98	7.33	2.24	4.85	100.00	100.00	0.00	31.02	27.42	29.38	25.66	20.74	23.38
1998-99	9.19	11.65	10.32	100.00	100.00	0.00	25.37	24.15	24.79	21.01	20.59	20.81

Source: Compiled from the date collected from the Sample Schools of Orissa and Tamil Nadu.

ANNEXURE-4.12

CASTE AND SEX-WISE DROPOUT RATE OF STUDENTS OF THE SAMPLE SCHOOLS IN DIFFERENT YEARS OF PURI DISTRICT AND ITS TWO SAMPLE BLOCKS

SATYABADI BLOCK

Year	SC			ST			Others			Total		
	P	*G*	*T*	*B*	*G*	*T*	*B*	*G*	*T*	*B*	*G*	*T*
1989-90	31.12	33.21	32.13	--	--	--	32.76	31.33	32.00	32.20	31.89	32.04
1990-91	28.36	33.34	30.14	--	--	--	35.33	33.75	34.50	31.78	33.61	32.61
1991-92	29.04	30.08	29.52	--	--	--	30.39	28.50	29.51	29.90	29.06	29.51
1992-93	24.03	28.79	26.34	--	--	--	26.36	29.33	28.13	25.55	29.19	27.60
1993-94	25.00	29.30	27.33	--	--	--	20.76	26.33	22.81	21.91	27.61	24.35
1994-95	20.36	26.37	22.86	--	--	--	22.33	21.56	21.95	21.47	23.32	22.32
1995-96	19.35	20.36	19.92	--	--	--	15.66	19.35	17.32	16.97	19.82	18.38
1996-97	21.33	18.36	19.81	--	--	--	17.33	20.22	18.42	18.59	19.40	18.93
1997-98	21.87	22.36	22.14	--	--	--	15.56	-3.45	7.08	17.58	7.39	12.64
1998-99	19.33	20.66	19.93	--	--	--	8.33	2.86	5.55	12.14	8.20	10.21

PURI SADAR BLOCK

Year	SC			ST			Others			Total		
	B	*G*	*T*	*B*	*G*	*T*	*B*	*G*	*T*	*B*	*G*	*T*
1989-90	34.55	36.78	35.58	--	--	--	30.59	40.28	35.03	31.15	39.78	35.11
1990-91	38.57	34.00	36.78	--	--	--	29.36	30.38	29.81	30.47	30.75	30.59
1991-92	37.23	37.54	37.36	--	--	--	37.77	36.35	37.04	37.65	36.55	37.11
1992-93	34.22	33.12	33.87	--	--	--	36.21	38.66	37.25	35.96	38.20	36.89
1993-94	38.58	39.78	38.98	--	--	--	35.58	40.55	37.81	36.02	40.48	37.96
1994-95	33.33	32.78	33.03	--	--	--	33.55	27.22	30.87	33.53	27.98	31.11
1995-96	26.33	22.33	24.89	--	--	--	17.32	20.69	19.04	18.46	20.81	19.62
1996-97	28.96	31.82	30.33	--	--	--	13.66	20.00	16.88	16.83	22.22	19.54
1997-98	21.36	23.02	22.22	--	--	--	24.10	15.73	19.77	23.68	16.84	20.14
1998-99	14.35	18.33	16.04	--	--	--	22.03	17.59	19.91	20.78	17.69	19.33

PURI DISTRICT

Year	SC			ST			Othes			Total		
	B	G	T	B	G	T	B	G	T	B	G	T
1989-90	32.72	34.80	33.70	--	--	--	31.17	37.35	34.14	31.49	36.84	34.05
1990-91	31.85	33.59	32.49	--	--	--	30.57	31.28	30.90	30.88	31.70	31.24
1991-92	33.02	33.42	33.20	--	--	--	35.21	33.93	34.57	34.59	33.81	34.22
1992-93	28.81	30.11	29.35	--	--	--	33.89	35.12	34.48	32.92	34.34	33.58
1993-94	32.19	32.67	32.41	--	--	--	31.24	37.32	33.84	31.42	36.37	33.56
1994-95	25.08	29.46	27.13	--	--	--	31.50	25.94	29.07	30.33	26.65	28.70
1995-96	22.37	20.85	21.62	--	--	--	16.90	20.41	18.64	17.99	20.49	19.23
1996-97	25.31	24.94	25.13	--	--	--	14.92	20.05	17.33	17.49	21.35	19.33
1997-98	21.63	22.65	22.17	--	--	--	21.52	11.02	16.29	21.54	13.79	17.62
1998-99	16.54	19.42	17.80	--	--	--	18.97	13.99	16.55	18.45	14.98	16.80

Source : Compiled from the date collected from the Sample Schools of the respective areas.

ANNEXURE-4.13

CASTE AND SEX-WISE DROPOUT RATE OF STUDENTS OF THE SAMPLE SCHOOLS IN DIFFERENT YEARS OF RAYAGADA DISTRICT AND ITS TWO SAMPLE BLOCKS

RAYAGADA BLOCK

Year	*SC*			*ST*			*Others*			*Total*		
	B	*G*	*T*	*B*	*G*	*T*	*B*	*G*	*T*	*B*	*G*	*T*
1989-90	--	-	-	61.29	70.97	66.13	61.67	75.00	67.00	61.40	71.79	66.34
1990-91	--	--	--	63.33	54.55	59.62	54.44	68.75	63.60	61.28	60.53	60.91
1991-92	100.00	--	100.00	55.00	55.26	55.13	53.33	65.67	59.50	55.47	57.76	56.58
1992-93	100.00	100.00	100.00	66.67	78.57	71.88	45.45	49.02	46.57	63.27	74.86	68.01
1993-94	100.00	100.00	100.00	77.78	78.57	78.05	48.36	47.50	47.98	73.99	72.43	73.43
1994-95	50.00	0.00	33.33	66.67	71.43	68.42	45.80	45.36	45.65	62.31	64.67	63.16
1995-96	--	75.00	75.00	65.71	42.86	57.14	40.00	41.75	40.29	62.50	53.40	58.83
1996-97	--	--	--	66.67	41.18	58.00	45.10	48.69	45.82	61.63	36.04	53.26
1997-98	80.00	40.64	42.31	42.86	46.15	44.12	40.00	41.12	40.42	52.78	56.93	54.48
1998-99	25.00	42.13	40.31	52.00	62.50	54.55	38.59	40.83	39.34	47.65	70.07	53.91

KOLNARA BLOCK

Year	SC			ST			Others			Total		
	B	G	T	B	G	T	B	G	T	B	G	T
1989-90	66.67	66.67	66.67	70.00	56.23	60.56	60.22	40.22	48.56	65.00	29.03	49.30
1990-91	50.00	66.67	57.14	11.11	48.55	38.28	-20.00	12.50	-3.78	18.18	13.79	15.69
1991-92	0.00	100.00	100.00	67.74	60.02	64.72	69.57	50.56	65.34	63.79	51.85	60.00
1992-93	66.67	100.00	86.59	61.54	70.35	69.33	52.66	78.26	68.45	56.86	76.92	65.56
1993-94	-300.00	66.67	-80.00	71.43	62.63	64.12	48.35	83.33	70.44	26.32	47.37	36.84
1994-95	66.67	75.00	70.00	50.00	53.94	46.37	70.00	66.67	68.75	60.71	37.04	49.09
1995-96	0.00	25.00	25.00	23.53	40.12	46.43	40.00	50.23	48.15	23.81	62.96	39.13
1996-97	12.50	57.14	39.47	58.33	36.81	35.94	35.66	35.21	35.23	51.06	69.23	57.53
1997-98	-40.00	25.00	-11.11	27.27	46.22	27.27	39.66	36.75	37.11	22.94	39.86	31.40
1998-99	-22.22	-100.00	-46.15	35.71	42.29	48.00	39.96	26.85	39.87	20.61	33.94	26.71

RAYAGADA DISTRICT

Year	SC			ST			Others			Total		
	B	G	T	B	G	T	B	G	T	B	G	T
1989-90	66.67	66.67	66.67	64.71	54.00	59.41	43.15	23.33	34.99	59.80	48.95	54.83
1990-91	50.00	66.67	57.14	51.28	35.14	43.42	18.57	23.25	21.52	43.61	33.70	38.42
1991-92	20.00	100.00	69.23	60.56	50.94	56.45	61.18	36.52	53.44	58.93	53.04	56.52
1992-93	70.59	100.00	80.77	64.52	71.74	67.59	35.24	72.71	52.53	59.40	75.46	66.18
1993-94	-100.00	75.00	-12.50	76.47	63.16	71.70	42.92	61.63	52.63	63.04	63.62	63.27
1994-95	62.50	60.00	61.54	62.50	47.37	55.81	60.38	59.00	59.89	61.98	50.75	57.30
1995-96	0.00	66.67	31.58	51.92	56.25	53.57	41.36	57.62	47.77	43.02	58.32	49.09
1996-97	0.00	42.86	20.00	63.16	53.57	60.00	58.60	73.96	63.54	56.11	56.04	56.09
1997-98	40.00	61.54	50.00	37.50	37.50	37.50	3.26	3.75	3.50	29.40	33.77	31.38
1998-99	-7.69	-14.29	-10.00	46.15	63.16	51.72	52.12	5.77	27.01	36.08	30.13	33.81

Source: Compiled from the data collected from the Sample Schools of the respective areas

ANNEXURE-4.14

CASTE AND SEX-WISE DROPOUT RATE OF STUDENTS OF THE SAMPLE SCHOOLS IN DIFFERENT YEARS OF MADURAI DISTRICT AND ITS SAMPLE BLOCKS

MADURAI EAST BLOCK

	SC			*ST*			*Others*			*Total*		
Year	*B*	*G*	*T*	*B*	*G*	*T*	*B*	*G*	*T*	*B*	*G*	*T*
1989-90	25.23	21.79	23.81	--	--	--	25.34	18.96	22.83	25.32	19.60	23.04
1990-91	18.61	16.45	17.53	--	--	--	22.44	14.63	18.76	21.68	15.03	18.50
1991-92	16.76	13.34	15.40	--	--	--	20.00	18.40	19.29	19.21	17.35	18.40
1992-93	13.80	-3.33	5.00	--	--	--	26.31	28.21	27.12	23.79	19.94	22.07
1993-94	24.12	13.67	19.18	--	--	--	18.66	19.20	18.91	19.88	17.93	18.97
1994-95	21.26	17.28	19.31	--	--	--	18.11	15.23	16.67	18.97	15.77	17.35
1995-96	17.47	9.68	13.62	--	--	--	16.87	11.46	14.65	16.99	10.98	14.41
1996-97	14.29	9.41	11.73	-	--	--	14.92	9.53	12.68	14.78	9.49	12.43
1997-98	16.41	6.70	11.41	--	--	--	12.46	8.77	10.93	13.35	8.14	11.06
1998-99	9.86	3.96	7.30	--	--	--	9.96	6.32	8.28	9.93	5.66	7.99

ALLANGANULLER BLOCK

Year	SC			ST			Others			Total		
	B	G	T	B	G	T	B	G	T	B	G	T
1989-90	31.12	34.34	32.87	--	--	--	27.98	21.45	24.98	28.78	25.65	27.27
1990-91	29.45	30.36	29.88	--	--	--	26.53	24.23	25.30	27.69	26.30	26.98
1991-92	23.59	26.09	24.85	--	--	--	25.70	21.46	23.68	25.01	23.10	24.08
1992-93	27.10	21.30	24.20	--	--	--	30.11	19.59	24.99	29.17	20.15	24.74
1993-94	33.66	24.86	29.38	--	--	-	28.23	16.77	22.34	29.92	19.10	24.45
1994-95	28.44	19.36	24.41	--	--	--	25.09	19.44	22.28	26.22	19.42	22.95
1995-96	23.76	17.09	20.15	--	--	--	23.70	10.19	17.78	23.72	12.82	18.57
1996-97	18.49	16.96	17.80	--	--	--	17.21	14.96	16.22	17.57	15.55	16.68
1997-98	24.37	8.73	15.86	--	--	--	16.22	13.23	14.76	18.99	11.46	15.17
1998-99	19.59	18.01	18.84	--	--	--	19.63	16.03	18.08	19.62	16.79	18.36

MADURAI DISTRICT

Year	SC B	SC G	SC T	ST B	ST G	ST T	Others B	Others G	Others T	Total B	Total G	Total T
1989-90	19.93	22.36	21.10	--	--	--	17.50	13.64	15.87	18.06	16.07	17.19
1990-91	24.81	21.35	23.14	--	--	--	18.17	16.04	17.10	20.11	17.52	18.83
1991-92	19.45	20.39	19.88	--	--	-	19.75	15.25	17.68	19.67	16.72	18.31
1992-93	23.16	16.39	19.74	--	--	--	22.74	15.54	19.46	22.85	15.79	19.54
1993-94	28.57	21.85	25.34	--	--	--	22.94	16.04	19.57	24.44	17.56	21.10
1994-95	22.61	16.69	22.01	--	--	--	21.89	19.32	20.61	23.34	18.59	21.02
1995-96	19.55	9.38	14.24	--	--	--	25.09	19.28	22.63	23.72	16.02	20.24
1996-97	17.80	15.27	16.57	--	--	--	18.54	16.51	17.67	18.35	16.14	17.37
1997-98	21.61	12.21	16.62	--	--	--	20.09	14.00	17.39	20.50	13.38	17.15
1998-99	22.47	19.78	21.25	--	--	--	22.79	17.75	20.53	22.69	18.41	20.77

Source : Compiled from the date collectedc from the Sample Schools of the respective areas.

ANNEXURE-4.15

CASTE AND SEX-WISE DROPOUT RATE OF STUDENTS OF THE SAMPLE SCHOOLS IN DIFFERENT YEARS OF VILLUPURAM DISTRICT AND ITS TWO SAMPLE BLOCKS

KOLIYANUR BLOCK

	SC			ST			Others			Total		
Year	*B*	*G*	*T*	*B*	*G*	*T*	*B*	*G*	*T*	*B*	*G*	*T*
1989-90	30.00	27.27	28.57	NE	NE	NE	3.49	37.35	20.12	6.25	36.17	21.05
1990-91	50.00	10.00	31.82	NE	NE	NE	-4.82	27.78	12.14	2.11	26.00	14.36
1991-92	25.00	22.22	23.53	NE	NE	NE	24.75	34.65	29.70	24.77	33.64	29.22
1992-93	0.00	33.33	17.65	NE	NE	NE	19.05	22.83	20.81	17.70	23.76	20.56
1993-94	33.33	35.71	34.78	NE	NE	NE	26.32	31.09	28.76	26.83	31.58	29.30
1994-95	0.00	80.00	50.00	NE	NE	NE	20.00	18.18	19.02	18.81	23.33	21.27
1995-96	-433.33	-160.00	-223.08	NC	NC	NC	32.91	39.81	36.81	14.63	22.12	18.97
1996-97	-266.67	-333.33	-300.00	NC	NC	NC	37.93	40.63	39.34	26.67	29.29	28.04
1997-98	-700.00	-333.00	-480.00	NC	NC	NC	44.44	46.07	45.21	29.70	31.52	30.57
1998-99	-109.09	-100.00	105.56	NC	NC	NC	25.33	29.67	27.71	8.14	18.37	13.59

THIRUNAVALUR BLOCK

Year	SC			ST			Others			Total		
	B	*G*	*T*	*B*	*G*	*T*	*B*	*G*	*T*	*B*	*G*	*T*
1989-90	51.61	37.50	44.44	100.00	100.00	100.00	50.00	56.10	53.09	51.33	51.30	51.32
1990-91	50.00	59.26	54.72	0.00	--	-100.00	53.75	62.50	57.89	52.34	60.61	56.31
1991-92	41.38	57.14	49.12	100.00	--	100.00	53.85	67.42	60.56	51.24	64.96	57.98
1992-93	18.18	50.00	30.91	--	0.00	0.00	12.50	22.22	17.65	14.81	29.87	22.15
1993.94	65.71	33.33	52.54	0.00	100.00	66.67	47.79	59.00	53.05	51.68	54.76	53.09
1994-95	24.00	41.67	32.65	50.00	50.00	50.00	47.00	49.32	47.98	42.52	47.47	44.69
1995-96	33.33	27.27	31.03	100.00	100.00	100.00	29.33	47.95	38.51	31.25	43.75	37.02
1996-97	41.38	40.00	40.74	100.00	100.00	100.00	46.48	52.87	50.00	45.54	50.88	48.37
1997-98	6.90	-11.11	2.63	100.00	100.00	100.00	54.41	46.77	50.77	40.82	40.28	40.59
1998-99	-16.67	5.26	-5.41	100.00	100.00	100.00	36.36	40.00	38.10	25.88	32.50	29.09

VILLUPURAM DISTRICT

Year	SC			ST			Others			Total		
	B	G	T	B	G	T	B	G	T	B	G	T
1989-90	46.34	34.88	40.48	100.00	100.00	100.00	25.90	46.67	36.25	30.62	44.50	37.56
1990-91	50.00	45.95	48.00	0.00	--	-100.00	23.93	43.21	33.54	28.71	43.22	35.91
1991-92	37.84	48.65	43.24	100.00	--	100.00	38.54	50.00	44.24	38.70	49.78	44.20
1992.93	59.09	34.21	47.56	0.00	100.00	66.67	37.00	43.84	40.36	40.44	42.86	41.62
1993-94	14.63	45.16	27.78	---	0.00	0.00	16.99	22.60	19.73	16.49	26.40	21.24
1994-95	19.35	52.94	36.92	50.00	50.00	50.00	33.85	30.60	32.28	32.02	34.25	33.11
1995-96	-2.56	-31.25	-15.49	0.00	100.00	50.00	31.17	43.18	37.58	24.23	32.06	28.29
1996-97	12.50	0.00	6.67	0.00	100.00	66.67	41.77	46.45	44.28	36.65	40.85	38.86
1997-98	-38.71	-91.67	-53.49	100.00	100.00	0.00	48.50	46.36	47.48	35.18	35.37	35.26
1998-99	-51.72	-23.08	-38.18	100.00	100.00	0.00	30.50	33.77	32.19	16.96	24.72	20.92

Note : 1.NE =No Enrolment.
2 NE= Not calculated because of the very negligible number of students.

Source : Compiled from the data Collected from the Sample Schools of the respective areas.

SELECT BIBLIOGRAPHY

1. A World Bank Publication: *Primary Education in India,* March, 1997.

2. Bedi, Daljit Singh and Pattnaik, Satyanarayan: "Universalisation of Primary Education—— A Myth or Reality", *Kurukshetra*, vol. XLV, No. 12, September 1997.

3. Devadas, Rajammal P.: *The School Lunch Programme—— Organisation and Outcomes,* Ministry of Education and Culture, Government of India, 1983.

4. Dhawan, G.: Education Policies since Independence—— Progress, Prospects and Challenges, *Kurukshetra,* vol. XLV, No. 11, August 1997.

5. George, Fort St: *Note on Puratchi Thalaivar M.G.R. Nutritious Meal Programme*, Social Welfare and NMP Department, Chennai, 9.

6. Harrissa, Barbara: *Child Nutrition and poverty in South India : Noon Meals in Tamil Nadu.* Concept Publishing Com pany, New Delhi, 1991.

7. Jeyapaul C. : Nutritional Support to Primary School", *Yojana,* Vol. 40, No.1, Jan., 1996.

8. Kumar, A. K. Shiva: "A Story of Betrayal", *Frontline*, Jan., 1 1999.

9. Madhya Pradesh Chronicle, *Irregularities Alleged in Mid-day Meal Scheme* 08.05.1997, p.6.

10. Madras Institute of Development Studies: *Tamil Nadu Economy: Performance and Issues*, Oxford & IBH Publishing Co. Pvt. Ltd., New Delhi, 1988.

11. Pandya, Rameshari: " School Dropouts Home-related Rea sons," *Kurukshetra,* vol, 46, No. 12, September 1998.

12. Rajan, S. Irudaya and Jayakumar, A. : "Impact of Noon Meal Programme on Primary Education An Exploratory Study in Tamil Nadu", *Economic and Political Weekly,* vol. XXVII, No 43 & 44, October 24-31, 1992.

13. Sobti, Renu: "Education and Nutrition". *Yojana,* Vol. 42, No. 10, Oct., 1998.

14. The Pioneer. *Mid-day Meals may be Scrapped,* 11.04.1997, p.6.

15. The PROBE Team in association with Centre for Development Economics: *Public Report on Basic Education in India,* oxford University Press, New Delhi, 1999.

16. The Telegraph: *Cooked Food for Students under Mid-day Meal Scheme,* 11.03.1997, p.15.

17. The Times of India: *MCD Plans detailed Mid-day Meal Policy,* 18.12.1997, p.4.

INDEX